## About the book

*Lost Battalions* is a remarkable story of men in combat. Two battalions, one German, one American, find themselves surrounded, deep behind enemy lines in late 1944.

The 1st Battalion, 141st Infantry ("Alamo Regiment"), had been cut off for six days and food, water, and ammunition were running out. Sent to rescue the "Texans" were the Japanese-American Nisei of the famed "Go For Broke" 100/442d Regimental Combat Team. At virtually the same time, only five miles away, a similar drama unfolded as the Wehrmacht's 201st Mountain Battalion attempted an equally desperate rescue of its sister unit, the 202d Mountain Battalion.

The weather was abysmal, the terrain virtually impassable. Some generals lost their sons there, other generals lost only their honor. Told by the soldiers, American and German, from both sides, *Lost Battalions* is an unforgettable account of courage, honor, and humanity.

# LOST

## Going For Broke in the Vosges, Autumn 1944

# BATTALIONS

## Franz Steidl

PRESIDIO

This edition printed 2000

Copyright © 1997 by Franz Steidl

Published by Presidio Press, Inc.
505 B San Marin Drive, Suite 160
Novato, CA 94945-1340

**Library of Congress Cataloging-in-Publication Data**

Steidl, Franz.
   Lost battalions : going for broke in the Vosges : autumn 1944 / Franz Steidl.
     p.   cm.
   ISBN 0-89141-622-6 (hardcover)
   ISBN 0-89141-727-3 (paperback)
   1. World War, 1939–1945—Campaigns—France—Vosges Mountains. I. Title.
D762. V67S74       1997
940.54'21438—dc21           96-54035
                                  CIP

Printed in the United States of America

*This book is dedicated to all who fought and sacrificed in the engagements described herein. I owe a large debt of gratitude to those who wrote this chapter in history with their own blood, and to the survivors who graciously consented to share their memories, often painful ones, with me.*

*To Joe Osamaru Hattori, Vitus Kolbinger, Marty Higgins, and Glenn Rathbun, whose dedication to family, friends and country made this book possible*

# Contents

# Part 1: The Race to the Vosges

# 1: Operations Meadow-Saffron and Dragoon

The summer of 1944 brought a series of stunning defeats to the Third Reich. June saw the Normandy invasion, July the attempt on Adolf Hitler's life, and August the Allied landings in southern France. In the East, the Russian summer offensive smashed Army Group Middle, and on every other front the Wehrmacht was either on the defensive or in a state of retreat. On 1 July the aging Feldmarschall Gerd von Rundstedt was relieved by Günther von Kluge as commander in chief West, who in turn committed suicide on 17 August when summoned to Berlin. Failing to push the Allies back into the sea and being implicated in the plot against Hitler were too much for Kluge (even though he had held out against the conspiracy until proof of Hitler's death was offered).

On 15 August, as thousands of Germans found themselves trapped in the Falaise pocket, the American Seventh and French First Armies landed on the Riviera. Allied plans had envisioned Normandy as the hammer that would smash the German army against the anvil mounted in southern France. Although the timetable had been changed several times, Operation Dragoon (earlier code-named "Anvil") caught the Germans completely off guard. While the Oberkommando der Wehrmacht (OKW) had every reason to expect such an Allied operation, and knew in advance, from aerial reconnaissance, that the invasion fleet was under way, it failed disastrously in attempting to deduce the target area of the attack. By the time the German Nineteenth Army recovered from the surprise of the landings between Cannes and points east of Toulon, it was too late. The shock of the assault by an airborne task force, three American and four Free French divisions, and commandos, and the resulting speed of their advance inland, so disorganized the coastal divisions that their commander, Gen. Friedrich Wiese, never succeeded in assembling the bulk of his forces to pose a serious threat to the beachhead.

General der Infanterie Wiese, who had assumed command of the army at the end of June, had been forced to release three infantry and his only panzer division to fight in Normandy, and his remaining nine divisions were understrength and ill equipped. Ironically, the 9th Panzer Division, which had left in early August, had been deployed within striking distance of the invasion beaches. The 11th Panzer Division, minus one of its tank battalions, arrived too late to stem the tide. By 20 August much of the 148th, 242d, and 244th Divisions had been cut off and destroyed between Toulon and Marseilles. Three days later Wiese ordered a large-scale withdrawal north along the Rhône.

During the first, critical days of the invasion the Luftwaffe was virtually absent, not even providing reconnaissance aircraft, while Allied fighter-bombers pursued the retreating Germans with devastating results. Even General Wiese's staff car was shot out from under him, without injury to its occupants.

The unhappy state of the Nineteenth Army was complicated even more by a grave shortage of motor vehicles and fuel, which forced large elements to rely on horse-drawn transport. Even the 11th Panzer Division had to move some of its grenadiers into battle by towing them on bicycles behind the few available trucks. Also, quite a number of soldiers were foreigners and prisoners of war pressed into German service. Once defeat appeared inevitable, its materialization was hastened by the low morale of the troop, and their fear of French partisans.

As the American 3d and 45th Divisions pursued the Germans up the Rhône valley, Task Force Butler and the 36th Division attempted to end-run General Wiese's army by racing north on Route Napoleon, through Digne and Gap. Their effort was partly successful. On 28 August, at Montélimar, Task Force Butler intercepted the bulk of the 198th Division. In the vise of three U.S. divisions the drawn-out columns east of the Rhône were decimated. Along a ten-mile stretch of road lay the carcasses of horses, burned-out trucks, and soldiers. More than two thousand motor transport, one thousand horses, and one hundred artillery pieces, including six huge railway guns, were captured, as was the division commander, Generalmajor Otto Richter.

Yet the German 189th, 338th, 716th, and 11th Panzer Divisions escaped and continued to withdraw toward Valence, Lyon, and Dijon before turning eastward in the direction of Belfort, near the Swiss border. They fought only when forced to, screening their withdrawal routes from Allied units racing north and east to cut them off. At the same time, a mass of German army, navy, air force, and administrative personnel began to evacuate central and southwestern France to escape the pincer movement of the U.S. Seventh and Third Armies closing in on Épinal.

By early September, the Oberkommando des Heeres (OKH) had completed substantial reorganization of Army Group "G," commanded by Generaloberst Johannes Blaskowitz, and ordered the formation of a new front running from Switzerland north along the western approaches of the Vosges and Luxembourg. While the early part of the month saw the Wehrmacht still retreating as rapidly as their inadequate transport permitted, the middle of September saw a sudden reversal of fortune, with German units defending, stubbornly and effectively, as hastily formed battalions turned and stood with their backs to the *Vaterland*, taking full advantage of difficult weather and terrain, as well as overextended Allied supply lines.

First signs of the new German tactics came on 1 September when the 11th Panzer Division attacked the U.S. 45th Division near Meximieux. The Germans surrounded the town held by the 179th Regiment, which was forced to use every available man, including kitchen personnel and clerks, to repulse the attack. But under the cover of darkness, the 11th "Ghost Division" slipped away once again.

The Commander of the American VI Corps, Maj. Gen. Lucian Truscott, viewed the battle as a positive sign—a desperate act by a severely crippled enemy. Lucian King Truscott Jr., the hard-hitting son of a Texas country doctor, who had led the 3d Division at Anzio, was known for his steely resolution, resilience, and decisiveness.

Truscott had been posted to Combined Operations Headquarters in London when America entered the war, giving him insights into the strengths and weaknesses of the British military. This, and a gift for diplomatic cunning, gave him an edge when he led his troops alongside the British while in Italy. At forty-nine, with graying hair, a gravely voice, and resolute toughness, there was no doubt in anyone's mind that his orders had to be obeyed at once.

Now, with the Germans trying to outrun him, he sent a special courier to his superior, the Seventh Army commander, Lt. Gen. Alexander M. Patch. The captain gave the following verbal message:

> During the battle, at least fifteen German tanks have been destroyed, and the enemy is disorganized and in full retreat along the west bank of the Saône.
>
> General Truscott asks to continue the relentless pursuit of the enemy on the axis Lons–le Saunier–Bescançon–Belfort in order to prevent his escape to Germany and inflict heavy losses upon him.

General Patch approved.

But General Wiese, whose divisions had barely escaped the trap at Montélimar, was not about to engage Truscott. Fifty-one-year-old Heinrich Friedrich Wiese was an ardent National Socialist who had risen from battalion commander to army commander within five years. Until 22 June, Wiese had commanded an army corps in Russia. On the day after his departure the Red Army's summer offensive had resulted in the total destruction of Army Group Center.

In his post-war writings General Wiese lamented the loss of his comrades.

> The General Command of XXXV Army Corps and its brave units fought tenaciously until the bitter end. They deserved a better lot. From the General Command, as far as I know, only three officers survived. I will always remember my corps with high respect and sorrow.

As his friends died or were marched off to Russian prisoner of war camps, Wiese had assumed command of an already stripped Nineteenth Army in southern France. Now, with the Allies racing toward Paris and up the Rhône valley, Wiese rapidly withdrew his battle-weary units north toward the Belfort gap, where, in the rugged Vosges Mountains stretching between neutral Switzerland and Strasbourg, he would make his stand.

To buy time, he again ordered Generalmajor Wend von Wietersheim and his trusted 11th Panzers to attack—this time the French I Corps near the Swiss border. The Ghost Division did so on 8 September, effectively grinding to a halt the drive for Belfort. With its left flank thus anchored, the Nineteenth Army pivoted northeast and turned its attention to the Germans and French collaborators trying to escape from southwestern France. Hastily formed task forces or "Kampfgruppen" and badly understrength units, like Generalleutnant Wilhelm Richter's 716th Division and the newly created 30th SS Infantry Division, were to hold the corridor open as long as possible. But the plan, hastily conceived and executed, was fraught with problems. For example, the SS Division, whose members were mostly Eastern Europeans, had little desire to die for Germany while fighting Americans on French soil. In one battalion, the Russians killed their officers and joined the French resistance.

Still, the German leadership hoped that by holding open the corridor, enough forces would be saved to establish a new front strong enough to hold the Vosges through the winter. But the withdrawal from southern and western France turned into a rout, costing the Germans more than a hundred thousand men—eighty-nine thousand of them prisoners.

Operation *Herbstzeitlose* (Meadow-Saffron)—the retreat from the Bay of Biscay and central France—did not start until three days after the Allied "Dragoon" landings in southern France. Against rapidly growing resistance mounted by the French Forces of the Interior (FFI), three march groups, each numbering between fifty thousand and sixty thousand and named South, Middle, and North, were to rush east toward the Belfort gap before the Allies could shut the corridor. March Group North, commanded by Generalleutnant Haeckel, consisted of an odd assortment of regulars from his 16th Volks-Grenadier Division, the 360th Cossack Regiment,

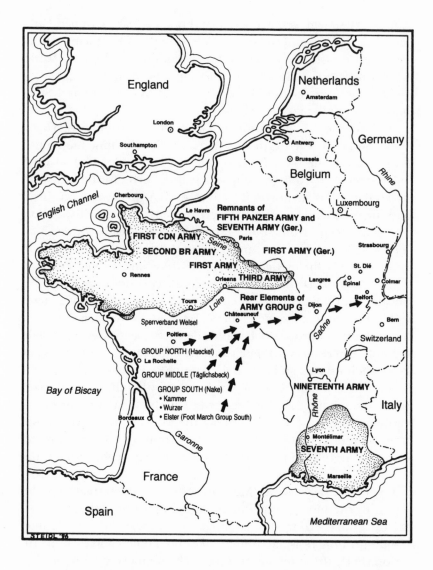

25 August 1944. As the Third and Seventh Armies were racing toward Dijon, threatening to cut off all escape routes, the Germans began their massive retreat. Operation Meadow-Saffron (Herbstzeitlose) was meant to save the bulk of the Wehrmacht, civilian personnel, and collaborators (some units held out on island fortresses for several more weeks).

12th Antiaircraft Brigade, the district commands of Tours, Angers, and Nantes, along with service, hospital, and railroad units, and collaborators who feared reprisals from their own countrymen. March Group Middle, led by Generalleutnant Täglichsbeck, was a hodgepodge of military and civil administration units, including the 950th Infantry Regiment "Freies Indien," comprised of East Indians who had been recruited to fight against the British. Similarly, March Group South, under Generalleutnant Nake, was composed of second-rate combat units, civil administration and service units, customs officials from Biarritz and Lourdes, and transport and hospital personnel from Bordeaux.

Each group was to place a reinforced regiment on its point, the mass of troops in the center, and a reinforced battalion at the rear. All possible weapons and matériel were to be brought along; everything left behind was to be destroyed, including bridges after they had been crossed. But to execute such a massive operation was problematic from the start. Road networks were wholly inadequate to handle such masses of people and vehicles, many of them horse-drawn, and what was left of the patchy telephone network was sabotaged by the French resistance. In addition, the Germans lacked adequate food and medical supplies and were at times reduced to living off the land—foraging, buying, and stealing whatever they could. This emboldened the French, who now blocked their advance wherever and whenever they could. Well supplied by the Office of Strategic Services (OSS) with weapons, ammunition, and radios, the FFI blew up railroad lines, laid mines and booby traps, and sniped at stragglers.

Thus harassed, and finding their escape routes narrowing day by day, the Germans adopted draconian measures—flying courtsmartial, executions of deserters, and ruthless treatment for captured resistance fighters. But the French were just as brutal, executing stragglers without provocation. The Germans knew this, and when given half a chance opted to surrender to the Americans or British. Generalmajor Ludwig Bieringer and his staff, for example, barricaded themselves in a villa at Draguignan and fought off partisans until the Americans arrived on 16 August. Then they readily surrendered and persuaded Gen. Ferdinand Neuling of LXII Corps to do likewise.

On 27 August, two days after the liberation of Paris, March Group South was approaching its third assembly area near Poitiers when ordered to further sort out all personnel into three subgroups: one combat group divided into slow-moving and fast-moving vehicles, a bicycle combat team, and a foot column. All motor vehicles and bicycles were to be turned over to these new formations without regard to property rights or prestige value. The former owners of these vehicles were to walk, and excess baggage was to be dumped on the road or destroyed. Horse-drawn transport of the infantry units was to be handed over to the foot columns for the transport of food and ammunition only. Despite the great difficulty of carrying out such orders while on the march, the subgroups, each named after its commander, did their level best to comply.

Generalmajor Botho Elster was left with the dregs: the nearly immobile, ill-armed, and largely helpless mélange of service troops. Unlike other groups bearing the names of their leaders, General Elster chose to disassociate himself from his bedraggled mass, renaming it "Foot March Group South." As he watched the combat units pull out on the last day of August, he wished his comrades godspeed, and then went about the task of getting his ragtag band to Poitiers before the FFI could cut them off. By 5 September, his long columns of marchers stretched out between Poitiers and Châteauroux. Surrounded and harassed by FFI units, strafed by Allied fighter aircraft, and short of food and gas for the few remaining vehicles, Elster knew that their days were numbered. But he did not want to surrender to the FFI, fearing retribution for German atrocities. Therefore, on 7 September, he sent parliamentarians toward Gen. George Patton's Third Army lines to inquire about terms of surrender. After contact was established with General Macon of the U.S. 83d Division, Elster called his senior officers together at Châteauneuf, and explained the hopelessness of the situation. When he asked for recommendations, heated arguments broke out, and his officers split into two opposing camps. With this unusual experiment in democracy a failure, General Elster distanced himself from his die-hard officers, and continued negotiations with the Allies. In the end his judgment prevailed, and terms of surrender were issued on 10 September.

1. The present military situation has resulted in the fact that it is no longer possible for Foot March Group South, abandoned as it is in central France without communications and supplies, to reach the German border.
2. Foot March Group South is not a combat unit. It is in no state to force its way back through regular troops by use of arms, equipped as it is with inadequate weapons and little ammunition. Completely defenseless, it is at the mercy of the enemy's air force. The two short air attacks of 7 September caused stunningly high casualties and severe damage to horses, vehicles, and trucks, as well as rations, weapons, and ammunition. The remaining rations are enough for only a few days. In brief, the situation can lead only to disintegration and disaster.
3. Being aware of the situation, the American Third Army, in position on the Loire, has made the following proposals:
   • All units will halt at the towns reached.
   • Units will march to designated assembly areas with weapons and full equipment.
   • Units will pass in review before an American Infantry Regiment at present arms.
   • German units will be admitted to American-occupied territory north of the Loire after they have laid down their arms. Third Army has given notice that all air attacks have been suspended for the duration of a short truce to consider these terms. It has also let us know that if the terms are rejected, its air force will bomb and strafe the column out of existence.
4. Realizing the situation, and the clear fact that to march on and join the German troops near Belfort as reinforcements would merely result in the useless shedding of priceless German blood, and out of consideration for each individual under my command, and to preserve the worth and honor of the German Army, I have been constrained to accept these terms.
5. As Commander of Foot March Group South, I order:
   • Suspension of the march.

- Suspension of hostilities against the regularly organized forces of the American, British, and French army and air force.
- Order, discipline, and especially obedience to all superior officers. The eyes of the German army are upon us all!

Elster, Brig. Gen.

On 13 September, in accordance with the agreement, the subgroups were dispatched toward the Loire at Orléans, Beaugency, and Mer. But the French population, which had already experienced the destruction and pillaging of the other retreating units, acted increasingly hostile toward the surrendering Germans. To relieve the strain, General Elster tried to make good some of the damage done by units like Regiment "Freies Indien" (Free India), which had plundered the area, by turning over eight million francs to the local prefect.

A few diehards, however, left their units, donned civilian clothes, and attempted to make their way back to Germany. Others ripped the national insignia from their uniforms, sang the Communist International, and deserted. Many of those caught were summarily executed by the FFI.

Finally, on 16 September, General Elster and his staff reached the Loire bridge south of Beaugency and surrendered—to the consternation of the FFI, whose leaders had pleaded with Patton to allow the French to accept the surrender. Once in American hands, Elster and his men were treated with such courtesy that it again outraged the French and strained relations between the Allies. Meanwhile, Elster issued his farewell message to his troops.

*I thank all officers, civilian employees, noncommissioned officers, and enlisted men for their exceptional accomplishment and the exemplary discipline maintained on the march. May the road through captivity back to our homeland be short.*

*Heil the Führer. Long live Germany.*

*Elster, Brig. Gen., March Group South*

The total number of prisoners admitted to the Beaugency cage was 19,605.

At the same time, oblivious to the plight of his still-retreating armies, Adolf Hitler devised a grandiose plan to attack General Patton's Third Army. According to Gen. Walter Warlimont, chief of the National Defense Section, OKW (Oberkommando der Wehrmacht), Hitler demanded that a strong offensive grouping be assembled on the Plateau de Langres. The force was to be created from parts of General Wiese's Nineteenth Army still moving up the Rhône, remnants of armored formations retreating from Normandy, two Panzer Grenadier divisions ordered up from Italy, and two newly formed armored brigades from Germany—all under the command of the Fifth Panzer Army. The initial task of this group was to stabilize the front west of the Vosges, with the subsequent and principal mission to attack the right flank and rear of General Patton's Third Army.

In his book *Inside Hitler's Headquarters 1939–45,* Warlimont states:

> These ambitious plans were another example of Hitler's disregard of the rules of time and space; moreover he took no account of the fact that the forces at his disposal were extremely weak. Under the pressure of fresh and severe reverses, of which the loss of Antwerp came as a particularly unpleasant surprise, Jodl managed on 6 September to get Hitler back to the view he had held on 19 August that 'a major decisive attack in the West is not possible before 1 November.' However he could not get Hitler to lift his order that Fifth Panzer Army was to make local counterattacks.

The plan may have looked good on a map, but it defied the reality at hand. As his regiments were running for their lives, Gen. Ernst Haeckel's 16th Volks-Grenadier Division was to be one of the pivotal units in Hitler's plan of attack.

Fifty-four-year-old Generalleutnant Ernst Haeckel, son of a chief railroad inspector from Gemünden, Bavaria, had served as an infantry platoon leader and staff officer in World War I and was experienced in both offensive and defensive operations from his three years on the Russian front. Detail-oriented and plodding, Haeckel was criticized for his tendency to get caught up in the minutiae of day-to-day activities, as well as his inability to react quickly and boldly to a rapidly changing battlefield. "Not a daring or strong leader," wrote General Heinrici, and his superior, General Burgdorf, praised him as "a fine training officer worthy of a replacement division, but not qualified for a combat command."

In 1943 Haeckel was put in charge of the 158th Training Division, stationed north of La Rochelle. But in the spring of 1944, Heinrich Himmler, head of the SS and chief of the Replacement Army, called for the formation of twenty-five new Volks-Grenadier divisions. And so, by merging the 158th Training Division with the 16th Luftwaffe Field Division, the 16th Volks-Grenadier Division was born, with Haeckel in charge. Life in France had been good to Haeckel, portly and afflicted with high blood pressure, who was to face the challenge of his life.

It wasn't until the Allies had already landed in southern France and taken Paris that General Haeckel got orders to withdraw from the Bay of Biscay. As in the case of the other march groups in the LXVI Reserve Corps, March Group North, placed in Haeckel's charge, had to make a run for it. As his three columns followed along the southern bank of the Loire between Nantes and Blois, through Poitiers, Bourges, and Dijon, Allied bombs and French resistance fighters extracted a heavy price of men and matériel. Haeckel remembers: "Partisans were all about. In Mirecourt we could determine the enemy's advance from the bells tolling in each village reached by the French units."

On the day General Elster surrendered his Foot March Group South, Haeckel's drawn-out columns, now approaching Charmes, found their way blocked by Gen. William Eagles's U.S. 45th Division coming up from the south, and General Leclerc's French 2d Armored Division and General Wyche's 314th Regiment just rushed in from Paris to the northwest.

The request made by Gen. Walter Lucht, to have Haeckel's division withdrawn across the Moselle, was denied, as it conflicted with Hitler's plans. Instead, two of three brand-new panzer brigades were to attack west toward Haeckel's beleaguered unit. Panzer Brigades 112 and 113 were equipped with the latest Panther, but the commanders hardly knew each other and their men, never having practiced together. The decision to form ever new units, rather than infusing men and matériel into battle-experienced divisions, proved to be a fatal mistake.

One of the battle-hardened commanders fighting alongside the 112th was Oberstleutnant Hans von Luck. Leading his 21st Panzer Combat Group, Luck, who had just received the Knight's Cross for his actions at Normandy, was once again ordered to do the near impossible.

"On the morning of 12 September, I received orders to support the Panzer brigade's attack, which was to thrust north ahead of me just west of Épinal against the 2d French Armored Division. Perhaps, remembering 1940, we underestimated the French who— supported by massive air attacks and excellent American artillery— were equipped with the best matériel and brilliantly led, moreover, by General Leclerc. Prisoners told us that French civilians had informed Colonel Langlade that German tanks had reached Dompaire, and that my combat group was on its way. So began the 'Debacle of Épinal.'"

As fighting raged in and around Charmes, General Haeckel and his staff left the division behind and drove to Bains-les-Bains and then Épinal to persuade LXVI Corps to allow the 16th VGD to withdraw across the Moselle. Lacking adequate communication gear, Haeckel didn't find General Lucht until 3 A.M., 13 September. But by the time he pleaded his case, it was too late.

"On the telephone, I issued orders for my units to fight their way back. I myself had orders to remain at Épinal to organize the resistance. Of the whole 16th Division only one infantry battalion at Charmes and some bicycle troops got to the east bank of the Moselle. Most of the division, with its artillery and fighting vehicles, was taken prisoner. They were missed in the upcoming fight from the Moselle to the Vosges."

Six weeks later Haeckel would have to defend his action before a court martial.

At dawn, Colonel Langlade's French armored formations cut the Dompaire-Épinal road, while Lt. Col. Jacques Massu (who years later staged the coup in Algeria) tore into the new German Panzers.

Colonel Luck remembers: "Langlade attacked the Panther group early on 13 September to separate it from the southern group,

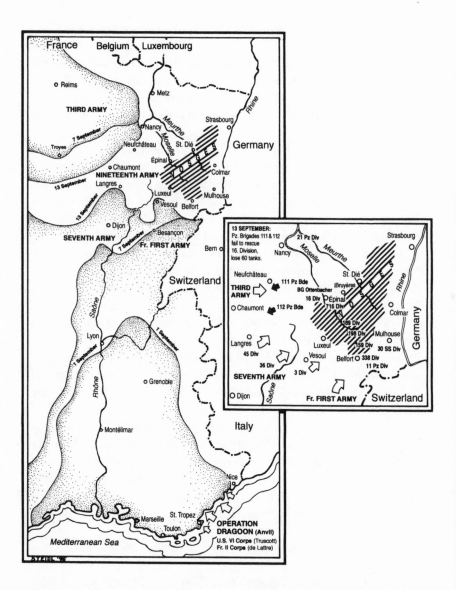

By late September fuel and ammunition shortages brought the Seventh Army's rapid advance along the Rhône and Saône to a sudden halt. After the "Debacle at Épinal," the German Nineteenth Army dug in along the Vosges, and by mid-October the American VI Corps set out to breach the "Vogesen Kammstellugen," with St. Dié, Strasbourg, and Colmar as objectives.

before I could come to its aid. The two Panzer groups lost 34 Panthers and 26 Panzer IV, and our infantry was decimated. To prevent a complete debacle, I attacked with my combat group late in the afternoon, but against strong resistance was forced to call off the engagement."

Thunderbolt pilots of the 406th Fighter-bomber Group, summoned all the way from Brittany, flew four missions and scored more than half of the hits that day.

"On 14 September, with the remaining seventeen tanks and only 240 Grenadiers and virtually no artillery support, we gained a little ground before American artillery stopped us in our tracks. We were finally ordered to withdraw toward Épinal; for we were to be 'spared,' so that we would be available for the attack on Patton's flank that Hitler was still planning. It proved impossible to free our 16th Infantry Division from the encirclement. Only 500 men reached our lines, and 7,000 died or were taken prisoner," Luck wrote.

Loss of the 16th Volks-Grenadier Division and most of Panzer Brigade 112 was but one more drumbeat in Hitler's version of Götterdämmerung, about to be played out in the Vosges and Ardennes during the freezing fall and winter months ahead. (Panzer Brigade 112 was replenished and continued to fight. Men and matériel of the two remaining brigades were distributed among the panzer divisions in dire need of both.)

From the one battalion that had survived at Charmes and some four hundred men who had managed to flee across the Moselle, General Haeckel rebuilt the 16th Volks-Grenadier Division at Épinal. Reserve, air force, navy, and rear echelon units were thrown together with Battle Group Ottenbacher and SS Polizei Regiment 19 from Lyon, bringing the total fighting strength to barely twenty-five hundred men. And the division suffered from an appalling lack of heavy equipment, artillery, and most important, radios and other communications gear.

Following the "Debacle of Épinal," OKH now called for holding the German Nineteenth Army front along the Moselle, Mortagne, and Meurthe rivers, each flowing parallel to the northwest. With the joining of the Allied Third and Seventh Armies, there now existed a continuous front line from Switzerland to the English Channel.

Flushed with his successful advance north along the Rhône and Saône Rivers, General Patch was bent on breaching the Vosges and crossing the Rhine with his Seventh Army before German resolve, reinforcements, and winter weather could stop him.

The son of a cavalry captain, Alexander McCarrell Patch Jr. was born at Fort Huachuca, Arizona, on 21 November 1898. A graduate of the U.S. Military Academy class of 1913, Patch had fought in World War I and made a name for himself by successfully prosecuting the Guadalcanal campaign in the Pacific (after the 1st Marine Division left; December 1942 to February 1943). He was given command of the Seventh Army on 1 March 1944. Outgoing and congenial, Patch had a special rapport with the troops he commanded and could often be seen rolling a cigarette from a sack of Bull Durham while chatting with his men. He believed that the essence of leadership is formed in character, and that the greatest attributes of a leader are honesty, courage of purpose, and an unselfish attitude.

First to cross the Moselle was the U.S. 36th Division. Guided by the sixty-year-old mayor of Raon-aux-Bois, a former French naval officer M. R. M. Gribelen, the 1st Battalion of the 141st "Alamo" Regiment took a forest shortcut near Éloyes, which led to a ford in the river that was unknown to the Germans. In spite of several determined German counterattacks, the 141st, as well as the 143d Regiment, had established a firm bridgehead by the afternoon of 20 September. The same was true for the 45th "Thunderbird" Division, which sent its 180th Regiment across against only light resistance. But that division paid its toll north of Épinal in a protracted contest lasting until 24 September. Once again General Haeckel turned out to be the loser.

> The police regiment at Épinal was a total failure. A counterattack, mounted in the afternoon of the 24th by one of our battalions, was unable to push the enemy back across the Moselle. General von Kirchbach, one of my subordinates, was shot in the stomach during the battle and died a few days later. It was clear to me that the next blow would be against Grandvillers and Bruyères which held the key to the les-Rouges-Eaux valley and its pass road to St.-Dié.

Haeckel's assessment was correct. The American "Thunderbird" Division was indeed heading north through Rambervillers and Baccarat in the attempt to breach the Saverne Gap between the Low and High Vosges. Similarly, in the VI Corps center, General Dahlquist's 36th Division was to rush north toward St.-Dié and the Saales Pass, considered the least demanding route through the High Vosges, and on to Strasbourg and the Rhine. The remaining VI Corps division, Gen. John W. O'Daniel's 3d, was to be inserted three weeks hence between the 45th and 36th, with its objective Rupt, Col de la Schlucht, and Colmar.

The fiasco at Épinal, with its considerable loss of men and matériel, was unfairly blamed on Generaloberst Johannes Blaskowitz. Blaskowitz, who at the beginning of the war had protested the atrocities in Poland, was never liked by Hitler. On 20 September, on the Führer's orders, he was relieved from command of Army Group "G" and succeeded by the general of Panzer Forces, Hermann Balck. Balck, the son of Gen. Wilhelm Balck, and a Hitler favorite, had spearheaded Gen. Heinz Guderian's assault beyond the Meuse in 1940, and later had led the 11th Panzer "Ghost Division" in Russia, as well as Panzer Division Grossdeutschland and the Fourth Panzer Army. His instructions from Hitler were clear—"Hold the Alsace and Lorraine at all cost!"

Balck made his assessment in a letter to Chief of Staff (WEST) Generaloberst Alfred Jodl, on 10 October.

> *In the most important sector, the human being, one gains the best perspective. The human factor is the most important in the jungle fighting of the Vosges and Lorraine Woods. If we do not receive replacements, we can calculate the time by which a front line will no longer be in existence, and, due to this lack of personnel, we will no longer have the reserves to stem the tide. I believe that the 12,000 men now plugged into our Army Group can hold. The front is now so torn and stretched that one has to wonder how these few exhausted men can master the situation.*
>
> *We urgently need mountain troops. Flatland troops are not suited to fight in the Vosges Mountains and are not properly equipped in comparison to the enemy's mountain troops.*

*While the 1st Army and 5th Panzer Army are in sorry condition, circumstances in the Nineteenth Army are pitiful in both matériel and personnel. Never before have I led such thrown-together and poorly equipped troops.*

*For us to take a stand and to dispatch the 3rd Panzer Grenadier Division to the north was only possible because of the poor and hesitant American and French leadership, and the willingness of our troops, including our thrown-together hordes, to fight. That which is accomplished here by general and soldier, both of whom often fight shoulder to shoulder on the front lines against superior and better equipped forces, is unbelievable. It is unfortunate that we cannot inform the public of this struggle because of the circumstances facing us. I am writing this to explain clearly what our situation is like, and to ask you to intervene personally to help us quickly.*

*Heil Hitler,*

*your servant, Balck*

In response to his letter, General Balck was to receive fewer than five thousand replacements and reinforcements in October—many of them elderly men and young boys. Altogether these twelve thousand combat effectives were about to take on Gen. Alexander M. Patch's Seventh Army, which outnumbered the Germans five to one (with U.S. replacements flowing at 3,500 men every ten days, and three fresh divisions due in late October).

Against these odds General Balck had to resort to a flexible defense, which for the Nineteenth Army meant ruthlessly stripping much-needed units from "quiet" sectors and throwing them into one hot spot after another—the so-called "fire brigades." To accomplish his mission, Balck and his subaltern, Wiese, had two significant allies—terrain and weather.

# 2: The Vosges

Nineteenth Army log entry:

The mountainous forests have an almost jungle-like character which swallows men. The individual fighting units usually have large sectors to defend, and contact is easily lost. Also navigating through these woods is very difficult. Communications between the various fighting units and command posts is problematic. Many of the incorrect or delayed messages can be explained by the difficulty messengers encounter in the deep ravines of the wooded thickets. By the time a messenger reaches the command post, the situation at the front usually has already changed.

The wooded heights of the Vosges Mountains gradually diminish toward the west. Two good pass-roads lead from west to east: from Bruyères to Brouvelieures-les-Rouges-Eaux to St.-Dié, and the other from Rambervillers over Brû–St.-Benoît to Raon-l'Etape. Also, higher roads are important and threatened by the enemy. The roads leading through the hilly, wooded countryside have sharp drops and are bordered on the other side by steep, wooded slopes. Traffic is only possible on the roads, and main attacks threaten along these roads. The enemy controls the streets through constant artillery harassing fire, which is directed by forward air controllers during the day. Therefore, our resupply convoys can only move by night.

The forests are pine and leafy trees with many thickets and fallen logs. Visibility is often no more than 50 meters. The enemy seems to appear everywhere. Because of this, and the tree bursts of the enemy artillery, our soldiers do not like to fight in the forests. Many of our fighting groups frequently have to set up defensive perimeters because a continuous front is impossible. Also, digging in is difficult because of the many roots, and because fortifications are only temporary.

The linking of the Third and Seventh Armies at Épinal marked the end of the pursuit phase for the Allies. The latter part of September ushered in what General Eisenhower would later call the "Battles of Attrition," a tedious slugging match along the front reaching from the Netherlands to the Swiss frontier. But after his remarkably rapid advance, General Patch was still convinced that war in Europe might end by December. On 19 September, Patch instructed Truscott to advance on the axis Vesoul–St.-Dié–Strasbourg—a fateful decision. Both General Patch and Gen. Jacob Devers commanding the newly formed Sixth Army Group did not understand how difficult the terrain was, nor could they know that winter was to arrive early that year. Two weeks later at Épinal, when Général d'Armée Jean de Lattre warned Patch about the steep, wooded mountains around Bruyères and suggested an attack toward Gérardmer and the Col de la Schlucht, General Patch good-naturedly brushed him aside. The die had already been cast (de Lattre knew the area from his days as a young lieutenant with the 12th Dragoons).

It rained again during the night of 22–23 September, as the battle of Épinal neared its peak, and the 45th and 36th Divisions encountered mounting resistance in the Vosges. By the following day the 36th Division had all three of its regiments, 141, 142, and 143, across the Moselle and was in continuous contact with German rear guards. Little headway was made in the mined woods as General Dahlquist found his men scattered over an eleven kilometer front and an exposed twenty-five kilometer right flank. To top it off, the Allies were experiencing critical shortages of gasoline and ammunition, due to production shortfalls in the United States and overextended supply lines. Scarce supplies were also being diverted to the

XV Corps (79th Infantry and French 2d Armored Divisions) which had just been attached to Seventh Army. These shortages, heavy rains, and a determined effort by the Germans to hold the new front in the Vosges virtually brought the Allied advance to a standstill.

The 36th "Texas" Division had a distinguished record. After landing first in North Africa and then Salerno, the unit had fought its way up the Liri Valley to Lungo, Hill 1205, and San Pietro. From there the "T-patchers" (their unit insignia features a T for *Texas* on an arrowhead) had battled their way to the heavily defended Rapido River, Cassino, and a freezing Italian winter, before the landing at Anzio and the battle of Velletri. Eric Sevareid, commentator at the time for CBS, had called this "the action which turned the key to the City of Rome and handed it to General Mark Clark." But then the battles at Magliano and Grosseto took their toll before the division was finally sent south to Paestum to rest and regroup. Eleven months on the Italian peninsula had changed the makeup of the division. Of eleven thousand casualties sustained, more than two thousand came from the original Texas National Guard unit that had been federalized in November 1940.

Once rested and replenished, the 36th Division participated in the 15 August landings in southern France, and from Cannes pushed north to Grenoble along the Route Napoleon. General Truscott, who had considered it politically expedient that the French take Toulon and Marseilles, had sent the "T-patchers" northeast across the foothills of the Maritime Alps, and then west to cut off the German Nineteenth Army escape route along the Rhône. Within eight days the division covered 250 miles before coming face-to-face with the retreating German divisions at Montélimar. At the place where Hannibal's army had once camped before ascending the Alps, the division fired more than seventy-five thousand artillery rounds, leaving a seven-mile path of death and destruction and taking fifteen thousand prisoners.

Commanding the 36th Division was forty-eight-year-old John Ernest Dahlquist of Minneapolis, Minnesota. Dahlquist, who like Truscott had been serving in England when America entered the war, had already proven his abilities as an exceptional planner and administrator on General Eisenhower's staff. But he was no armchair general. Brash, aggressive, and impetuous, he was the first division commander to hit the beach at Nice. Throughout the race north he had spent most of his time on the front lines of the "Texas" Division, which he had taken over from Gen. Fred Walker two months earlier. But his short temper and single-mindedness proved to be his Achilles' heel. More often than not, Dahlquist made snap decisions that came back to haunt him. His scowl, lack of humor, rudeness, and tendency to brood made him an unattractive figure, generally disliked by his own officers and men. Entering the Vosges was a homecoming of sorts for the general who, some twenty years earlier, had "kept watch on the Rhine" as a member of the American army of occupation, and, for a spell, served as the appointed mayor of Mayen, near Koblenz. But now shortages of fuel, ammunition, and men forced the 36th to pause.

On Sunday, 24 September, General Dahlquist wrote into the small book he carried in his breast pocket:

> Visited all three regiments. 142d and 143d very tired, wet, and discouraged. Practically no progress being made. In afternoon, began receiving several small attacks on overextended right flank. Several roadblocks broken through. Finally got Corps to release all troops in Remiremont. Turned them over to 142d."

> Monday, September 25:

> Rumored enemy attack did not take place. 143d improved its position. 142d drew back during the night to a more defensible position. Enemy shelled CP this morning. . . . Troops are very wet and disconsolate and morale seems to have gotten very low. . . . 142d still hanging on for grim death.

Both entries foreshadowed what awaited the exhausted regiments—a tedious and costly slugging match between Americans and Germans determined not to give any more ground. The 142d Regiment alone, "hanging on for grim death," had sustained more than nine hundred casualties in nine days. Most of its companies were down to fifty or sixty men, and spirits were low. The type of tactics the Americans were encountering were not unlike those experienced a generation later in Vietnam, with ill-defined front lines in heavily wooded, mountainous terrain where small units battled each other at point-blank range. From lessons learned in Russia, the Wehrmacht kept the initial fighting line only sparsely manned, with the mass of troops two or three kilometers farther back. This defense in depth was intended to waste the attacker's energy and ammunition on minor targets, while allowing German commanders more flexibility to meet the main attack. Numerically inferior, the Germans placed an ever-increasing reliance on mines, mortars, and machine-gun battalions (twenty battalions for Army Group G) to impede Allied movements. With mass-produced, rapid-fire MG42's and mortars, one German squad could hold back a platoon of Americans, but in the long run, shortages of ammunition and trained infantry eroded this advantage.

One of General Dahlquist's junior officers was a twenty-seven-year-old lieutenant from Jersey City named Martin Higgins, who by month's end would briefly stand in the limelight of history as the nominal commander of the so-called "Lost Battalion." Two of Higgins's predecessors, Captain McNeil and Lieutenant Daugherty, had been killed in action, and the reluctant company commander who followed them had just been relieved. In the middle of the battle for St. Amé, First Lieutenant Higgins found himself in charge of Company A, 1st Battalion, 141st "Alamo" Regiment.

According to Higgins, "I knew that my platoon would follow me, but I didn't know about the rest of the boys. I just went ahead and they followed. My men outflanked the Jerries, and we killed quite a few. The rest took off. But we were exhausted by then, and the weather was miserable. I figured if I was going to get killed, I'd rather get it sooner than later. But I couldn't tell anybody, not even in my letters to my young bride, Marge. I had to keep my chin up, and encouraged my men to do the same."

Mindful of his soldiers' pitiful condition, General Dahlquist asked his superior, Truscott, for permission to call off the attack on Herpelmont set for 4 October, and requested that the troops be used to relieve his battered 142d Regiment. But his request was denied. As ordered, the "Alamo" Regiment attacked Herpelmont, just four kilometers south of Bruyères. But in the days to follow, German

infantry, tank destroyers, and self-propelled guns wreaked havoc with
Col. Clyde Steele's men. Unable to breach the German defenses, Maj.
Roswell Dougherty, intelligence officer for the regiment, requested
FFI teams with radios to report on German movements and gun em-
placements.

Their reports eventually confirmed that German infantry and artillery were well entrenched at Champ le Duc and Bruyères. During
the month ahead, FFI teams were to prove extremely valuable to the
Americans, pinpointing more than fifty German artillery positions
and the transport of two mountain battalions toward les-Rouges-
Eaux.

The first ten days of October saw the American 36th Division tan-
gled up in the Bois de Chamont and Bois de Lacet between Herpelmont and Jussarupt, harassed by S-mines, booby traps, mortars,
machine guns, and artillery ranging to 170mm guns, and counterattacked again and again by German infantry and armor. Every company in the "Alamo" Regiment took a beating, mostly from tree bursts
showering the men with searing hot steel and equally lethal wood
splinters.

As one observer put it:

> These high velocity 88s, bursting in the treetops, added to
> the hail of shell fragments descending upon us. The night only
> served to illuminate the reddish glare of the shell bursts and to
> magnify their explosive crash against the trees, causing them
> to appear closer to us than they usually were. The darkness of
> the evening filled the forest with a dreaded stillness which was
> irregularly broken by those weird and nerve-wracking noises.
> The pine trees, swaying in the wind, whistled eerily, much as ar-
> tillery shells skimming overhead. Branches fell from the aging
> trees and knocked against tree trunks and limbs on their way
> to the ground, much as spent shell fragments would batter
> against the trees around us. Twigs would snap and leaves would
> rustle on the ground, suggesting the tread of approaching feet,
> but more often than not it would be merely the wind playing
> with the forest. The night seemed to delight in playing tricks
> on us. Sometimes the trees, silhouetted against the skyline,

would dress up like humans with log bayonetlike limbs ready to strike us down. Every twig seemed to conceal a Schuh mine, every bush a sniper. Nighttime seemed an infinity."

The attacking infantry suffered. Company F, for example, took so many casualties that it was merged with Company E. (Company E, originally a National Guard unit from El Paso, Texas, had been virtually wiped out while crossing the Rapido River in Italy.)

When Generals Marshall, Devers, Hardy, and Truscott came to visit the division on 10 October, Marshall praised the men of Company L, 142d Regiment, who had gone through hell since crossing the Moselle. Marshall understood that the Texans had sustained more casualties than any other division in VI Corps and promised Dahlquist first pick of the replacements and reinforcements already on their way from Marseilles.

Anticipating renewed American attacks, General Haeckel's 16th Volks-Grenadier Division evacuated Brouvelieures that day to block the entrance to the les-Rouges-Eaux valley. The town of Bruyères and points south were held by its southern neighbor, the 716th Volks-Grenadier Division, with the boundary line between them stretching from Bruyères toward Belmont and points east (also the boundary between General Werner Gilsa's LXXXIX Corps and General Helmut Thumm's LXIV Corps of the Nineteenth Army).

Commanding the 716th Division was a capable artillery officer, fifty-two-year-old Generalleutnant Wilhelm Richter, from Hirschberg, Silesia. The son of the mayor of Frankfurt on the Oder had learned his craft as a battery commander in World War I and, some twenty years later, mastered it in Poland and Russia. But the division he now commanded was only a shadow of the 716th Infantry Division mauled during the Normandy invasion. On that longest day, 6 June, only one of his four German and two Russian battalions had escaped the horrific British airborne and seaborne onslaught at Caen. Also, three quarters of his artillery and antitank weapons were destroyed, along with sixty-five percent of his antiaircraft contingents.

When Oberst Hermann von Oppeln-Bronikowski led his Panzer Regiment 22 against the British, he had encountered Richter "visibly shaken, telling me, 'My troops are lost. My whole division is finished.'" Bronikowski asked what he could do, pointing to his map and asking for the general's positions. But Richter just shook his head. "I don't know. I just don't know."

One of Oppeln-Bronikowski's men was nineteen-year-old Werner Kortenhaus, a radio operator in the 4th Tank Company. "We were alerted early that morning, but didn't attack until afternoon. By then there wasn't much left of General Richter's division, which had been subjected to terrific air and ship bombardment."

A few years earlier, Kortenhaus's father, then Richter's operations officer, had been instrumental in organizing the coastal division. On 6 June, the son witnessed its destruction. At the end of June, from a core of 350 survivors—mostly staff officers and engineers—the division was rebuilt near Perpignan in southern France. When the Allies landed on the Riviera, Richter had only five thousand men and was still woefully short on artillery pieces and communications gear. On 18 August, Richter's division began its retreat on the west side of the Rhône, avoiding major engagements and suffering only moderate losses due to air attacks. But on 3 September, Richter's division was committed at Chalon to hold open a gap for the retreating columns, including General Haeckel's 16th Volks-Grenadier Division—an effort that came too late.

Upon reaching the Moselle, the 716th received new artillery pieces for its seven batteries, horses, and communications equipment to defend the Vosges winter line (Vogesen Kammstellugen). Still, by early October, Richter's division, like most others along the Nineteenth Army front, had the strength of a reinforced regiment, barely 2,000 men with replacements barely making up his losses.

Meanwhile his adversary, General Dahlquist, received the reinforcements he so desperately needed to breach the defenses at Bruyères.

Thursday, 12 October, was a partly cloudy day, with a cold wind blowing from the east, as 3,313 men and 193 officers of the 100th Battalion/442d Regimental Combat Team left Charmois-devant-Bruyères for their assembly area to the east. They were in high spirits, laughing and waving at T3g. Tom Gerzen of the 163d Signal Photo Company, who had been assigned to film their progress. Burdened with gear and weapons, one company after another loaded onto deuce-and-a-halfs that would take them to the woods west of

Bruyères. From there they moved in double file to their assigned bivouac areas, pitched their tents, and did what soldiers do—they waited. Some of the boys from Hawaii played their ukuleles and sang songs from the islands; others played poker, cleaned weapons, stood in chow lines, and wrote home. For most of the mainland boys, "home" was one of ten relocation centers set up after the attack on Pearl Harbor to confine some 120,000 "enemy aliens"—residents and American citizens of Japanese descent.

The 442d Regimental Combat Team, distinguished by the red, white, and blue shoulder patch showing the Statue of Liberty's extended arm holding the torch, was made up almost exclusively of Japanese Americans and led primarily by Caucasian officers. The Japanese Americans had already proven their mettle in North Africa and Italy (initially as the 100th Battalion). At Anzio, Cassino, and Hill 140 they had fought with distinction, as attested by the 676 replacements needed to fill the ranks before the unit was shipped to France.

Unlike mainland Japanese Americans, most in Hawaii had escaped internment. To incarcerate them would have been logistically difficult and would have severely impacted the operation of docks and other military and civilian facilities.

"When we got to Camp Shelby, we didn't know that many of the mainland boys had volunteered from inside internment camps," said Daniel Inouye, then a platoon sergeant in Company E. "We Hawaiians, 'Buddhaheads,' who had darker skin and spoke pidgin—while they often spoke better English and Japanese—at times thought they were looking down on us. One thing led to another, and there was a lot of conflict between these two groups. We were the ones beating up the mainlanders, and that's how the name 'Kotonk' came up—every time a guy hits the ground he goes 'kotonk!'

"Finally somebody had the bright idea to send some of us noncoms to visit the Rohwer internment camp in Arkansas. We were prepared for a fine weekend of 'Kotonk' girls and food, but, when we saw the barbed wire and machine-gun towers, we realized for the first time what our brothers had gone through and looked at them with respect and pride."

Another of the "Hawaii boys," Sgt. Peter Kawahara, had been a young draftee on Oahu when Japanese fighters strafed Schofield Barracks on 7 December 1941. Like most American soldiers of

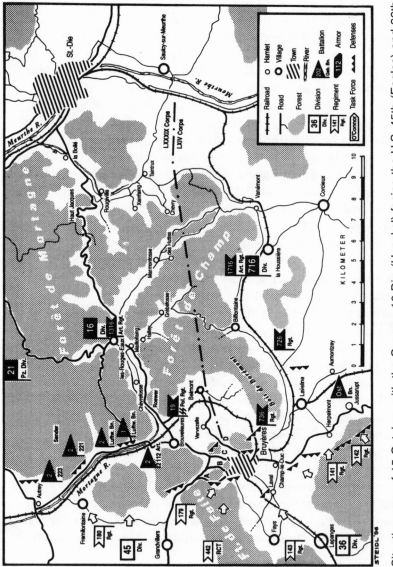

Situation map of 15 October, with the German 16 Div. (Haeckel) facing the U.S. 45th (Eagles) and 36th (Dahlquist) Divisions. The German 716 Div. (Richter) is holding Bruyères and points south.

Japanese descent, he was reassigned to the mainland and given menial tasks. But when he heard that a unit was being formed of Japanese Americans, he joined up. As a member of the 100th Battalion he had already fought in North Africa and Italy before being shipped to France. On his way to Bruyères he wrote to his brother Bill.

> *They transferred some of us old-timers from the 100th to this rookie 442d outfit. Somehow I can't seem to get the idea that the 100th is part of the 442d because we have done something unique, and these new boys are mainly riding the gravy train. . . .*
>
> *Italy and Africa are memories now. . . . Man is a pretty infinitesimal object against the tremendous forces of nature and the world about him. Certainly, in my case, I have been greatly affected by the great forces of love, hate, prejudice, death, life, destruction, reconstruction, treachery, bravery, comradeship, kindness, and by the unseen powers of God. I guess most people really get to appreciate life when death lurks around close. But that is not good talk.*

The 100th Battalion was permitted to retain its distinctive unit designation when integrated into the 442d Regimental Combat Team, in effect serving as its 1st Battalion. What Peter Kawahara didn't know was that the combat team was about to face its most difficult test, one that would dramatically balance the fighting record between Kotonks and Buddhaheads.

One of the mainland boys, or Kotonks, was Pfc. Joe Hattori, A Battery, 522d Field Artillery Battalion. Joe had lost his father when he was only five. On the way to a Fourth of July picnic in Long Beach, their family car had crashed head-on into another, killing the father of eight. As was the case with most Japanese immigrants, or Issei, Joe's father had come to the United States alone, looking for work, and sent for his family once he had established himself. His wife, Kien, arrived in 1924, leaving their youngest boy behind with relatives in Japan. The Hattoris worked side by side in their small *senbe* (rice cracker) shop in downtown Los Angeles, when Osamaru "Joe" came into the world—their first child born in the United States—a Nisei, followed two years later by his only sister, Yaeko (the eighth one). The children grew up in Boyle Heights, a part of Los Angeles that at the time was home to a large number of Japanese, Italian, and Jewish immigrants, now supported by their brothers and whatever handicrafts their widowed mother could sell.

Joe was a junior at Roosevelt High, a football player with hopes of going to college, when Pearl Harbor forever changed his life. In the spring of 1942, President Franklin D. Roosevelt signed Executive Order 9066, the deportation decree that sent residents and U.S. citizens of Japanese descent to ten "relocation camps" throughout the country. Like other Issei and Nisei, Joe and his family were allowed to take only a few personal belongings and were removed from their home to the horse stables at the Pomona Fairgrounds. Then, by summer's end, all were shipped to some unknown destination—for the Hattori family a desolate region of Wyoming, called Heart Mountain. What awaited them was a camp made of flimsy tar-paper barracks, surrounded by barbed-wire fences and guard towers, icy cold winters, hot and dusty summers, and the monotony, uncertainty, and fear that comes with prison life.

Joe was only seventeen when he heard that a Japanese American unit was being formed, and like many other Nisei was determined to prove his loyalty to his country. *"Hattori no namae wo haji kake na!"*— "Don't disgrace the Hattori family name and reputation," his older brother, Fred, told him as he cosigned the enlistment papers. In Japanese culture, to bring dishonor to the family is simply unacceptable, and in the case of the Japanese American regiment, it was a powerful force to do well, to not let one's buddies down.

After his training, when Joe was about to be shipped overseas, his sister Yaeko handed him a *senin-bari*—a sash embroidered with one thousand stitches. Each cross-stitch of red yarn had been carefully made by a different woman at the camp, except for those born in the Year of the Tiger—who, like Yaeko, could stitch the number corresponding to her own age: sixteen. Now in France, Joe wore the sash under his uniform, a talisman to protect him in the battle ahead. "A bad battle," Joe would recall half a century later.

# 3: The Battle for Bruyères

Nestled in a picturesque valley, on the western edge of the Vosges, lies the small town of Bruyères. Roman artifacts found nearby date its origins to the fourth century A.D. Two centuries later, Ambron, son of Clodion-the-Long-Haired, built a castle on one of four surrounding hills. In the fall of 1944 a new chapter was to be added to the history of Bruyères, one written in the blood of Americans, Frenchmen, and Germans locked in fierce combat on those four hills and the mountains stretching east toward St.-Dié.

With the liberation of Paris on 25 August, and the drive up the Rhône Valley by the U.S. Seventh and French First Armies, the citizens of Bruyères were praying for a speedy and safe delivery from their German occupiers. But their hopes dimmed when the fall of Lyon brought French SS, militia, and SIPO-SD (Reich security police) to their small town. Among the uninvited guests were French collaborators Marcel Bergier, Charles Marandin, and Klaus Barbie, still limping from his foot injury. Years after the war, Barbie, the "Butcher of Lyon," would be implicated in the deaths of hundreds of maquis, the torture and death of underground leader Jean Moulin, and the deportation of French Jews to the Auschwitz death camp.

In early September, Reichsführer SS Heinrich Himmler came to inspect the Vosges fortifications, conferring with his subcommanders at the Villa Chevalier at Lake Gérardmer. Himmler had just assumed command of Army Group "Oberrhein," which was to hold the Colmar bridgehead (Colmar Pocket) against American and French forces until February 1945.

In early October, all Frenchmen born in 1922 were pressed into forced labor service, and civilians were evacuated from the western and southern suburbs, while roving tanks and self-propelled artillery drew fire. Soon the Bruyères hospital was filled with casualties. One of them, fifteen-year-old Serge Carlesso, had been picking potatoes when an American shell flung him into the air. A German soldier, who had come to the aid of his comrades, noticed the blood-covered boy in the field. According to Carlesso, "He took me to an army aid station, and from there I was brought to the hospital. Many Germans were wounded, but the surgeon operated on me first because my wounds were so serious. When the Americans came, they found me lying in the cellar, and evacuated me in an ambulance."

As rumors persisted that Bruyères would fall within days, the resistance stepped up its sabotage effort. But each act was met with swift German reprisals. Farms were burned, hostages taken, and more civilians forced into labor gangs to construct defenses. Most valuable to the Allies was the continuous flow of intelligence provided by French resistance fighters. Max-Henri Moulin (alias Joe II), Albert Mercier, Gaston Perrin, Raymond Georges, André Ferry, André Villaume, Father Thiry, and others risked their lives gathering information about German troop movements and fortifications and relaying it to the Allies. In one instance Mlle. Odette Genuée and a friend stuck pillows under their overcoats to suggest they were pregnant. Instead, they were carrying maps and information between FFI commanders and Allied intelligence and OSS (Capt. Justin Greene for this sector and Col. Ed Gamble for the Seventh Army).

On 29 September, anticipating the American attack, the Germans blew up the railroad tunnel on the Bruyères-Épinal line and set the station on fire. That same day American artillery shells began to fall on the town and surrounding hills—the first of thirty thousand.

VI Corps Field Order No. 4, to be carried out commencing 15 October:
The 36th Inf. Div. will lead the attack with Bruyères as its objective. The 45th Inf. Div. will be on the left flank and take the high ground north of Bruyères.

In the gray hours of Sunday morning, 15 October, the town crier was admonishing the citizens of Bruyères to observe curfew when American artillery shells suddenly rained down. As the townspeople took to their cellars, one building after another was hit, including the hospital and the watchtower, which served as a German observation post. Meanwhile, in the forests to the west, two American divisions advanced while a third was secretly moved up to assist in the drive toward St.-Dié. Spearheading the drive was the 442d Regimental Combat Team, led by fifty-year-old Charles Wilbur Pence of Hoopeston, Illinois. Pence had fought in World War I as a lieutenant with the 39th Infantry Regiment and, after accepting a Regular Army commission, had served a tour of duty in China. In February 1943 he had assumed command of the newly formed Nisei regiment at Camp Shelby, Mississippi. Pence was a strict disciplinarian who gave each newly assigned officer a choice—to serve without prejudice toward the Japanese Americans or ship out.

At 0800 hours, Lt. Col. Gordon Singles's 100th Battalion and Lt. Col. James Hanley's 2d Battalion crossed the line of departure. Ahead of them, like forbidding sentries rising a thousand feet from the valley floor, stood four strategic hills designated A, B, C, and D. The 100th Battalion's objective on the far left was Hill A (Buemont), while Hill B (le Château) half a mile south was the goal of the 2d Battalion. The first soldiers encountered by the Nisei were Russians in German uniforms, who offered little resistance.

The situation was far more difficult for the men of the 100th Battalion, up against SS Polizei Regiment 19. The police regiment's forward observers spotted the Americans, who at once became targets for German artillery bursting in the tall pines, showering the Nisei with searing-hot steel fragments and lethal wood splinters. First Lieutenant Sam Sakamoto's Company A, in reserve, was just digging in when a mortar barrage killed one and wounded nineteen. Ahead, the attack companies encountered minefields, roadblocks, and withering machine-gun fire from the police regiment, Grenadier Regiments 736 and 223, and Fortress Machine Gun Battalion 49. Originally intended as garrisons for the West Wall, five of these machine-gun battalions were committed against the Seventh Army—

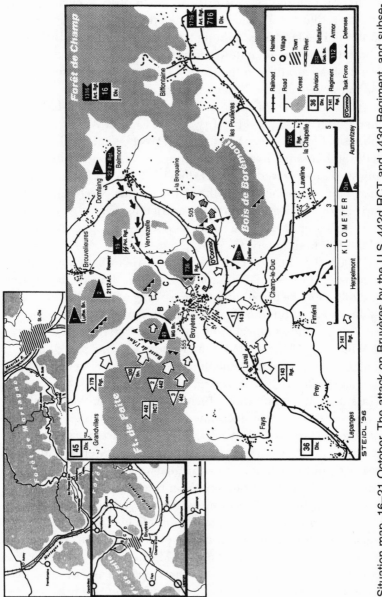

Situation map, 16–21 October. The attack on Bruyères by the U.S. 442d RCT and 143d Regiment, and subsequent breach of the German lines (Task Force O'Connor) south of Belmont.

clear evidence that the Germans intended to hold the Vosges before falling back on the Siegfried Line.

By mid-morning Capt. Sakae Takahashi's Company B and Capt. Joseph Hill's Company F were embroiled in heavy firefights with German infantry on a ridge line preceding Hill A. The Germans had constructed dugouts, carefully concealed with brush and mutually supported by machine guns and snipers. During the fight Lt. Yeiki Kobashigawa, leading the first platoon of Company B, crawled up to a German machine-gun position, pulled back the overhead logs, and killed its crew. But this was to be one of few successes. Even though Companies C and E were committed, the regiment gained barely five hundred yards by the end of the day.

With the American drive blunted at Bruyères, two kilometers south, the 143d Regiment took Laval and then turned north toward Champ le Duc.

Reports Maj. Robert Lee O'Brien, adjutant of the 143d:

As scheduled, the attack on Bruyères and surrounding areas began at 0800 hours 15 October 1944, with a fifteen-minute hammering by attached artillery units. Jumping off from the north-south road leading through Fays, the 1st and 3d Battalions advanced abreast, the 1st Battalion contacting the 442d RCT on the left. At the outset, Company A faced little opposition, but as they climbed Hill 479 west, they received direct artillery fire from Laval and engaged enemy infantry in a firefight. The 3d Battalion (minus Company L in regimental reserve) moved around the southwest shoulder of the hill, meeting small arms and moderate artillery fire. While mortars poured a smoke curtain, Companies I and K fought into the center of Laval. At this point, Company A, pushing to cut the Bruyères-Laval road, engaged in a fierce firefight astride the railroad tracks, receiving 20mm fire from a flak wagon.

Cracking the opposition, the 1st Battalion on the left took sixty prisoners, including the commanding officer. One of the POWs gave a complete sketch of the Bruyères defenses.

Throughout the day the Germans sought to break the 143d's hold on the approaches to Bruyères by heavy concentrations of mortar and artillery fire. Our artillery retaliated, flattening those parts of Bruyères that the Germans sought to defend. Eight-inch howitzer fire was trained on the railroad tunnel which had been shelter for the enemy.

During the night of 15–16 October, patrols proceeded to Champ le Duc and Bruyères. Second Lieutenant O'Dean T. Cox of Waco, Texas, a Company K platoon leader, led his patrol into Champ le Duc and engaged thirty enemy in a small-arms fight. After killing or wounding four Germans this patrol knocked out a machine-gun position with hand grenades. Scouting to within 200 yards of the outskirts of Bruyères, a Company I patrol clashed with a German eight-man patrol, scattering the enemy with M-1 and .50-caliber fire.

Although receiving fire from the woods, the 3d Battalion by early morning, 16 October, had completely cleared all points of resistance in Laval, taking fourteen prisoners, knocking out an antitank gun, and preparing to resume the attack. The 1st Battalion was occupied by clearing well-fortified houses on the Bruyères-Laval road and along the railroad tracks.

That same day, the 141st Regiment reached Herpelmont and the 142d Champdray.

With the 442d Regimental Combat Team hung up on the German defenses at Bruyères, General Dahlquist shifted most of his division artillery and tanks to them.

A hard rain was falling as the 100th and 2d Battalions jumped off again at daybreak, 16 October. As Companies E and F fought their way toward Hill B, Capt. Pershing Nakada's engineers tried desperately to clear the roadblocks and profusion of mines ahead. But when the two attack companies reached open ground, they were again pinned down by murderous fire from Hill 555 and Hill B.

The same was true for the 100th Battalion on the left. After Companies A and C cleared their sector around Hill 555, they were stopped short at the open valley known as Basse de l'Âne (Donkey Flats). It was to be an all-day effort, through cold rain and relentless German pounding, before Company F finally took Hill 555 with its commanding view of Bruyères and surrounding the hills. But as an evening mist began to cloak Donkey Flats, the Germans launched a counterattack. Supported by artillery, mortars, self-propelled guns, and a platoon of tanks, the full force of the attack hit Company E. American artillery and mortars saved the day, but from their slit trenches Capt. Tom Atkins's men fought on into the eerie half-light before the German grenadiers finally pulled back.

According to General Haeckel, "Again and again we had to use alarm units made up of rear echelon contingents to fill the gaps. And almost daily, local breakthroughs had to be closed with counterattacks. Forces available for this task were insufficient. The wooded ridge, which extends from the northwest of Bruyères to Grandvillers, defended by SS Polizei Regiment 19, was heavily contested."

In February 1944 after fighting Yugoslav partisans in Upper Kraina, SS Polizei Regiment 19 had been subordinated to the Befehlshaber der Ordnungspolizei, Paris, and sent to southern France. Its ranks filled with more than six hundred new replacements, the regiment was sent to eradicate the maquis and FFI, or "bandits," as the Germans preferred to call them, in the Lyon region.

Although they bore the SS designation, police regiments were not part of the Waffen SS. They were part of the Ordnungspolizei, whose mission it was to keep order in the occupied territories, safeguard strategic installations, and during the latter part of the war stem the groundswell of partisan activity. It was not until February 1943 that the police regiments were permitted to use the SS designation "in recognition of their especially brave and successful engagements." By then many of the police regiments and battalions had fought alongside the Wehrmacht and Waffen SS, and bled like them.

In his insatiable quest for power, Reichsführer SS Heinrich Himmler had wrested all police powers from the German ministry of the interior—first, over Göring's protest, the Gestapo, and in 1936, over Reichsminister Frick's vehement objections, the remaining law enforcement branches, making him the chief over all German police forces. Himmler also saw to it that police recruits met the same stringent physical (including height—170cm) requirements as the Waffen SS, and on more than one occasion had police officials and complete units, along with their equipment, transferred to the SS.

SS Polizei Regiment 19, established in 1942 in Vienna, was fully motorized and organized into three battalions, a headquarters company, and an antitank company with a total strength of two thousand men. The antitank company received one additional platoon in June 1944. But the regiment's retreat up the Rhône, and the bloody engagements at Langres and Épinal, had taken their toll.

German commanders had standing orders, issued by Hitler, to meet any breakthrough with an immediate counterattack or be subject to court-martial. Hitler's threatening orders, which had become standard fare ever since Stalingrad, were taken seriously by all commands. How many courts martial, reductions in rank, transfers to *Bewährungseinheiten* (punishment battalions), executions, or other forms of punishment resulting from this can only be estimated.

Also several *Kampfgruppen* had been dispatched to the Bruyères sector to support the German 716th and 16th Infantry Divisions. Panzer radio operator Werner Kortenhaus wrote:

At the beginning of October, the center of fighting for the 21st Panzer Division shifted from the right wing to the left wing where its neighbor, the 16th Infantry Division was located. The region of Rambervillers and farther south was under heavy pressure by the slowly advancing Americans in the difficult, forested region.

Strong pressure of the 3rd, 36th, and 45th U.S. Infantry Divisions against the weak positions of its left neighbor (German 16th Division) in the direction of St.-Dié, forced the army to continuously seek new remedies.

The loss of Rambervillers on 30 September forced the Army Corps to attach ten companies from the 21st Panzer Division to its left neighbor in the Mortagne sector. These companies from Panzer Regiment 22 with fifteen tanks, and Panzer Grenadier Regiment 192, often no stronger than fifty to sixty men, were almost continuously in heavy combat during ever cooler, rainy weather. The nights were very cold, and the soldiers hadn't had a roof over their heads for weeks on end, and no opportunity for the most basic personal hygiene. Nevertheless, the division had surprisingly few losses due to illness. Under these circumstances the formation of reserves was nearly impossible. Emergencies forced commanders to improvise. Most found their reserves among the older men and boys of the

Volkssturm or the support services. Organized as 'Alarm Companies,' they were quickly brought into action.

In the "Alamo" Regiment, Lieutenant Higgins's Company A, and Company B commanded by his friend Harry Huberth, and three tanks made little progress on their way toward Jussarupt—met by violent artillery and machine-gun fire as they attacked late that afternoon. The story was little different for the French First Army near Moselotte. In addition to extensive minefields and guns, the North African troops fell victim to the weather. The 3d Algerian and French 1st Armored Divisions took such high losses that Gen. Jean de Lattre called a halt to the attack and had his forces go on the defensive.

It was still raining at dawn, 17 October, as a frustrated General Dahlquist urged his 143d Regiment to take Champ le Duc, defended by Grenadier Regiment 736. But, once again, the Americans were welcomed by an artillery barrage—fifty well-placed rounds and concentrated machine-gun fire from the stone houses. Undaunted, the engineers went ahead to clear the mines, allowing Companies I and K to fight their way house to house into town.

At the same time German infantry resumed their counterattacks against the Japanese American 100th and 2d Battalions. For more than an hour Nisei and SS were locked in a bitter struggle at close quarters. Finally, the SS police pulled back, regrouped, and attacked again with tanks in the lead. Unable to maneuver their own antitank guns through the forest, Colonel Hanley's men formed six bazooka teams, which finally broke the German assault.

The second German counterattack hit the 100th Battalion just as its forward platoons were jumping off. The SS succeeded in breaching the American positions, and for some time both sides fought small unit actions at point-blank range. The Hawaiians eventually turned the tide and, with the Germans off balance, resumed their offensive. But as soon as the lead elements reached Donkey Flats they fell victim to devastating enfilade fire from atop Hills A and B, and the stone houses below.

The Otake brothers, Masayuki and Masanao, from the island of Maui, were serving together in the regiment—Masayuki was a sergeant in the 2d Battalion near Hill B; his older brother, a lieutenant in the 100th. Lieutenant Masanao Otake, one of the original members of the 100th Battalion, had received his battlefield commission at Anzio. On that cold and rainy Tuesday, as his kinsmen tried to break through the SS machine guns and antitank guns, Lieutenant Otake's platoon stood in reserve. General Dahlquist appeared on the scene and demanded to know why the men were not participating in the attack. Dissatisfied with Otake's answer, the general ordered the lieutenant to send a reconnaissance patrol to the houses at the base of Hill A. Otake decided to lead the small group himself, and veiled in fog, reached the nearest house. As an experienced soldier he knew the likelihood of an ambush and decided to go ahead on his own. He was spotted, and in the ensuing melee fought until a burst from a machine pistol cut him down. Otake, a formidable football and baseball player (Aloha Team), was twenty-four. For his gallantry he received the Distinguished Service Cross posthumously.

The rains did not let up on the fourth day of battle, 18 October, when the heaviest barrage to date was unleashed on Hills A and B and Bruyères itself: five battalions of artillery—sixty guns firing at maximum capacity, plus forty 37mm antiaircraft guns blasting from Fiménil and Beauménil. The 442d RCT attacked with eight companies abreast—Lt. Col. Alfred Pursall's 3d Battalion making a wild dash across Donkey Flats, now blanketed by a heavy smoke screen.

On the regiment's left flank the men of the 100th Battalion silenced the machine guns inside the farmhouses where Lieutenant Otake had been killed, and just before noon Companies A and B scaled their objective, while Company C pressed the attack on the battalion's right. Close combat continued until mid-afternoon when Hill A was secure. Some seventy Germans were taken prisoner.

In the regiment's center, Companies F and G were less fortunate. At noon they were still pinned down between their line of departure and Hill B. Not until their 60mm mortars knocked out the key machine gun in the German defenses did the 2d Battalion gain a toehold at the foot of le Château. When Capt. Joseph Byrne's Company I managed to circumvent Hill B, fighting its way up the steep southern slopes, the defenders shifted some of their forces away from the

2d Battalion's frontal assault to plug the gap. But after a six-and-a-half-hour fight, Hill B was taken.

Meanwhile, the men of Company L were fighting house to house at the northern approaches of Bruyères. Monique Carlesso was only eight years old when Nisei soldiers entered her parents' home. After searching for "Boche," one of them gave her a chocolate bar while another shared his leftover bread. "It was soft, just like cake, and tasted heavenly."

At noon the 143d Regiment also breached the German defenses at the southern part of town. Captain Thomas Brejcha's Company A was mopping up the industrial sector when his riflemen were caught in a hail of mortar fire. "The savagery with which the Germans fought was illustrated by the fact that they would not permit our aid men to administer first aid or evacuate the exposed wounded. By 1600 hours, the 1st Battalion had swung away from the cheese factory where it had been receiving fire and had moved under the protection of a ridge to reach the road junction in the heart of Bruyères," Brejcha said.

By late afternoon Company C of the 143d Regiment met the Nisei of Company L. Bruyères had fallen. Only on Stanislas Square did a group of Germans hold out until midnight. The last big explosions came when Capt. Pershing Nakada's 232d Engineer Company blew up the concrete barricades around the town hall.

The 442d captured 134 Wehrmacht members, among them Poles, Yugoslavs, Somalis—and East Indians of the Regiment "Freies Indien," who had plundered their way across western France. Most prisoners were part of 2d and 3d Company, Füsilier Bataillon 198 (Hauptmann Schreiner), Grenadier Regiment 736, and Panzer Grenadier Regiment 192, sent from the 21st Panzer Division to the north, as well as men from various battle groups hastily formed to stem the American tide.

Stunned by days of shelling and hunger, some four thousand French civilians emerged from their basements to greet their liberators. Eduard Canonica was surprised when he saw "the short Asian men who showed such extraordinary kindness to the towns-people." The French offered their gratitude, some sharing the little food and wine they had saved for the occasion, while others invited the liberators into their homes. The following day, not far from the schoolhouse that Colonel Singles used as his temporary headquarters, citizens celebrated in another way. They shaved the heads of four prostitutes who had consorted with Germans and paraded them down the street as onlookers jeered and spat on them.

With Bruyères in American hands, the next objective was Hill D (Avison) east of town. With the 100th Battalion in reserve on Hill A, Companies E and G attacked at 1000 hours, 19 October. The Germans continued to pour artillery onto the town, wreaking havoc among civilians and the attacking Nisei. One shell exploded near Sgt. Edward Okazaki, wounding him and four other men. In spite of his injuries and the continuing shell fire, he dragged each of his men to the safety of a nearby building and administered first aid. When an aid man arrived, he refused medical attention until each of his men had been cared for. Only then was it discovered that he had been hit once in his arm and twice in his left leg. For this, Sergeant Okazaki from the island of Maui received the Silver Star.

Despite German opposition, Avison fell at noon, and before sundown the 2d and 3d Battalions reached the railroad embankment on the edge of the Bois de Borèmont. Commanding the 2d Battalion was Lt. Col. James Hanley from North Dakota. Hanley's father, while commanding a battalion under General "Black Jack" Pershing, had taken eight-year-old James along on the so-called "punitive expedition" to find Pancho Villa. Like his father, James pursued a career in law and joined the army reserves. And like his father in World War I, he was destined to fight near St.-Dié. As Hanley describes it:

> The railroad embankment was perhaps ten feet high. The Germans had it fully covered with automatic fire. Late in the afternoon the battalion staff and I followed the leading companies. Not knowing precisely where the line was, we moved north along the road, away from Bruyères, and within a hundred yards found trees on each side of the road with dynamite strapped to their trunks.
>
> We came to a German command car which had hit one of their own mines, destroying the car and killing its three occupants. I was reminded of Hamlet: 'For 'tis the sport to have the engineer hoist with his own petard.'

By nightfall Companies E and G had dug in west of the railroad embankment; Companies I and K, between the Belmont road and a minefield in back of them. During the night General Richter's 1716th Artillery Regiment fired on Bruyères. By now sustained shelling from both sides had damaged three quarters of all buildings, including the hospital, and twenty-three houses burned completely to the ground.

Two German fighters strafed the 36th Division during the night of 19–20 October. Captain Chris Keegan was operations officer for the 2d Battalion when an urgent message came in. One of his supply parties was pinned down at a wooded ridge near La Roche. Keegan said, "I picked troopers from 3d platoon of Company H and the A & P platoon of Headquarters Company, about thirty men led by Lieutenant Farnum. My instructions were to clear the trails leading to Companies E and G, while both companies attacked west along the Belmont road with their reserve platoons."

The rain had stopped when Lieutenant Farnum's group left at daybreak. A few minutes later they were ambushed by German infantry and a half-track. In the firefight SSgt. Robert H. Kuroda led his men against one of the German machine guns, killing its crew and three riflemen, while Lieutenant Farnum ran along the top of the ridge firing his tommy gun. A bullet through the throat killed him instantly.

When he saw that Farnum was dead, Kuroda picked up the lieutenant's gun and knocked out another machine-gun emplacement with hand grenades. But as he turned to fire on the supporting rifleman he, too, was killed by a sniper.

Colonel Hanley said, "Both Farnum and Kuroda received awards for their heroism—a Silver Star for Farnum, and a Distinguished Service Cross for Kuroda from Hawaii. The Battalion had recommended a DSC for Farnum, but the recommendation apparently did not have the right adjectives. The award of combat medals too often depends upon the writer of the recommendation."

For the first time in five days the sun rose against a blue sky, bolstered by billowing white clouds. Less than a mile from where Farnum and Kuroda lay dead, Captains Bill Aull and Tom Atkins tried to get their men across the railroad tracks. But each rifleman who had reached the top of the embankment was hit by machine-gun fire.

For the time being all they could do was wait—wait for artillery, air support, or darkness to provide sufficient cover for another attempt.

Staff Sergeant Yoshimi Fujiwara's squad was already embroiled in a firefight, when two panzers, supported by artillery and infantry, probed the 2d Battalion's left flank. Fujiwara climbed a small knoll and fired several antitank grenades—without effect on the heavy German armor. He got hold of a bazooka, fired again, and scored a partial hit on the lead tank. But the tank kept coming, raking Fujiwara's position with machine-gun fire. Finally, his fifth rocket stopped the tank in its tracks, prompting the other tank and infantry to withdraw. Staff Sergeant Fujiwara was credited with preventing a breakthrough in Company G's sector, and for his courageous action was awarded the Distinguished Service Cross.

At the same time, Company F was trying to dislodge a German company that had infiltrated Hill D (Avison) during the night. The fight was at a deadlock when TSgt. Abraham Ohama went to the aid of a fellow soldier. Disregarding his white flag, the Germans continued to fire, wounding Ohama. When a team of litter bearers tried to get to both of them, another volley wounded the men with the Red Cross helmets and killed Ohama. At that moment, without a word or command, every man in Company F got on his feet and charged the German positions in what was later called the "banzai charge." Captain Hill's men gave no quarter. They fought with such ferocity that soon more than fifty grenadiers lay dead, and seven survived only by hiding until the following morning.

Michio Takata recalls "We devastated the Germans. By that time they were using boys, sixteen or seventeen years old. They had run out of manpower. It was a pity to see young Germans yelling, getting shot, and asking for mercy. It was pitiful. I remember our company commander, Captain Hill, trying to apply first aid to a sixteen-year-old boy whose testicles were blown away. A sixteen-year-old kid. I remember the captain with tears in his eyes, trying to help that boy."

That same morning Colonel Singles moved his 100th Battalion north to attack Hill C (Pointhaie). Along the way Captain Takahashi's Company B ran into German infantry. In the ensuing firefight, now joined by 1st Lt. Sam Sakamoto's Company A, the Nisei pushed the Germans back up the steep, wooded slopes. Tanks were useless in the dense forest, but an artillery strike from the 522d Battalion decided the action. By noon Hill C was in American hands. Korean American Young Oak Kim, operations officer for the battalion, was watching General Haeckel's infantry massing for a counterattack when General Dahlquist called. Kim remembers, "I was on the radio when Colonel Pence gave the order to clear the hill immediately. 'A direct order from the general.' We could have held it, or turned it over to another unit, but instead we handed it back to the Germans."

Later that day Hill C was retaken by the 7th Regiment of the 3d Division, which had just joined the attack. Lieutenant Colonel Clayton Thobro's 2d Battalion lost several men, including Capt. Frank Williams of Company E.

The battles between Bruyères and Brouvelieures left an indelible impression on General Haeckel.

> The wooded high ground stretching from Bruyères to Grandvillers, defended by SS Polizei Regiment 19, was bitterly contested. By the 17th this important line was in enemy hands, including the ridge overlooking Bruyères. Defense of Bruyères was assigned to our neighboring division to the south (Richter's 716th), which fell to the enemy by the 19th. The battles around Grandvillers, and in the forests west of the Mortagne River, were very costly to our division. Our active battalions and inexperienced air force regiments suffered the most, and the Polizei Regiment was pulled out of the line to be used elsewhere. [SS Polizei Regiment 19 was withdrawn on 22 October and sent back to fight partisans in northern Yugoslavia.]
>
> Alarm units, formed from the rear echelon troops, stragglers, and convalescing soldiers, had to fight with insufficient equipment and few if any antitank weapons. And because leaders and their men hardly knew each other, units often disintegrated after an attack.

Also on the afternoon of 20 October, air observers spotted a German tank column moving from Belmont toward the 442d Regiment's left flank. To meet this threat Colonel Pence dispatched armored Task Force Felber on the Bruyères-Belmont road. But before the two units clashed, a flight of Thunderbolts bombed and strafed the column of Panzer Regiment 22, reporting seven hits.

By the fall of 1944 the Allies had achieved undisputed air superiority, with 4,700 fighters, 6,000 medium and heavy bombers, and 4,000 reconnaissance and transport planes. But in October this advantage was of little consequence, as bad weather grounded planes for days on end.

Finally, after a twenty-minute artillery barrage, the 2d and 3d Battalions managed to cross the railroad embankment by late afternoon. But on the other side fields of S-mines, dug-in infantry, and approaching darkness once again ground the attack to a halt.

Among those opposing the Japanese Americans was an eighteen-year-old Luftwaffe airman from Heek, Westphalia—Joseph Schwieters, who had just been assigned to the infantry. On the day Paris was liberated, 25 August, Schwieters's Luftwaffe contingent had still been stationed on the Atlantic coast near Bordeaux. Then came the retreat—hasty, poorly organized, and subjected to daily harassment by the French resistance and Allied air power. With resupply poor to nonexistent, Schwieters, and his friend Hans-Paul Geiger, had been reduced to foraging for fruit and vegetables on farms they passed along the way. When his unit reached Gérardmer on 20 September, Schwieters, Geiger, and their compatriots were pressed into Füsilier Bataillon 198. According to Schwieters, "At 9:30 A.M., October 20, our attack began whereby a railway line was the target. We managed to break through, but to advance beyond was simply impossible. The fighting was fierce. We repelled attack after attack made by the Americans. About twenty meters ahead of me, one of our machine gunners was hit, and his partner took over. But I will never forget the cries of that gunner, 'They shot off my leg, I'm bleeding to death. Please take me off the embankment!' In the evening our wounded were picked up at the railway line and brought back."

Not far from Airman Schwieters's position, at the edge of the Bois de Belmont, stood a farmhouse that served as the Füsilier Bataillon 198 command post. At dusk the Nisei of Company K spotted a soldier exiting the building and shot him. When Lt. Robert Foote's men reached the Oberleutnant (first lieutenant), they found maps and documents in his briefcase. Division intelligence determined that the officer had been the battalion adjutant, and that the plans showed the German defenses (Germans usually marked their units right on the map whereas Americans used translucent tissue overlays). Armed with this information General Dahlquist and Colonel Pence decided on a simple but risky maneuver. During the night Companies F and L would infiltrate the German lines and attack from behind, while the 2d and 3d Battalions mounted a frontal assault.

Major Emmet O'Connor, executive officer of the 3d Battalion, was well aware of the risk involved when he was chosen to lead the task force. If discovered, his men would become easy targets for German artillery, or worse, be cut off.

Task Force O'Connor left in the early hours of 21 October, with two FFI guides and a minesweeping team on point, and a radio/telephone crew laying wire along the way. Moving silently east along the same railroad embankment that had been such a formidable obstacle, they cut deep into the German main defense line, and at dawn reached Hill 505. At that moment the 2d and 3d Battalions attacked the fortified positions of Grenadier Regiment 736, while O'Connor's men came in from behind. The artillery fire directed by forward observer Lt. Albert Binotti found its mark with such devastating accuracy, soon eighty grenadiers lay dead and another fifty-four surrendered.

By mid-morning resistance waned, and by noon Companies I and K reached the crest of Hill 505. On its march the 2d Battalion also engaged German armor with artillery fire, and by mid-afternoon the battalions caught up with the task force at a hamlet called La Broquaime. By then O'Connor's men had already dislodged a tank from cover, swept aside all German resistance—including the remnants of Airman Schwieters's Füsilier Bataillon 198—and driven them up the valley toward Belmont. In addition to three ammunition carriers and one antitank gun, a large quantity of small arms were captured. For their outstanding performance Task Force O'Connor was awarded a Distinguished Unit Citation.

The German Nineteenth Army log read:

Infiltration of strong forces of the U.S. 36th and 45th Infantry Divisions in the dense forest brought about large gaps in the German lines. There were many stragglers and missing, including those who surrendered to the other side.

Battles under these circumstances were heavy and took a large toll. The enemy was able to use air observers, or the superb work of surveyors with optical or acoustic measuring equipment that could quickly pinpoint suitable targets for artillery or air bombardment.

Karl Schmid, a gunnery sergeant with the 4th Battery, 1716th Field Artillery, experienced the effectiveness of American counterartillery fire outside Bruyères. Schmid recalls, "We had just begun to fire, when a smoke shell fell in front of our gun barrels. I immediately told my men to take cover in the barn cellar nearby. Moments later a volley ripped the courtyard apart. A short time after that our battery commander joined us because another volley was sure to follow. We had two dead, a fellow from the Rhineland and a miner from Silesia, who had made the retreat with us all the way up the Rhône Valley. It was a shock for us, and everyone thought, 'Who will be next?'"

# 4: Biffontaine

As Task Force O'Connor breached the German main defense line west of Belmont, the 100th Battalion proceeded east through the Forêt de Belmont and along the ridge reaching toward the village of Biffontaine. Their objective was the high ground east of the Belmont-Biffontaine road, from which the link between the German 16th and 716th Divisions could be severed. This move would force the contingent in Belmont to surrender or retreat north into the arms of the U.S. 7th Infantry Regiment.

The companies advanced in columns, and twice the Germans hit the rear guard made up of Company B. Other than that, there was no more organized resistance. Captain Sakae Takahashi remembers capturing a bespectacled ex-policeman from Munich and his teenage son, who had been drafted just weeks before (Hitler's decree forming a German home guard, or *Volkssturm*, had been issued on 25 September).

Also on 21 October, the U.S. 7th Regiment pushed through General Haeckel's "Alarmeinheiten" at Brouvelieures and Mortagne. Casualties were appalling. Haeckel, and a few hundred men remaining of his 16th Division, retreated east to escape complete annihilation.

The German Army log assessed the situation realistically:

On 19 October, the enemy attacked with a very heavy artillery and mortar barrage, including white phosphorous, in the 16th Division sector, inflicting heavy casualties. The next three days, 20–23 October, with clearing and then pleasant fall weather, brought heavy battles east of Bruyères against the 16th Division, including the losses of the towns of Brouvelieures, Vervezelle, Domfaing, and Belmont. The Americans now stand at the Mortagne sector, entrance to the 14km long, wooded pass road to St.-Dié.

Aware of his neighbor's plight, General Richter knew that he alone could not hold the line stretching from les Poulières to Biffontaine and la Houssière.

Richter wrote, "Crisis situations were the rule in all our engagements. Our front lines were overextended and manpower insufficient. My infantry no longer consisted of grenadiers, but mostly of rear echelon soldiers, air force battalions, navy, and replacement units."

But Richter was not yet ready to evacuate Biffontaine.

On Sunday, 22 October, Rev. Hiro Higuchi held services before the 2d Battalion headed east again. Christians and Buddhists prayed side by side, reflecting on their own lives, mindful of the irony inherent in fighting for a country that kept their families in internment camps, and stamped the Buddhists' dog tags "Protestant" as a matter of expediency.

Later that morning Companies E and F engaged a company of German bicycle troops who had infiltrated the Col de Arnelle during the night. After a sharp firefight, General Haeckel's men cleared the field, leaving a number of dead and six prisoners. And while the 3d Battalion mopped up pockets of resistance near Belmont, the 100th Battalion established itself on the high ground overlooking Biffontaine. Company B had already cut the eastern approaches to the village and shot up a German truck convoy, when Grenadier Regiment 736 counterattacked. With the 716th Division command post only two kilometers away at la Houssière, the Germans used every available means, including the dreaded "screaming meemies," and 8.8 flak to stop the Americans. Soon firefights were raging on three sides of the American battalion, but the German thrust was not strong enough to penetrate its defenses. The protracted fighting left the Nisei short on ammunition and water, and their medical facilities overwhelmed with casualties.

To make matters worse, a supply column from Belmont was ambushed in the hills just south of town. Lieutenant David Novak's infantry platoon, mounted on five light tanks, made easy targets for the German machine guns. The Americans lost three killed and several wounded in the initial burst, and as they tried to turn, Lt. Raymond Gainey's tanks became mired in mud. Staff Sergeant Itsumu Sasaoka, himself seriously wounded, covered the withdrawal with a steady stream of fire from his turret machine gun. But as his tank lurched forward he fell off and was later listed as missing in action. For his heroic act Sergeant Sasaoka was awarded the Distinguished Service Cross.

Lieutenant Milton Brenner and a platoon from Company L finally succeeded in making their way through the difficult terrain, bringing much-needed water and ammunition to the beleaguered 100th Battalion.

At his 22 October staff meeting, General Dahlquist told his deputy, Brig. Gen. Robert Stack: "The 442d RCT, just as soon as it finishes the job it is now doing, will stop as they have been fighting for eight days, and have been fighting all the way. They have not had a man missing in action yet. This is a fine record. Yesterday, they had one enlisted man and one officer missing, but they are fighting in heavy woods, and there is a possibility that these men have been killed and their bodies have not yet been found."

Part of the job the Nisei had to complete was the capture of Biffontaine.

"A worthless tactical objective," according to Capt. Young Oak Kim. "The only radio within range was that of the artillery, which required a generator. We would have been far more effective by continuing along the top of the ridge."

Captain Chris Keegan, operations officer for the 2d Battalion, agrees. "Biffontaine was not a logical tactical objective. . . . It should have been cutting the St.-Dié–Corcieux road and seizing the high ground to the east."

Had their advice been heeded, the 100th Battalion might have reached the heights above la Houssière ahead of the German reinforcements about to arrive in two days' time.

On the morning of 23 October, the 100th Battalion descended on Biffontaine, an L-shaped village of about three hundred souls. When the men of Company C ran across M. Henry's field, the speed of the assault caught the Germans by surprise. Against only light resistance the Hawaiians managed to capture several houses and twenty-three retreating troops, including the major in charge of the 716th Division signal unit, who proved to be a valuable intelligence asset. Captured small arms and ammunition were distributed among the rifle companies, and the men braced for counterattack.

Meanwhile, Companies B and D had cut the eastern and western approaches to the village. Captain Sakae Takahashi, commanding Company B, remembers: "Some German vehicles tried to get through, but we blasted them. One of the trucks carried food. I had fresh peaches for breakfast that morning."

But Takahashi's pleasure was short-lived. "The Germans countered with an artillery barrage, very effective, with shells bursting on impact. That's when a number of my men and I got hit."

Late that afternoon, Captain Kim and Lieutenant Pye of Company C were watching a German tank from inside the village church, oblivious of a German soldier watching them. "He'd been hiding in a barn, under a trapdoor covered with straw. When he spotted us he aimed his Schmeisser at Bill Pye but hit me instead."

Kim, who had already earned a Silver Star and DSC in Italy, sustained serious injuries to his right hand and lost a considerable amount of blood. He was under sedation when General Richter's men counterattacked from three sides during the night, using 8.8mm and 20mm antiaircraft cannon, tanks, and infantry. With ammunition nearly exhausted, the Nisei fought back with all available means. Holed up inside the solid stone buildings, they used captured weapons, and in some instances even threw flowerpots and rocks at passing tanks. But bravado wasn't enough. As casualties mounted, the dead and dying were stacked inside Paul and Josephine Voirin's home at the edge of the woods. Chaplain Israel Yost recalls, "I was furious when I saw the life draining out of the young men in Biffontaine, and at seeing them pushed toward annihilation in the forest."

In spite of German exhortations to surrender, the village remained in American hands. The next morning a litter train was assembled to evacuate the wounded. Made up of medics from the 100th and 3d Battalions, along with German prisoners acting as litter bearers, the group set out with Lt. Sam Sakamoto up front and Lt. James Kanaya and his medics bringing up the rear. But they had barely left Biffontaine when a German patrol intercepted them. A tug of war ensued, with Sakamoto demanding that the Germans surrender, while the same was demanded of him. As it became clear that the larger German patrol would prevail, Captain Kim rolled off his litter and escaped into the woods, along with Richard Chinen, a medic. The remaining twenty men, including medics Kanaya, Fuji, Uchimura, and the wounded Sam Sakamoto, were captured.

To meet the American breakthrough at Biffontaine, General Richter received reinforcements from the 198th Division on his left—namely Battle Group Eschrich. Thirty-three-year-old Maj. Walter Eschrich was an artillery officer who had come up through the ranks of the horse artillery, an athlete and fervent equestrian who eventually commanded a battery and a section in Russia. There, with the 26th Panzer Division, he had earned the Iron Cross and the Assault Badge and had been singled out for his personal courage and calmness in the face of the enemy.

Now, supported by panzer grenadiers, Eschrich's self-propelled artillery and assault guns attacked the village, firing point-blank at the houses defended by Company C. As the fierce 88's hammered the stone houses the Americans took to the cellars, but each time the grenadiers attacked, the Nisei emerged and threw them back. Probes during the night culminated in one last, desperate infantry charge at dawn, which broke against the 100th Battalion's first line of defense.

The Daily Summary of the Wehrmacht describes the day's events:

> Our own counterattack to close the gap between LXIV (64th) and LXXXIX (89th) Army Corps to correct the enemy breakthrough at Biffontaine was met by renewed enemy attacks and remained mired along the line 1.5 km northeast of Biffontaine. The village itself was lost by evening. Our own forces, in the forest southwest of Biffontaine, were thrown back across the southern bank of the Neune River.

After ten days of continuous battle, the Nisei were relieved on 24 October and sent to Belmont, where they received dry clothes, hot food, baths, and much-needed rest. The intensity and duration of the battle had been worse than anything they had experienced in Italy, where resistance had usually waned after two or three days, followed by a planned German withdrawal. But at Bruyères there had been no letup. The German 16th and 716th Divisions had fought day and night with the desperation of men whose backs were against the wall.

But at General Dahlquist's headquarters the mood was optimistic. Ever since the fall of Bruyères, and the success of Task Force O'Connor, the prevailing opinion was that the German resistance had been broken. At his 22 October staff meeting, General Dahlquist gave his assessment: "General O'Daniel's 3d Division is attacking this morning along the road to Mailleufaing, and the 442nd RCT has the job of cleaning the area inside the blue line. When we have that, we have gotten our first objective, and we might be able to walk into St.-Dié. This position on the west bank of the Meurthe River is going to be a holding position for us to regroup and proceed north or to Strasbourg. If this thing goes through, he [General Truscott] wants the 36th Division to carry out the mission of going over the mountain. There is a good trail leading over the mountain from Belmont."

Dahlquist faced Col. Carl Lundquist of Grand Rapids, Michigan, who now commanded the "Alamo" Regiment. "If Corps says that we attack tomorrow, the 141st will do the job. Plan to make the attack with two battalions tomorrow, if the order comes through."

Turning to his operations officer, Lt. Col. Fred Sladen: "Do you have the map with the overlay?"

"No, but we have a copy of the overlay. Our objective is here." Colonel Sladen pointed to the high ground above la Houssière. "It will be made with one regiment. The 442d RCT will remain in assembly area in the vicinity of Belmont and, if the route is clear, will follow along the same trail as the attacking regiment."

General Dahlquist: "We've taken six hundred German prisoners in the past six days, not counting the number of men we have killed or wounded. We have either broken his line, or he has completed another one here [pointing to the Meurthe River]. General Truscott is trying to make up his mind this morning about the attack. If we break through, we will not have to fight terrain and enemy; we'll just have to fight terrain."

Colonel Sladen: "Major Reese (G-2) is getting guides and wood-cutters who know the area, and they will act as guides."

But that evening the general recorded his doubts in his pocket notebook:

> Truscott wants to push attack now instead of waiting. Late in the afternoon ordered 2d Bn, 141st to move to Belmont area, prepared to move on next objective: ridge overlooking Houssière. Ted Brooks [about to assume command of VI Corps] spent most of the day with me. He is for just pushing on. I fear he has discounted the terrain obstacle of the Vosges Mountains.

Neither General Brooks nor his predecessor, Truscott, knew that Gen. Friedrich Wiese held captured American maps showing the American advance, called "Operation Dog Face." The Nineteenth Army commander had no intention of giving up the forests between Belmont and St.-Dié without a fight. Instead of pulling back to the Meurthe line, as the Allies suspected, both Generals Haeckel and Richter were about to receive three thousand reinforcements within four days, turning the Forêt de Champ and the mountain pass at Haut Jacques into a trap for the Americans.

As both sides regrouped, another kind of war, a clandestine one, was being waged behind Allied and German lines. With the front stabilizing in late September, German intelligence services reestablished their espionage and sabotage efforts. In the month of October, the Allied Seventh Army netted twenty-five German agents, whose missions ranged from infiltrating intelligence agencies to acting as stay-behind agents operating radio sets in Allied territories. One, a Sicherheitsdienst stay-behind agent in Épinal, was arrested while waiting for his radio transmitter to be delivered in a suitcase. Another, dressed as a priest, was turned over to the French and summarily executed.

Most interesting, perhaps, was the case of a Swiss national with the mission of blowing up Allied fuel pipelines. The plan, conceived by General Schellenberger of Amt VI, Reichssicherheitshauptamt, failed, however, when the agent and his accomplices were apprehended by military police manning a roadblock. Hidden sabotage dumps with explosives, weapons, and food had been especially set up for this purpose, and when caught, the agents were carrying several million francs in a suitcase.

Reports also persisted that the Sicherheitsdienst had targeted General Eisenhower and other Allied military personalities for assassination. If true, none succeeded.

At the same time masses of French collaborators were streaming toward the Rhine. Members of the Milice Française, the Légion des Volontaires Française, the Parti Populaire Française, the Francisme Movement, and numerous smaller groups provided the German Wehrmacht and intelligence services with a ready-cut crop of new recruits and potential agents. Members of the Légion Volontaires Français were incorporated into the Waffen SS, and many of the twenty-five thousand Miliciens who left the Schirmeck and Natzwiller-Struthof concentration camps were sent to the espionage and sabotage schools at Wiesbach, Osnabrück, Hundsbach, Hubacker Hof in the Black Forest, and Freiburg im Breisgau. The Hubacker Hof school specialized in training young Frenchmen and parachuting them and their radio transmitters behind the Allied lines. The largest school, predominantly for the Milice, was located in Freiburg. Just before their retreat into Germany, large numbers of PPF had been assembled at St.-Dié, then headquarters of the Abwehr Office III and Frontaufklärungstrupp 353, where they were organized into teams who would cross the lines and form a chain of agents reaching from the Vosges to Paris. As part of their ruse, the Abwehr also freed members of the French resistance and mixed agents among them as they tried to reach the Allied lines.

Meanwhile, in the interior of France arrests of suspected collaborators reached a frenzied pace—more than thirty thousand for the months of September and October. In Paris alone, thirteen thousand prisoners awaited trial, which had to be repeatedly postponed due to a shortage of transportation and courtrooms. But once judgment began, it was swift and harsh—sixty death sentences in October alone, ranging from Vichy Premier Pierre Laval (sentenced in absentia) to bar owner Marie Balaretti, nurse Paulette Raymond, and Marie Borot, a dancer, all of whom were executed 9–10 October, in Marseilles.

In spite of their diligent efforts, German intelligence never matched the successes achieved by the Office of Strategic Services, in conjunction with British intelligence and FFI. OSS chief Gen. William "Wild Bill" Donovan, a World War I veteran and recipient of the Medal of Honor and the DSC, took every chance to go into the field—which, in most cases, meant behind German lines—to spur his men on. One such occasion came in early September, as the Seventh Army moved up the Rhône Valley. Master spy Allen Dulles (brother of John Foster Dulles), under orders from Washington, had crossed from Switzerland into France and was taken to a secret location near Lyon to join a maquis group (*maquis* is a Corsican term meaning "men of the underbrush"). While waiting for a clandestine flight, he was unexpectedly met by General Donovan, and together they flew to London to finalize plans for the end of the "Thousand Year Reich."

OSS teams had been parachuting into France and other parts of Europe for more than a year to execute their delicate and dangerous missions, living with partisan fighters determined to liberate their country from fascist domination. OSS teams had dropped into France, weeks ahead of the Overlord and Dragoon invasions, to supply much-needed intelligence and direct sabotage operations. Thousands of supply sorties were flown to provide essential weapons, explosives, and radios to the French. In the south, where the resistance was strongest, as many as seventy-five thousand armed men and women controlled large sections of what was Vichy France. In spite of the lore surrounding this effort, there was nothing romantic about operating in German-held territory. If caught alive, torture and almost certain death awaited them—a fate OSS operatives were to avoid by taking poison. Donovan's men and women were recruited from all walks of life—Ivy League schools, socialist groups, trade unions, and the military. The OSS was also one of few agencies that made effective use of Japanese Americans in the Far East at a time when these loyal Americans were confined to detention camps.

# 5: Lost Battalions

At dawn, Monday, 23 October, the American 45th, 3d, and 36th Divisions jumped off in a coordinated attack aimed at the German main defense line running from Rambervillers to Biffontaine. As the 7th Regiment in the center spearheaded the 3d Division's drive through the les-Rouges-Eaux valley, General Dahlquist moved his 141st "Alamo" Regiment into the Forêt de Champ just east of Belmont. Going on the assumption that the German main defenses now ran along the Meurthe River, division intelligence told the 1st Battalion commander, Lt. Col. William Bird of Barberton, Ohio, to expect only light to moderate resistance. Led by FFI guides Henri Grandjean and Pierre Poirat, the 1st Battalion set out along the heavily wooded ridge stretching southeast from Biffontaine into the valley between Corcieux and St.-Dié, unaware that they were heading into a trap.

The commander of the Nineteenth Army, Gen. Friedrich Wiese, already knew of the American attack.

> Through agent reports and captured maps, the enemy's intentions were known—to cut across the Vosges passes into the Alsace in the sector le Thillot, la Bresse, le Tholy, Gérardmer, Bruyères, and the area west of Baccarat, west of St.-Dié.

Log entries of 23 and 25 October, confirm that OKH was in possession of captured maps showing specific attack routes of the American divisions. To counter the threat, General Wiese committed

Grenadier Regiment 933, Mobile Battalion 602, and Mountain Battalion 202 followed by 201.

Backed by Reserve Battalion 285, which had been rushed in from the Czech Protectorate, Col. Walter Rolin's Grenadier Regiment 933 moved into the forest on the morning of 24 October. Rolin wrote, "During mid-October our regiment was withdrawn and, by truck convoy, via Colmar, attached to General Richter's division to counterattack the adversary who had broken through east of Bruyères in the Forêt de Champ. Our mission was to attack in the vicinity of Biffontaine, les-Rouges-Eaux, to close the gap and hold the positions. At the time the regiment had a fighting strength of about 350 men."

As soon as it crossed the line of departure, Colonel Lundquist's "Alamo" Regiment ran into trouble. In the densely wooded hills, two kilometers east of Belmont, Maj. Walter Bruyere's 3d Battalion immediately locked horns with Schnellabteilung (Mobile Battalion) 602 and Heeres Gebirgsjäger Bataillon (Mountain Battalion) 202.

On the morning of Tuesday, 24 October, TSgt. Charles Henry Coolidge was digging in on Hill 623 when he saw German soldiers coming up the wooded slope on his right. "We were just putting our guns in when I saw them. I had one trooper who spoke German, George Ferguson from Queens, New York. I told him, 'Hey George, ask them if they want to surrender!' He went up and talked to them for about five minutes. I thought things were looking pretty good, but then one of the Germans pointed his rifle at George, like he was going to shoot him, and that's when I opened up with my carbine, wounding one of them. The Germans fired back with their burp guns, and pretty soon we were in the thick of it. Then there was a lull, and George tried to talk to them again, but a bullet shattered his left arm. I dragged him back over the crest of the hill to our foxholes."

Since no officers were present, the twenty-three-year-old sergeant from Signal Mountain, Tennessee, took charge of some green troops from Company K, and with this group of twenty-eight men, made his stand.

His citation reads:

Unmindful of the enemy fire delivered from close range, Sergeant Coolidge walked along the position, calming and encouraging his men and directing their fire. The attack was thrown back. Throughout 25 and 26 October the enemy launched repeated attacks against his combat group, but each was repulsed due to Sgt. Coolidge's leadership. On the third day, German infantry, supported by two tanks, made a determined attack on the position.

Coolidge remembers: The hatch popped open and the tank commander spoke to us in perfect English, "You fellows want to give up?" I stood up and told him, "No, Mac, you've got to come and get us." Then he fired at us at point-blank range, five shells—trees shattering all around. One fragment cut off the top of my boot. And the troops kept on coming. I picked up a bazooka, but it misfired. I had two cases of hand grenades though and kept lobbing them past the tank at the infantry. We battled them for nearly an hour until we ran out of ammo. I hollered to my men, 'You all better withdraw.' Other than those who were killed, I got everyone out, except for a fellow who was only fifteen feet from the tank and a medic. Both got captured and survived the war."

For his steadfast action Technical Sergeant Coolidge received the nation's highest award, the Medal of Honor.

While the situation was tenuous on the 141st Regiment's left flank, it was disastrous on the right. Late on the twenty-fourth, Lt. Col. William Bird's 1st Battalion had traversed the narrow ridge above Biffontaine, only half a mile from their objective above la Houssière, when Marty Higgins's Company A encountered the grenadiers of Regiment 933. Higgins moved his men and antitank platoon forward to attack. But in the ensuing fight the battalion's command post was overrun, and 275 men of Companies A, B, C, and a platoon from Company D were cut off two kilometers behind friendly lines.

That night, the trapped battalion sent a coded message over the artillery radio net, relayed to their regimental headquarters. "No rations, no water, no communications with battalion headquarters; four litter cases."

German Nineteenth Army log, Wednesday, 25 October read:

A captured map confirms the intent of the enemy to attack with the 36th Division toward Vanemont–la Mossière, alongside

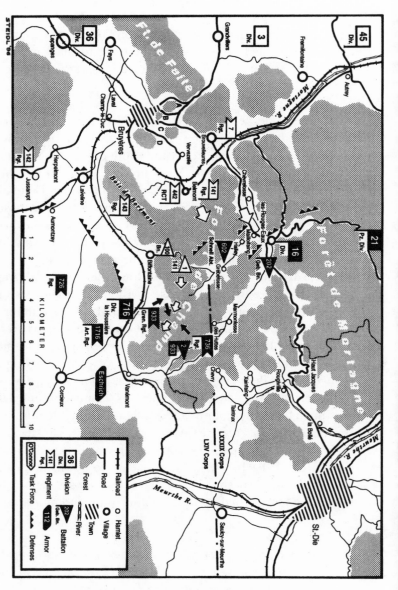

Situation map, 23 October. The 100th Battalion has taken Biffontaine while the 1/141 heads into the trap sprung by Grenadier Regiment 933. As the rest of the "Alamo" Regiment tries to breach the German fortifications south of Halley, the mountain troops of Gebirgsjäger Bataillon 202 struggle against the U.S. 7th Regiment at les-Rouges-Eaux.

the American 3d Division at the Mottagne sector, direction St.-Dié. Resistance by Bataillon 202 has temporarily prevented a breakthrough. Among the enemy is also a Japanese regiment.

In addition to Mountain Bataillon 202, Army Group G has also committed Grenadier Regiment 933 to attack in the vicinity of Biffontaine, les-Rouges-Eaux and close the gap and hold the positions.

General Haeckel wrote: "After the Mortagne line was breached, it became the mission of the division to tie down the enemy as long as possible in the forests north and south of the pass road to St.-Dié to allow completion of the Meurthe line. From 10 October to 11 November, the division was under the command of General Gilsa's LXXXIX (89th) Corps, with the division command post at les-Rouges-Eaux and then Rougiville. As reinforcements the division received two mountain battalions and two probation battalions that fought very well, along with a few tanks and 8.8 Flak.

"The area les-Rouges-Eaux and Rougiville apparently was a center of French resistance, because division command posts in both towns received heavy fire in cooperation with American forces."

The men of the 442d Regimental Combat Team had barely rested a day when Lieutenant Colonel Hanley was alerted to move out again. Still exhausted from eight days of continuous fighting at Bruyères and Belmont, the 2d Battalion left at 3 A.M., Thursday, 26 October. No one knew what lay ahead as the men stumbled through the pitch-black night, until at day's first light the men found themselves deep in the Forêt de Champ on the division's left flank. By mid-morning the Nisei passed through Maj. Walter Bruyere's 3d Battalion of the 141st Infantry, but managed to go no more than two hundred yards in the direction of Langefosse before Schnell-abteilung 602 opened up with machine guns and mortars.

*Colonel Hanley:*
   *While moving into position, we became engaged in a firefight with about 100 Germans entrenched on Hill 617—a long, sloping ridge honeycombed with foxholes and trenches. They were well trained, some of them snipers who wore camouflage uniforms with hoods fitting over helmets to break the outline. . . .*

At 1030, Gen. Lucien Truscott (who had just turned over command of VI Corps to Maj. Gen. Edward H. Brooks) arrived with General Dahlquist and his chief of staff, Col. Charles Owens. With the 1st Battalion cut off, an angry General Dahlquist confronted his regimental commander, Lundquist. "Why aren't you using artillery on the enemy?"

"Because artillery shells have landed too close to the 'Lost Battalion.' They've suffered casualties on account of tree bursts."

"Then have your 1st Battalion attack to the rear immediately! I can't believe that you let this thing go on for thirty-six hours while four battalions are sitting around doing nothing!"

Colonel Lundquist's 2d and 3d Battalions had, in fact, tried to break through but suffered heavy casualties. At the time, Lieutenant Colonel Bird and his staff were not with their cutoff 1st Battalion, and an interim commander had not been appointed, nor had orders for a breakout been issued. General Dahlquist sent his deputy, Brig. Gen. Robert Stack, to the front lines to take charge, but the attack never got off the ground. Furious, Dahlquist ordered Hanley to attack.

Colonel Hanley denies that he refused the order. "Our battalion was too close to the enemy positions to chance an artillery barrage and to make a frontal attack; charging up such a steep slope against heavily entrenched forces would have been very costly."

It was General Truscott who suggested that Hanley take his 2d Battalion east, while tanks went head-on against the roadblocks, and the 141st and 143d Infantry would outflank the Germans. Dahlquist accepted his superior's advice and gave Hanley permission to operate on his own. Hanley states: "I ordered Company G to hold the enemy in position while the other two companies moved north and then up to the ridge to Halley, then back on the other side of the ridge to the enemy's rear."

While Company G engaged the Germans, Companies E and F, commanded by Captains Tom Atkins and Joseph Hill, headed north along the road from Grèbefosse to Mailleufaing. From there they intended to swing east and then south across Hill 585 (Grands Vitourneurs) to attack the Germans from behind. But the terrain was exceedingly difficult, and as night fell the Nisei companies were scattered all along the ridge running north from Hill 617, loosely connected by a forest path that had been revealed by German prisoners.

After being dressed-down by General Dahlquist, Colonel Lundquist again ordered his 3d Battalion to break through to his trapped 1st Battalion. Tanks were loaded with K rations, water, and ammunition, and each rifleman was told to carry extra rations for their encircled comrades, who had not eaten in two days. As darkness fell, Lundquist insisted that his commanders push on through the night—an all but impossible task, given the terrain, fresh minefields, and tenacious Germans who had already knocked out two of his tanks. His company commanders balked, and word came from Company E that the company commander and every platoon leader and noncom had been killed or wounded.

With his other regiments already committed, and faced with the potential annihilation of one of his battalions, General Dahlquist had no other option but to call up the Nisei 100th and 3d Battalions.

After two days' rest at Belmont, the 100th and 3d Battalions left at 4 A.M., Friday, 27 October. Led by officer-guides from the 141st Regiment, they moved silently through the night and steady, cold rain— each man holding on to the backpack of the trooper in front of him, until at daybreak they found themselves deep inside the forest. The 442d Infantry was to attack at 1000 hours with Major Bruyere's 3d Battalion of the 141st furnishing a base of fire. But the attack was delayed when friendly artillery fell short near the 141/442d command post. General Dahlquist visited the CP and remained all day. A scheduled air drop of food, medicine, and ammunition for the trapped men of the 1st Battalion had to be canceled due to fog. But by early afternoon, all three Nisei battalions were on line: the 100th on the right, 3d in the center, and, separated by steep ravines and wooded hills, the already committed 2d Battalion on the far left.

The regimental combat team had the direct support of two tank companies and one tank-destroyer company, heavy mortars, and the 522d and 133d Field Artillery. But the attack made little headway against General Richter's entrenched infantry and artillery. By midafternoon Companies I and K in the center were counterattacked by four German tanks and a half-track supported by infantry. Most of the thrust fell on Company K on the left. Fighting was fierce as the

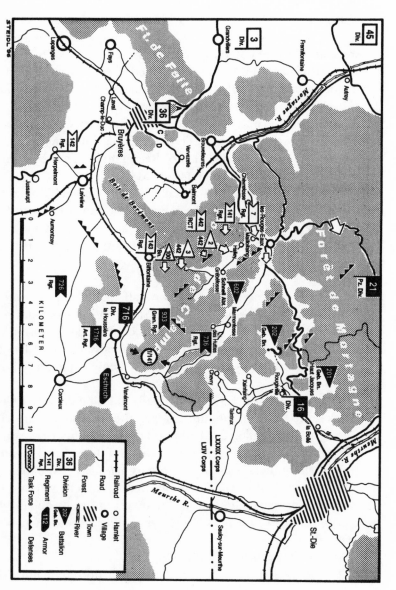

Situation map, 26 October. As the 2d Battalion 442 outflanks the German defenses in the Forêt de Champ, the 100th and 3d Battalions begin their push toward the "Lost Battalion." At les-Rouges-Eaux, Gebirgsjäger Bataillon 202 has been swept aside by the U.S. 7th Regiment, and advance elements of Bataillon 201 have just arrived at Haut Jacques.

tank rolled to within seventy-five yards of the company and fired at point-blank range.

Private First Class Matsuichi Yogi, armed with his bazooka, crawled toward one of the tanks, and, disregarding exploding shells and small-arms fire, exposed himself to score a direct hit. Then, spotting two German antitank gunners, he killed one with a rocket and drove the other back with rifle fire. Yogi, who was later killed in action, received the Distinguished Service Cross.

Late that afternoon, Lieutenant Colonel Bird, who had been cut off from his 1st Battalion, was relieved of his duties and replaced by his executive officer. The "Alamo" Regiment itself was placed under the command of Colonel Pence, 442d RCT.

Four days earlier, as the 100th Battalion defended Biffontaine and the 141st Regiment entered the Forêt de Champ, German Heeres Gebirgsjäger Bataillon 202 had arrived at les-Rouges-Eaux to block the American advance. At the time, Gerwin Eder was a runner for the communications platoon:

> During the night our battalion staff, Staff Company, and 1st Company were brought in from St.-Dié on charcoal-gas powered trucks. We were assigned to General Haeckel's division and thrown into the battle without reconnaissance or adequate preparation. It was as though we were being led to the gallows.

Only eight days before they arrived, and nine days after General Balck asked for mountain troops, the thousand-man Heeres Gebirgsjäger Bataillon 202 had stood muster on the parade grounds of Salzburg's Glasenbach Kaserne. General Julius Ringl greeted his "mountain hunters" with the customary *"Heil Jäger,"* and then called out, in Austrian dialect, "Come on over, boys!" The veterans of the Russian, Norwegian, Italian, and Yugoslav campaigns, and the young conscripts, broke ranks and formed a circle around their beloved general.

"You're going into the Vosges!"

This surprised the men, who knew that no mountain divisions fought in that part of France.

"You're probably going up against the Moroccans we fought at Cassino," Ringl continued, assuring them that they had little to fear. The mountain troops had, in fact, been earmarked to fight against General de Lattre's Moroccans, just south of the 36th Division. But when General Wiese learned of the Americans' intentions to break through to St.-Dié, he shifted the mountain battalion north.

Ringl continued: "The war has reached a critical stage. The enemy stands at our door, and you already know what to expect from the Bolshevik workers' and peasants' paradise, and the British and Americans who are bombing our cities."

Ringl was referring to the American bombing raid, one week earlier, in which Salzburg's twelve-hundred-year-old cathedral had been destroyed. "The Führer has promised us new weapons of unbelievably destructive power, but our country needs time to complete them. You, my young comrades, must buy that time for our Fatherland."

Bataillon 202 was an independent unit directly under OKH control, much like the Nisei 442d RCT was under the control of an army command. The battalion from Salzburg was made up of a staff and supply company, three line companies, a weapons company with heavy machine guns and mortars, and one platoon each of artillery, engineers, communications, and medical personnel. Most of its members came from Wehrkreis 18, the mountain region of Austria, but it also included volunteers from northern Yugoslavia and the Sudetenland. Mountain troops were an unusual lot. To withstand the rigorous combat training in the Alps, each man had to be in excellent physical condition. Officers and soldiers carried their own gear, shared the same simple food, and climbed the same mountains. All mountain troops shared a strong esprit de corps , but Gebirgsjäger Battailon 202 had been assembled very quickly, and the veteran officers and NCOs and the new conscripts did not know each other well. Also, during its two-month existence the battalion did not get the opportunity to train as a complete unit.

Orders to leave came suddenly, so sudden in fact that most men did not get the chance to test-fire their Model 44 assault rifles, or zero in the heavy machine guns—a circumstance that was to prove fatal. During the night of 19–20 October, the first of three trains left

Salzburg, one of which was strafed by American fighter-bombers, bringing about a number of casualties. As the first train waited outside Offenbach, some of the machine-gun crews were able to zero in their weapons. Then, in the cover of darkness, the steam locomotives left again, pulling their heavy load of men and equipment across the Rhine and into France.

From the start, Bataillon 202 was beset with problems. SS Polizei Regiment 19 had already begun its withdrawal on 22 October, and the next day the arrival of the first two Austrian companies was announced by an FFI radio team. A spell of pleasant fall weather had set in, allowing Allied spotter planes to pinpoint the mountain troops' movements, and the artillery strikes that followed proved lethal. A direct hit on the battalion command post at Mailleufaing killed most of the staff and the battalion commander, Capt. Erich Maunz. From a nearby ditch General Haeckel and Colonel Röwer witnessed the death and destruction wrought by the Americans' "fiery steam roller."

The Austrians, who had been thrown into battle without proper reconnaissance or time to set up, not only found themselves in the middle of a major attack, but also realized too late that many of the firing pins in their brand-new assault rifles were too short. Gerwin Eder clearly remembers one wounded Oberjäger, and two of his men, presenting their useless Model 44s at the command post. "But all they got was an admonition. 'Go back to the front. You've got a better chance of finding a weapon there.'" Some of the mountain troops indeed defended themselves with captured weapons, but at the end of the day, 23 October, most of 1st Company and Staff Company had been surrounded, killed, or captured.

Arriving one day later, Companies 2 and 3 were also thrown piecemeal against the U.S. 3d and 36th Divisions. In the three days that followed, most of Bataillon 202 was bypassed and cut off by the American 7th Regiment. Still, the mountain troops continued to fight, as their wounded and dying lay in a narrow draw, screaming from lack of morphine, attended by one lone medic who did his level best to care for them and the wounded American prisoners.

At dawn, 24 October, the tables turned briefly as Maj. Clayton Thobro's 2d Battalion found itself encircled by mountain troops they had bypassed the day before. Sharp engagements were fought, and Companies L (Capt. Ralph Yates) and I (Capt. Edward Just) were rushed up to relieve the hard-pressed 2d Battalion. Moving through the narrow valley at Halley, they were caught in the crossfire of a Panzer IV and machine guns, and by early afternoon, Company K had to be committed. When its commander, Capt. George Lauderdale, was hit, Lieutenants Vladimir Dostal and Ralph Payne continued with the assault. After four hours of fierce fighting, backed by tanks and tank destroyers, the hamlet of Mailleufaing was in American hands.

During the night of 24–25 October, small groups of German mountain troops infiltrated the "Cotton Balers," 2d Battalion, prompting several firefights and even fistfights. The next morning, as Major Thobro's men continued into the Forêt de Champ, the 7th Regiment's command post at Mailleufaing was pounded by artillery and rockets *(Nebelwerfer)*, which killed and wounded a number of men and destroyed all communication lines. Les-Rouges-Eaux had already been evacuated by the Germans, but east of town, Companies I, K, and L were drawn into one firefight after another, and Capt. William Dieleman's battle patrol had to fend off three separate counterattacks by mountain troops who refused to surrender.

By Friday, 27 October, Lieutenant Colonel Hanley's Japanese Americans reached Hill 585, which had just been cleared by the 7th Infantry. As Companies E and F tried to get behind Schnellabteilung 602, they got embroiled in a firefight with the mountain troops of Heeres Gebirgsjäger Bataillon 202. After four days of relentless battle, out of food and ammunition, and with no relief in sight, the battalion adjutant and twenty of his men finally surrendered.

By now the German High Command was utterly confused about the disposition of Bataillon 202, listing it as *verschollen* (lost) and placing a question mark on the map. Major Eisenhart, adjutant of the 16th Volks-Grenadier Division, and three of his companions fell victim to this confusion when their amphibious Volkswagen was racing toward les-Rouges-Eaux in the mistaken belief that the fighting was still confined to Bruyères. An American bazooka round abruptly ended their journey. The driver and a captain were killed, and Majors Gehring and Eisenhart were wounded. Eisenhart told the interrogator that they had been on their way "to visit old friends."

Another officer taken prisoner was Hauptmann Schötzler of Bataillon 202. Against Hitler's orders, he and his men had tried to break out of the trap. Like the American "Lost Battalion," his company had gone for five days without resupplies of food, water, and ammunition. Others were less fortunate. Some twenty mountain troops, taken prisoner by "Red Spaniards" fighting with the French resistance, were executed by their captors.

Remnants of the Austrian battalion continued to hold out against the 7th, 141st, and 442d Regiments for more than a week. Lieutenant Oskar Peuser's 3d Company was still fighting in the Forêt de Champ when he was wounded on 4 November. But for all intents and purposes, Heeres Gebirgsjäger Bataillon 202 ceased to exist as a cohesive fighting unit by 26 October. Like the American "Lost Battalion," the men from Salzburg went on fighting small actions until killed or captured. Only a handful, like Joseph Breiteneder, made their way back to St.-Dié, where they were collected at the Tirpitz Kaserne, to be thrown into the fray once again. On 5 November, near Rougiville, Breiteneder lost his leg to a grenade—one of very few to escape death or imprisonment. Most of his comrades, like Gerwin Eder, were captured and sent to Marseilles, where they spent the rest of the war unloading Allied ships, digging up mines, or working for French farmers as a means of reparation for the devastation done to the country.

But the Austrians had bought enough time to allow Gebirgsjäger Bataillon 201 to seal off the pass at le Haut Jacques. And so, in a curious twist of events, two battalions, one American and one German, found themselves cut off at the same time in the Forêt Dominale de Champ. And as Gebirgsjäger Bataillon 201 from Garmisch tried to aid its sister battalion from Salzburg, the Nisei 442d Regimental Combat Team set out to rescue the 1st Battalion of the "Alamo" Regiment.

After their arduous trek through the mountains east of Belmont, the Japanese Americans, led by Captains Tom Atkins and Joseph Hill, finally reached a point east of Grébéfosse from which they could attack Hill 617. At its southernmost extension, Schnellabteilung 602 was still locked with Company G when the Nisei stormed down from the high ground, taking the defenders by surprise. One of the attackers, SSgt. Tsuneo Takemoto, rushed toward a group of Germans, shouting and shooting as his platoon followed behind. When the Germans counterattacked, Sergeant Takemoto led another charge, routing the defenders and taking thirty-four prisoners. For his gallantry Sergeant Takemoto received the Distinguished Service Cross. The violence of the attack ended in a rout for the Germans. By mid-afternoon the fighting ebbed, and when Company G came up the front slope to join the rest of Colonel Hanley's battalion, it was all over.

In the early hours of Saturday, 28 October, General Dahlquist called Lieutenant Colonel Pursall: "Are you attacking?" The commander of the Nisei 3d Battalion answered, "Very slowly. It's so dark you can't see your hand in front of your face. I don't want to walk blindly into them."

"You've got to attack!"

By this time Colonel Pursall's Companies I and K had reached the easternmost point of the 36th Division, and indeed of the Seventh Army. Henry Nakada, Esuke Asato, and Nobuo Amakawa were scouting about a hundred yards ahead of Company I, straining their eyes to see through the half-light, moving silently from tree to tree, when German machine guns opened up at close range. Amakawa was killed instantly; Asato was wounded, while Nakada managed to scramble under a holly bush.

Nakada recalls, "One machine gun nest was about 20 feet above me, and I could hear them talking all afternoon. I stayed under my bush until it got dark, and then quietly crawled back toward what I hoped was our lines. When I was challenged I didn't know the password, so I said, *'Bakatare'* (stupid idiot). It got me through and back to Company I where I finally sacked out."

Earlier that day Company K had run into the first of a series of roadblocks. Each of these antitank barriers was manned by a company of infantry armed with automatic weapons. At one barrier SSgt. Gordon Yamashiro crawled ahead to scout the German positions, and along the way emerged victorious in a sniper duel. He then knocked out a machine-gun position with his BAR, and when another machine gun opened up, he killed its crew. As he covered his squad coming up from behind, Sergeant Yamashiro was killed by a sniper. But his valiant action left a gap in the German defenses through which Company K could now advance. Yamashiro was awarded the Distinguished Service Cross posthumously.

Throughout the attack, German mortar fire tore into the American ranks. When SSgt. Etsuo "Etchan" Kohashi called on his BAR-man, Kiyoshi Yoshii, to bring up his weapon, Yoshii ran and jumped into a half-finished foxhole. As he leaned forward to adjust his pod, a mortar round blew off his left arm and seriously injured his right, ending his dream of becoming an architect after the war. Mortar shrapnel also took Sgt. Shiro Kashino out of the fighting—the second wound he had sustained during the drive.

Lieutenant Colonel Pursall called for counterbattery fire—the tedious task of locating German guns in the wooded hills. Don Shimazu was part of such an artillery survey team, which served alongside the riflemen. Shimazu said, "Our commanders didn't know where our forces were. We went through countless enemy minefields and weren't aware of them until we read *'Achtung Minen!'* on the other side. And as we came near our infantry, we saw all the casualties. Men helplessly watching their buddies fatally wounded and dying."

On the right of the 3d Battalion, Colonel Singles's 100th found that the German grenadiers had withdrawn to the next ridge line. But as Companies B and C descended into the draw, artillery and mortar shells poured in, killing and wounding twenty men. Private First Class Joe Hattori, from Boyle Heights, was carrying the radio for the forward observer team attached to Company C. Hattori recalls, "It was cold and raining, and the Germans fired their mortars at us—tree bursts. There was this clearing we had to cross, and a Panther Mark V down this gully covering it. We had to time ourselves to get across, one by one, between that eighty-eight shooting at us— swoosh bang! I remember when it was my buddy Ukida's turn. He got up and ran just as the tank fired. 'I'm hit, I'm hit,' he yells! Turns out that a tree splinter went right through his jacket. He was okay, but we took a lot of casualties."

By evening the 100th and 3d Battalions had gained only a few hundred yards. Still, through dogged determination they had managed to take seventy prisoners from Grenadier Regiment 933 and Füsilier Bataillon 198.

The "Alamo" Regiment took a beating that day, forcing Lt. Col. James H. Critchfield, the commander of the 2d Battalion, to lead his own Company G. After the Americans were repulsed a third time, General Dahlquist took charge of a platoon, which eventually knocked out two machine-gun emplacements. For his participation the general was to receive the Silver Star.

General Ernst Haeckel also received a medal that day, at his Rougiville command post—the Iron Cross to the Knight's Cross—while his battalions were being decimated.

# 6: The "Alamo" Regiment

While the situation was precarious for the 442d RCT, it was desperate for the men of the 1st Battalion of the 141st Regiment. On the narrow ridge leading from Biffontaine toward Vanèmont, Lt. Marty Higgins had warned Lt. Col. William Bird that their battalion might be cut off. Bird had agreed and told Higgins that his orders were to proceed some four miles through dense woods with visibility less than fifty yards.

"Remember the Alamo" was the battle cry of the fledgling Texas Republic one hundred years earlier. For two weeks in 1836, the defenders of San Antonio's Alamo Mission stood firm against the Mexican army of General Santa Ana. Among those in the fortified mission were 189 settlers from east of the Mississippi who had come with the promise of free land, native Mexicanos, fourteen women and children, and one free black man and one slave—the servant of Colonel William Travis. Others were the famed Indian fighter and former congressman Davy Crockett, and Jim Bowie, now sick with fever.

On the night before the Mexican army attacked, Colonel Travis drew a line in the sand and gave his men the choice to stay or leave. All stepped across the line. Under the cover of night Santa Ana drew up his battle lines, and just before daybreak three thousand men attacked. No quarter was given. As the soldiers scaled the north wall and flooded into the compound, the Texans fired their cannon and long rifles until overrun. As the sun rose over the south Texas prairie, six hundred of Santa Ana's men lay in the fields and courtyards of the Alamo, and all but eight of its defenders were dead. "These are but chickens," the Mexican general is reported to have said. "But the battle is over. It was but a small affair." Then he had seven survivors shot. Only Louis Rose, who had slipped over the wall during the night, lived to tell his story.

The Alamo story is synonymous with the creation of Texas, and is a long-standing symbol of American freedom and self-sacrifice. And those of the "Alamo" Regiment saw themselves as the guardians of that legacy.

Since its founding in 1836, the "Alamo" Regiment had seen action in the War of 1848 and the American Civil War, under famed Texas general John Hood. The men of the Lone Star State also fought in the Meuse-Argonne campaign of World War I, and, when the drumbeat of war again resonated close to America's shores, the National Guard Regiment from San Antonio was federalized on 25 November 1940. New conscripts joined the regiment at Camp Bowie, near Brownwood, Texas, where the year 1941 was ushered in with "the Parade of the Wooden Soldiers." The nation, on the edge of war, was unprepared. Everything was simulated, from cars dressed up as tanks to wooden guns. Only the spirit and enthusiasm of the officers and men was genuine.

After Japan's attack on Pearl Harbor, the 141st continued to train with the 36th Division. Then, on 2 April 1943, the men from Texas sailed out of New York Harbor—destination Algeria.

Following lengthy amphibious training, the 141st landed at Paestum, just south of Salerno, on 9 September 1943—the first American regiment to set foot on the European mainland. But German artillery fire was deadly accurate. Several boats were sunk, and only three of seven scheduled waves were able to land on Blue Beach. As soon as it landed, the 3d Battalion was hit by panzers, and American howitzers fired point-blank to stop the attack just short of the division command post.

After nine bloody days the Battle for Salerno was over, with the Americans and British emerging victorious. But those who thought they had seen the worst were sadly mistaken. The Battle for San Pietro was followed by disaster at the Rapido River in January 1944. Even though more than thirty-one thousand rounds of artillery prepped the assault, the rubber assault boats proved inadequate for the swift currents, and many were destroyed by German fire. Once across, minefields and carefully registered mortar and artillery fire wreaked havoc among the Americans. Shattered and broken by the unbearable intensity of German fire, units began to lose all signs of organization; and the commanders and second in command of both the 2d and 3d Battalions, together with all the company commanders, had either been killed or wounded. Then the Germans counterattacked. Small-arms fire could be heard until midnight, 22 January, when most of the veteran fighters had disappeared into the blazing muzzle of death. It is said that one of the last orders transmitted across the river was, "You stay there until you die." They did.

On the morning of 25 January, American aid men carrying Red Cross flags crossed the Rapido. They were met by German officers and aid men who agreed to a truce to remove the dead. Once that sad task had been accomplished, fighting resumed in the late afternoon. What remained of the regiment continued on to Monte Cassino, then Anzio, and the successful campaigns at Velletri, and finally Rome. And then came France.

At 0800 hours, 15 August, the 1st Battalion of the "Alamo" Regiment was first to hit Blue Beach near the village of Dramont, and routed the German defenders from the slopes overlooking the beaches.

In a bold move the 36th Division covered 250 miles in eight days to cut off the escape route of the German Nineteenth Army at Montélimar. While the operation turned out to be a brilliant maneuver by General Truscott, his advance units were not strong enough to contain the retreating Germans. Once again the brunt of the fighting fell on the "Alamo" Regiment, as elements of the 11th Panzer and the 198th Divisions hacked away at the overextended regiment. Fighting was furious. More than seventy thousand rounds of artillery were lobbed in support of the 36th Division, with every available man on the firing line. The Germans bled heavily, losing more than ten thousand men killed, wounded, or taken prisoner, including Generalmajor Otto Richter, commander of the 198th. Also, loss of matériel was staggering—two thousand vehicles, one thousand horses, and six huge railroad guns. But then came the Vosges.

At noon, Monday, 23 October, the 1st Battalion, with Lieutenant Higgins's Company A in the lead, had passed through the lines of

Company K, 442d RCT, east of Belmont, heading up into the steep, wooded hills of the Forêt de Champ. An hour later they were followed by Major Bruyere's 3d Battalion. By 1817 hours Company A had its first contact in the Forêt de Champ, and throughout the night German artillery continued to harass the Americans.

The next morning, Tuesday, 24 October, Bravo Company got into a firefight with Frenchmen wearing civilian garb. Lieutenant Colonel Bird thought they were FFI, a claim rejected by Division G-2, who believed them to be German collaborators. At 1030 hours General Dahlquist arrived at the regimental command post and assured Colonel Lundquist that he didn't need to worry about his left flank, because the 7th Regiment was about to cut all roads coming down from the north. At 1100 hours German artillery intensified, and the Americans moved eight tanks up from Belmont to support the "Alamo" Regiment's drive.

But by 1400 hours came the first counterattacks against Company A, B, C, and 1st Battalion headquarters. At the time the steep mountains and the distance disrupted all radio contact with the regiment, and it wasn't until 1730 hours that Colonel Lundquist received word that the 1st Battalion CP had been overrun. As Lieutenant Colonel Bird and his staff fought their way back, Colonel Lundquist ordered his 2d Battalion to proceed north from Biffontaine to join the fight. By nightfall the 1st and 3d Battalions had dug in, bracing themselves for the artillery and infantry attacks that were sure to come.

One of the units that barely eluded the trap was Company E of the 2d Battalion. Originally Company E was made up exclusively of Mexican Americans from the El Paso region. Spanish was the primary language spoken by its men and officers—several of whom received battlefield commissions after the bitter fighting at Salerno and the Rapido River. One fourth of the company had been lost during the Italian landing, and, after the disastrous crossing of the Rapido, only twenty-three of the original group remained. First Sergeant Alfonso Mojica was one of the few who made it all the way through the war, and Gabriel Navarrete rose from corporal to captain, earning the DSC, two Silver Stars, and seven Purple Hearts.

By Wednesday morning, 25 October, it became clear that the Grenadier Regiment 933 had indeed cut off the 1st Battalion by erecting roadblocks covered by machine guns and artillery forward observers, and that they were surrounded by freshly placed mines. A strong combat patrol sent out by the 3d Battalion was thrown back with heavy casualties. When the "Alamo" Regiment's S-2 gave the situation report to Division G-2, General Dahlquist and his chief of staff came to the forward CP to assess the situation.

Among the trapped was SSgt. Jack Wilson of Newburgh, Indiana, a veteran of the Rapido River and Cassino battles, who was now calmly preparing his heavy machine-gun section to repulse a superior force, as the men of the Alamo had done 108 years earlier.

This was to be some of the worst combat that I had been in—no place to get away from the tree bursts, heavy sniper- and machine-gun fire. But we finally broke through and went three or four miles before we realized we were cut off. I guess we tried to push too far too fast, and the enemy closed the hole behind us.

When we realized we were cut off, we dug a circle at the top of the ridge. I had two heavy, water-cooled machine guns with us at this time, and about nine or ten men to handle them. I put one gun on the right front with about half of my men, and the other gun to the left.

We cut down small trees to cover our holes and then piled as much dirt on top as we could. We were real low on supplies, so we pooled all of our food. We had one 400 radio on which we called in once a day, and they tried to get some (supplies) in to us. The first try was to shoot smoke shells loaded with D-bars (hard chocolate) to us. But we took some casualties from these, so we radioed to stop the shelling. The next try, they dive-bombed us with spare gas tanks from P-47s. Most of these fell outside of our perimeter, and we had to fight for what little we got.

We realized what trouble we were in when we sent out patrols to make contact with our people, and none came back.

Henri Grandjean, one of two FFI guides, was carrying a pistol along with the M1 rifle he'd been issued. "There was no way out for me. I wouldn't have committed suicide, but I would have fought to the bitter end. They wouldn't have caught me alive."

By late morning the "Lost Battalion" had buried three of its dead and dug in deep, waiting for the German counterattack. Colonel Lundquist moved his "Alamo" Regiment's command post up to the front lines just north of Biffontaine and dispatched eight tanks and infantry with food, water, and ammunition for the encircled 1st Battalion in the woods above la Houssière. When the attempt failed, General Dahlquist called on the Nisei 442d RCT to finish the job.

On Thursday, 26 October, the forward observer, 2nd Lt. Erwin Blonder of Shaker Heights, Ohio, sent a message from the "Lost Battalion."

Out of food and water, and critically low on ammunition. Medical supplies next to nothing; wounded need attention. No way to evacuate them.

This was followed by another call at 1 P.M.

Contact with enemy forces at three different points. Twenty-eight wounded. Request artillery on enemy positions in Bois de Biffontaine, southeast of Devant le Feys.

In a coded message, Colonel Lundquist ordered Lieutenant Higgins to break out of the encirclement and move his men west toward Company K, one kilometer north of Devant le Feys. Higgins, the senior lieutenant, chosen by his peers to lead the cutoff battalion, pushed for the breakout but was voted down by the other lieutenants. The argument was that it would be too difficult to carry nine litter cases along with the walking wounded. Instead, it was decided that a combat patrol should try to get out. At dusk, fifty-three volunteers filed through the perimeter and down the narrow path toward their front lines. But a short time later the staccato of German machine guns, flares, and tracers betrayed their fate. Only five men returned to the "Lost Battalion." The rest were killed or captured. One survivor, Pvt. Horace Male of Allentown, Pennsylvania, alone managed to get past German sentries and minefields. He was found five days later wandering aimlessly in the forest.

The *Wehrmacht Daily Summary* describes the action:

In the sector northeast of Biffontaine our own attack against strong enemy resistance succeeded in closing the gap between the valley 2 km southeast of Erival and east of Biffontaine. In the process the commanding hill 2 km north of Biffontaine was retaken. Several enemy attacks in the sector were repulsed, and sixty prisoners were taken.

By Friday, 27 October, the "Lost Battalion" reported seven more casualties and requested an air drop of ammunition to make a retrograde operation possible. Through a crack in the clouds American spotter planes located the unit on the ridge line. But by the time the four planes from the 371st Fighter-Bomber Group arrived with belly-tanks full of food, medical supplies, ammunition, and radio batteries, heavy clouds again obscured the drop zone. Still the pilots released the belly tanks, hoping for the best. But on the ground, the men could hear as most of the containers crashed into the German positions.

At noon, at the "Lost Battalion," Lieutenant Blonder radioed back to headquarters:

"Weather is clear now. Please do something!"

Arthur Rodgers, the other heavy machine-gun team leader, remembers. "We were always wet and hungry. Do you know what happens when you go without food for four days? Your stomach shrinks. That's all we talked about—food. I had some fruit bars saved up and gave them to the medic so he could mix them with water and spoon-feed them to the wounded. We and the Germans got water from the same spot."

Jack Wilson recalls: "We did have a muddy water hole on the edge of our perimeter. From time to time, one of us would crawl up there and fill our canteens. The Germans also used it. In fact, one of my men shot a German, and he fell into the water. Most of us thought we were sure to be killed or captured because we knew that all attempts to come to us had failed.

"On the last patrol out, I was told to send three of my men. I knew they didn't have much of a chance of making it back. I sent Bob Camiani, Tillman Warren, and Bert McQueen. The last two fellows were born and raised in Kentucky in country like this. My thoughts were that if anyone can do it, these boys can. And after a day or two, these three did make it back, also bringing a prisoner with them."

According to Arthur Rodgers: "The Germans didn't use tanks against us, only a 170mm self-propelled gun, 88s, and regular artillery—tree bursts. We'd always try and dig in a little deeper."

Wilson agrees: "They didn't press us too hard. They knew we were trapped with nowhere to go, so why lose any more of their people; starve us out."

Finally, by late afternoon, Saturday, 28 October, four radar-equipped aircraft managed to drop some supplies inside the 1st Battalion's perimeter, at the cost of one plane shot down by friendly anti-aircraft fire. Also, division artillery had devised a method of fitting supplies into shells—chocolate bars and medicine to be fired just before dark. But most of the shells buried themselves deep in the ground or missed the beleaguered unit altogether.

One of those receiving the "fruits of heaven" was German Airman Schwieters, who now shared a foxhole with his old friend, Hans-Paul Geiger. Schwieters recalls, "We didn't know that we had surrounded the Americans until they were being supplied by air. One of the supply containers, dropped by parachute, landed near us. The packages were divided up among us. Ever since Saint-Jean-d'Angély we had been fed only sporadically, so that the food falling into our laps was most welcome. Even toilet paper was included. Thanks to our knowledge of English, we knew exactly what to do with the little bags of instant coffee altogether unknown in Germany. Real blended coffee was the high point of that quiet day in our foxhole."

With the 442d RCT still bogged down, and the possibility of losing his battalion growing ever stronger, General Dahlquist again came out to the front lines and fired his 141st Regiment commander, Lundquist, replacing him with his chief of staff, Col. Charles Owens of Tacoma, Washington. His orders to both Owens and Colonel Pence of the 442d were clear.

"I want the men to crawl and run forward because that's the only way to push the enemy back. Battalion and company commanders are to go up front and drive their companies!"

# 7: Banzai Hill

Frost turned the grass to silver as the sun rose on a fateful Sunday, 29 October. Airman Schwieters, whose platoon had spent the night in a farmhouse at des Huttes, took up his position north of la Houssière when suddenly, wild shooting broke out.

It was early in the morning, our first enemy contact, when I saw a couple of American soldiers seeking cover in the brush about 100 meters ahead. Hans-Paul jumped into a half-finished foxhole, and I took cover behind a tree trunk. As I cocked my rifle, I took a heavy, painful blow to the chin. Blood flowed. I crawled back over the hill and noticed that I couldn't move my left arm. I didn't know it then, but the same bullet had shattered both my jaw and left shoulder joint.

On the other side of the hill, a medic bandaged me and asked if I could still walk. I said yes. I had to cross an open field which obviously lay in the Americans' sights. But they didn't shoot at me, perhaps because of my bandages. Later, I thought that it was very sporting of them.

Airman Schwieters had once again encountered the "iron men" of the 442d RCT, now only half a mile from the "Lost Battalion." Numb with pain, he walked back toward the farmhouse where he had found shelter the night before, past rows of German corpses from the previous day's mortar attack, to the aid station where a German orderly refused to attend to him because he was from another battalion. "I could have murdered that orderly." Mustering all the energy he had left, Schwieters finally reached a farmhouse near Marmonfosse where other wounded lay on straw in the barn.

"After a while, a Frenchwoman, about forty years old, who had been watching me brought me a thick feather pillow, which she placed carefully under my head," Schwieters recalls. "After that she stroked my cheek. This was a unique experience for me which I shall never forget. With all the hatred in the world at that time, I could hardly comprehend so much goodness and sympathy."

A mile away, the Japanese-American battalions again ran into the mined and fortified positions of Oberst (Col.) Rolin's Grenadier Regiment 933. Forty-seven-year-old Walter Ernst Emil Rolin was a Prussian career officer, son of the foreman of a noble estate near Posen. At eighteen he had volunteered to fight in World War I, winning the Iron Cross 1st and 2d Class at Verdun and the Moselle, and by the time Germany attacked Poland in 1939 he was a lieutenant colonel. In 1943 as a colonel, he had assumed command of Grenadier Regiment 933 at Marseilles, which then had counted 2,950 men. But with the Allied invasion and subsequent retreat up the Rhône valley, the motorized regiment had become a moving target.

Rolin recalls, "Absolute Allied air superiority and favorable weather brought about heavy losses. The almost unceasing activity of the enemy fighter-bombers had a decisive influence on the tempo and maneuverability of the motorized formations. Here, the columns of service troops and later those of the fighting troops, moving in rows of four, had run into one another and become defenseless victims to the enemy planes. Losses in men, animals, and matériel were very heavy."

While assigned to the 338th Infantry Division, commanded by Generalmajor Réné de l'Homme de Courbière, Rolin's regiment was involved in heavy rear-guard action north of Montélimar. Like Courbière, Rolin was the descendant of French Huguenots who had found refuge in Germany during the wars of religion and had contributed many fine officers to the Prussian army. On 30 August, after escaping the American trap, Rolin's regiment had conducted a successful night attack to break through the Allied lines in the Forêt de

Marsonne. But now, as they climbed into the Forêt de Champ, 350 combat effectives were all that remained of Grenadier Regiment 933. Their mission was unambiguous: "Stop the Americans at all cost!"

The ridge on which the Nisei advanced was barely wide enough to accommodate two companies, with steep slopes on either side. While the 100th Battalion managed to skirt the minefield on the right, the 3d Battalion had to advance straight through it. They were met by murderous artillery and rifle fire, and Company K was thrown back with heavy losses. To make matters worse, the rugged terrain and tall trees made it nearly impossible for American forward observers to adjust artillery. Most rounds sailed over the German positions or crashed into the treetops above, showering friendly troops with deadly debris.

After Captain Kim was wounded at Biffontaine, 1st Lt. James Boodry took over as intelligence officer for the 100th Battalion. Boodry and 1st Lt. Bill Pye, commanding Company C, were huddling over a map when a tree burst split open Boodry's head. Pye, himself wounded by the blast, looked in disbelief on his fallen comrade, saying to himself, "If I have to get it, I'd rather get it now." The six-foot-two Pye, down to 110 pounds, kept his company moving until an hour later, when his legs were shattered by a German shell. At that point, Pye, from San Antonio, was less than half a mile from his fellow Texans of the "Alamo" Regiment.

Trying to make some headway, Colonel Pursall called on his tanks to fire point-blank into the German positions. The men of the 752d Tank Battalion were considered the best the Nisei soldiers had ever worked with. Through the most difficult terrain and against a tenacious enemy they went as far as they could, and then some. The Germans, too, respected the combined infantry and tank effort.

> With tank attacks, the escorting infantry covered dead angles of the tanks by escorting them on both sides. It was rarely possible to separate tanks from the infantry, thus allowing the enemy to penetrate deeper and deeper into the forest. In this for tanks difficult terrain, the American Sherman tank's drivability proved superior to our Panzer IV.

As the Shermans blasted away, Companies I and K gained some ground before antitank rockets, mines, and interlocking machine-gun fire stopped them once again. By now the strain of protracted combat was beginning to take its toll. Cold, rain, lack of sleep, and the sudden shock of battle brought on a sense of indifference for life, manifesting itself in the "thousand-mile stare" and sudden, irrational actions, like wandering off aimlessly, or simply shutting down. But there was to be no respite. General Dahlquist again came to the front lines "to get the attack going." Private First Class Matsui "Mutt" Sakumoto of Company I remembers: "On the third day General Dahlquist showed up and asked why we were sitting down, doing nothing. We told him, 'We're the reserve platoon,' and he said, 'Don't let the other boys do all the fighting—flank the enemy.' With the general was his aide, a tall, clean-cut young fellow with a lieutenant bar shining on his helmet."

Even though he had been warned about the German machine guns, the general insisted that the troops move out. Within seconds, guns and snipers opened up, killing his aide, 27-year-old Lt. Wells Lewis. Lewis, the son of Nobel prize–winning author Sinclair Lewis, died in the general's arms.

Still shaken by his aide's death, General Dahlquist called for an artillery strike. But the request was aborted when the forward observer and the 522d fire direction team realized that the coordinates given were right on top of the "Lost Battalion."

With a break in the weather, the trapped battalion was again promised help from the XIIth TAC. The men tore maps, underwear, and parka liners into long strips to mark the target area. This time they also tied smoke grenades to bent saplings, which were released as the planes approached late in the morning. With white puffs of smoke above the treetops, the Thunderbolts released their belly tanks right on target—nineteen planes dropping canisters filled with K rations, medical supplies, water, ammunition, and radio batteries.

"It was like something you see in the movies," Lieutenant Higgins recalls. "Shells falling with food, planes zooming and dropping parachutes, and belly tanks loaded with supplies—it was really something. Most of the men cried like kids. You just can't put into words how we felt.

"I ordered all the food brought to one point for a breakdown and equal distribution. And not one man stopped to eat anything. They brought the food, piled it up, and looked at it. It was the strongest discipline I ever saw. Some of the men had to shoot their way to the rations as they landed near the Jerries who tried to grab them first. We had the same sort of trouble near the water hole. Jerry placed snipers there."

At 1450 hours General Dahlquist advised the "Lost Battalion" that the Nisei were only seven hundred yards away, and that patrols should be sent out to make contact along the trail, and if necessary attack the Germans from the rear. But half an hour later the answer came back that only three thousand rifle rounds and eight hundred rounds of carbine ammunition had been recovered, and that not enough men could be spared, due to German counterattacks. Also, many of the men, suffering from trench foot, were barely able to walk. A message followed at 1645, informing the general that a patrol had been sent out along the trail, but that it had run into mines near the designated contact point.

Late that afternoon a furious fight broke out as Colonel Pursall's 3d Battalion charged uphill against Regiment 933. Just what sparked this third and last "banzai" charge is still the subject of discussion among the survivors. Some eyewitnesses claim it started of its own accord, while others attribute it to the courage of a few men. But, singly or in groups of two or more, Companies I and K started to move against the Germans solidly entrenched on top of the hill. Artillery and mortar rounds dropped into their ranks, and machine-gun fire cut them down, but still they kept moving from tree to tree, shooting and lobbing hand grenades.

Staff Sergeant Fujio Miyamoto, of Company K, crawled ahead to pinpoint a German machine gun when he was wounded in the forearm. Disregarding his injury, he kept crawling until he could kill the machine gunners with his own tommy gun. In the two-hour battle that followed, Miyamoto killed five more men, refusing medical treatment until the objective was taken.

At the same time Pvt. Barney F. Hajiro, of Company I, forged ahead, firing his Browning Automatic Rifle. Hajiro had only recently received a summary court-martial for helping a Nisei soldier in a street fight with an Italian civilian. As a result his pay had been for-feited, and he had been reassigned from Company M to I. At the time of the attack, Hajiro was disgusted with life, K rations, cold wind and rain, and the court-martial which he considered unjust. According to John Tsukano, he had nothing left to lose and decided to "go for broke." With his BAR slung around his shoulder, Hajiro moved for-ward, killing the gunners of two machine-gun positions. Then he killed two snipers before he and the men behind him overran the German positions.

Francis Tsuzuki distinctly remembers Colonel Pursall, pistol in hand, participating. "He was telling everybody to charge, the so-called 'banzai' charge. Hey, I'm an artillery man. I don't have to charge, but like a damn fool, I charge up the hill. You couldn't see the Germans, you could only hear the loud fireworks."

Richard Kurohara agrees: "It was Indian warfare, dodging bullets from tree to tree."

Private First Class Jim Y. Tazoi, a radioman with Company K, was alone up front when he decided to assault a German machine-gun position. Hit by a sniper's bullet along the way, he managed to kill two grenadiers before a grenade knocked him down. The first thing he saw when he came to, was the Red Cross helmet of a medic ex-amining the intestines protruding from his abdomen. Hajiro, Kuro-hara, and Tazoi received the Distinguished Service Cross.

Colonel Rolin's grenadiers put up a desperate fight, but nothing could stop the Nisei rushing up the steep slopes, shouting, firing from their hips, and lobbing hand grenades into dugouts. Finally the Ger-man defenses broke, and the surviving grenadiers fled in disarray. But that afternoon the American aid stations were crowded with casual-ties. The 2d platoon of Company I had only two men left, and the 1st platoon was down to twenty men. Company K's losses were equally heavy, including all officers. But for once there was no counterattack, only the relentless pounding of American and German artillery.

"Oh God, so many of our guys wounded or killed," Francis Tsuzuki remembers. "The Germans too. Their wounded cried out, '*Wasser, Wasser*' water, water. What can I do? We had our own wounded to care for. We couldn't wander off. We followed a trail marked with toilet paper, left by whoever cleared the minefield."

Near the top of the hill, Tsuzuki and Kurohara came to a foxhole. "Two German soldiers were there—one dead, the other a mortally wounded officer," Kurohara recalls. "Francis commanded the officer to hand over his gun belt. The German died soon after."

"He was in a beautiful foxhole," Tsuzuki remembers. "They had time to dig these nice foxholes. A medic was going to remove him to attend to his injuries, but the German refused. He probably knew he was going to die. He looked up at me and smiled. *'Nein, nein'*. He actually smiled at me. I can't forget that."

"The American attacks were so strong that we had to pull back at first," wrote Airman Schwieters's friend, Hans-Paul Geiger. "But then we were ordered to counterattack. It was in the afternoon when the Americans made their heaviest thrust, so strong that we could not resist it. The American infantry fought bravely and tenaciously. They took not a single backward step. So we had to pull back once again. One of our squads, with a machine gun, got orders to stay behind to cover the withdrawal—to defend the rock to the last bullet. They were a suicide squad. I assume that all died."

Lieutenant Scherer's 2d Company, Füsilier Bataillon 198, sustained heavy losses that day, as did Colonel Walter Rolin's Regiment 933. After it was all over, Rolin described the 442d as "an extraordinarily tough and hard-fighting adversary." His use of *adversary* rather than *enemy* suggests that he respected the Japanese Americans' skills as "mountain fighters." After the rescue of the "Lost Battalion," Rolin counted only eighty grenadiers left on the line.

Regimental staff and part of the regiment was pulled out as *abgekämpft*, (no longer combat effective) and temporarily detailed to brigade staff. Later, we were detailed to the 16th Volks-Grenadier Division (Haeckel) to rebuild the shattered unit and form Volks-Grenadier Regiment 221.

Late that afternoon there was one more casualty. Colonel Charles Pence, commanding the 442d, was seriously injured when he slipped and fell down a dugout. His executive officer, Lt. Col. Virgil R. Miller, assumed command of the combat team.

In his diary, General Dahlquist noted about the Nisei attack: "Late in the evening a furious fight developed which I believe was the crisis." Then he wrote to his wife Ruth:

*The past week has been a very difficult and anxious one, and the strain will not be over for several days yet.*

*Yesterday, or rather last night, in a dark and dank dugout, I got my last reports and issued my orders for today. One youngster, a major commanding a battalion, came with his colonel. I had a question to ask him and turned around to look for him. Up stepped a black-bewhiskered guy whom I did not even recognize. I had to ask him if he really was Bruyere [Major Walter Bruyere III, of Montclair, New Jersey, had been commanding the 3d Battalion of the "Alamo" Regiment for only nineteen days].*

*It astounds me how the men are able to stand the physical and mental strain under which they are constantly living. It is almost beyond comprehension that the human being can stand so much. I had a battalion commander crack the other day, and it was really pitiful. I had not seen him for several days or knew anything about his condition, and as soon as I did, I shipped him to the rear to the clearing company for a rest.*

*Charlie [Colonel Charles Owens, who replaced Colonel Lundquist] has a regiment [141st]. I do not know if I will leave him there or not. He, of course, is ready to do anything, and jumped right in. He took a terrific beating yesterday and today, but tonight, when I left him, he was just as chipper and alive as ever.*

*Last week Sandy Patch [Seventh Army Commander] came down one afternoon, presumably to visit one of my regiments. I took him up there and he went around talking to men. I am sure he was trying to keep his mind occupied. His boy had been killed the day before and buried that morning."*

[Captain Alexander M. Patch III., 315th Infantry Regiment of the 79th Division, was killed in action on 22 October, during the battle of Parroy and buried the following day at Épinal. General Cuthbert P. Stearns, G-5 SHAEF, lost his son also, 1st Lt. Cuthbert P. Stearns Jr., killed by an antitank mine on 19 October, near Épinal].

German Nineteenth Army log, 30 October:

After two clear days, hazy weather again. The enemy's main thrust is in the area of the 16th Infantry Division south of the road les-Rouges-Eaux to St.-Dié.

Attacking with superior forces, the Americans were able to break through in several areas.

Airman Hans-Paul Geiger, and the survivors of 2d Company, were pulled off the line at 4 A.M. for a brief rest. They were deloused, got hot showers and food, and received their first change of clothing in two weeks.

General Dahlquist's orders were the same as the previous day's. "Outflank the roadblocks and destroy the enemy!" The "Lost Battalion" was notified to split up, leaving only the weapons platoon with the wounded and prisoners, while the rest of the men fought their way back toward the Japanese Americans.

Shortly after 1000, Lieutenant Higgins requested a halt to the air drops because they were giving away his positions. Half an hour later the Germans began to lay smoke east of Biffontaine, which the Americans mistook for an all-out assault against the "Lost Battalion." In fact, the smoke screen was intended to mask the German withdrawal.

Just before noon Higgins radioed that he now had twenty-two litter cases, eleven trench foot cases, and ten walking wounded, and that German patrols with automatic weapons were probing his perimeter, complicating any attempt at a retrograde operation. General Dahlquist was not satisfied. At 1135 he again ordered Higgins to send a patrol to make contact with the advancing units. Higgins had just finished a brief note to his wife when his camouflaged foxholes were attacked. But Sergeant Wilson's and Sergeant Rodgers's heavy machine guns, and two artillery strikes, scattered the small force.

By this time the American attack companies were only five hundred yards from the encircled battalion. But their ranks had thinned to less than half. In the 100th Battalion, for example, Company B had only forty-three men on the line; A and C, only sixty-six; and D, fifty-

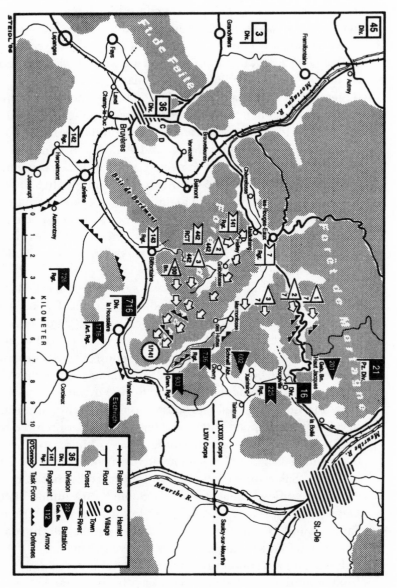

Situation map, 29–30 October. After the "Banzai" charge, the Nisei of the 442d RCT reach the "Lost Battalion." At the pass road west of Haut Jacques, "Cotton Balers" of the 7th Regiment battle, the "Mountain Hunters" (Gebirgsjäger) of Bataillon 201.

seven. In addition the battalion had lost nearly all of its officers: Sakamoto, Takahashi, Pye, Kim, and Boodry, and most of the platoon leaders. When Colonel Singles called for his company commanders that day, only two second lieutenants and two sergeants showed up.

With Company I down to forty men, Capt. Joseph Byrne was himself carrying a BAR that morning. Just after noon, when he received a call to come to the battalion command post, he asked commo sergeant Bert Akiyama to come along. The two men set out through the woods, and when they reached a narrow logging road, Byrne took the lead. Suddenly there was an explosion, and the captain slumped to the ground without uttering a sound. An antitank mine had ended the life of one of the most respected officers in the regiment. The six-foot-four, blond, blue-eyed Byrne, who had fought shoulder-to-shoulder with his men, was a giant in their eyes for more than just his physical stature. He had served in Hawaii as an enlisted man, and gone to OCS before joining the 442d. He knew many of his men from Schofield Barracks on Oahu, and as some put it, "was one 'haole' who could pronounce Buddhahead names."

Sergeant Akiyama took his captain's death very hard. He wrote, "We had lost our company commander—a man all of us in Company I had so much respect for. Joe Byrne was not only a good leader, he was an understanding and compassionate man, second to none in any endeavor. All of us believed that fate controlled our destiny, and that somewhere out there was a bullet with our name on it. After all the battles that moment had arrived for Joe Byrne."

By afternoon TSgt. Takashi Senzaki took out a patrol in an attempt to contact the trapped battalion. Henry Nakada, who two days earlier had survived German machine guns by hiding under a holly bush, and Matsui "Mutt" Sakumoto, were on point. Sergeant Akiyama had given Sakumoto a 300 radio with instructions not to break radio silence unless contact was made. Some twenty minutes later the patrol was approaching a wooded knoll known as "Trapin des Saules," and Sakumoto called, "We've contacted the enemy!" Akiyama waited to hear rifle fire, but there was none.

It was mid-afternoon when Private Sakumoto cautiously stepped from behind a tree. Sakumoto recalls, "In the distance I could see one or two persons moving about. But when I told Henry Nakada and Sergeant Senzaki, they didn't see any movement. The next time I looked ahead, I saw this GI looking straight in my direction. I kept looking until he motioned to his buddies. Then everybody started yelling to come out."

Sakumoto shouted into his radio, "We've contacted the Lost Battalion!"

Sergeant Edward Guy of New York City was on the perimeter next to a light machine-gun crew, when he noticed the American coming toward him. "I recognized a GI in the trees ahead and jumped up, and shouting and laughing ran down the slope toward the 442 trooper."

At that moment Mutt Sakumoto casually asked, "Need any cigarettes?"

"It was one of the happiest days in my life," according to Buck Glover. "The Japanese Americans were the most pleasing sight in the world—this short, dark-skinned kid coming up, wearing an American helmet several sizes too big. Did that matter? No. Here was a brother of mine coming up to save my life. . . . As long as I live, I will never forget the soldier who asked Eddie Guy, 'Need any cigarettes?'"

Jack Wilson said, "The Germans would have succeeded in starving us out if it hadn't been for the 100/442d boys. To me there was no finer bunch of troops in the U.S. Army."

After he was taken out with his comrades, Wilson was diagnosed as suffering from pneumonia, trench foot, and a serious concussion from a shell that had exploded near him. He was sent to a hospital at Fort Carson, Colorado, where a few days later he was joined by "Mutt" Sakumoto, who had been first to reach the "Lost Battalion."

At 1600 Lieutenant Blonder radioed his last message from the no longer trapped battalion. "Patrol from 442d here. Tell them that we love them!"

It was near dark as the main body of the Nisei regiment passed by the men of the "Alamo" Regiment, exchanging brief greetings, food, and cigarettes. Of 275 men cut off six days earlier, only 211 remained. Among them were Lieutenants Joseph Kimble, Harry Huberth, George Nelson and Erwin Blonder, who had chosen 1st Lt. Marty Higgins to lead them in their desperate effort. But with the relief complete, there was no time to celebrate. All were exhausted

from days of fighting, hunger, and exposure to the elements. Trench
foot was a serious problem. Standard issue boots with their rubber
soles were partly to blame for this, as they conducted cold and
caused feet to sweat. Under normal circumstances GIs would remove their boots, massage their feet, and change socks. But slugging
through cold mud, barely able to sleep in water-filled foxholes or
above ground, and under continuous bombardment, the Nisei began to suffer from this debilitating disease. Skin turned a pasty white
as it deteriorated, causing feet to swell and crack. Removing
shoelaces to accommodate swollen feet no longer worked, and in
some cases, boots had to be cut off. Constant exposure to weather
and death left the men dulled in spirit and indifferent toward life.
The conventions of civilized society no longer mattered, and the
only way out was "a million-dollar wound."

When Sgt. Shig Doi took a poncho from a dead German at the
water hole, one of the Texans hollered, "Hey, you can't do that!" But
Doi, who came from California's gold country, just shrugged and
draped the cloth over his own foxhole. "I didn't care. By that time I
couldn't feel anything anymore."

By late afternoon, as the 100th and 3d Battalions reached the far
end of the ridge overlooking la Houssière, General Dahlquist made
a brief entry into his notebook: "The 442nd finally broke through
to the 1st Battalion, 141st, late in the afternoon. Most of the resistance had been broken the day before."

And the *Wehrmacht Daily Summary* records:

> Connection between 716 and 16 Divisions again disrupted.
> The enemy breakthrough 2 km north of la Houssière could not
> be closed. Attacking southeast, the enemy reached the north-
> ern edge of Vanemont.

That night Assistant Division Commander Robert Stack wrote to
his brother Jack:

> *We've had a 'Lost Battalion' for six days. It was sent out as a cov-
> ering force to seize a mountain. They got there, but the 'Boche' came
> in behind in real strength. The terrain was rugged, heavily wooded,*

*plenty of rain, no roads and heavily held by Jerry with beaucoup ar-*
*tillery. . . . One of our battalions got to them this afternoon.*

*The Division Commander's aide was killed yesterday by a machine-*
*gun burst. He was a very nice young man, intelligent, spoke perfect*
*French, and a gentleman. He was the son of Sinclair Lewis, the nov-*
*elist. Dahlquist says the MG burst would have killed him if Lewis had*
*not been in the way.*

# 8: Mountain Hunters and Cotton Balers

As the men of the "Alamo" Regiment's 1st Battalion were being evacuated to the rear, splinter groups of the German "Lost Battalion" were still fighting for their lives west of Col du Haut Jacques.

Major Glenn Rathbun of the U.S. 7th Regiment remembers:

> Ken Wallace had just taken over the 1st Battalion and was on my immediate left. I was sitting on the front slope of a hill watching my troops clean out the village of Marmonfosse. I could also see the 442d keeping pace with my troops, and was about to move up when the phone buzzed between my feet. It was General O'Daniel, or 'Iron Mike' as we called him—a grouchy old cuss, but respected. He growled, "What are you doing?"
>
> I was watching my battalion and the Japs kick the hell out of the Krauts, and told him we were progressing. He said, "Don't you get tangled up in that brush like the 1st Battalion." I said, "Okay, General, no danger of that." He snorted, "Good," and hung up. Colonel Harrell had been on the line all the time, as I suspected, and I said, "Did you hear that, Colonel?" and he said, "Yes." The line of command was always respected in the 3d Division, as it should be.

The "Krauts" that both the Cotton Balers and the Nisei were battling that day were members of Lieutenant Höss's 2d Company,

Heeres Gebirgsjäger Bataillon 201, who had arrived only five days earlier. But the tables were soon to be turned on the "Cotton Balers." As Maj. Clayton Thobro's 2d Battalion followed the serpentine road leading up to the Col du Haut Jacques, his men were met by ever-increasing mortar and machine-gun fire.

"It was the toughest fighting since Anzio," according to Thobro, of Rock Springs, Wyoming. "We had never run into anything like that. They were a pretty tough outfit. I didn't sleep for three days and nights as attack followed counterattack."

Vitus Kolbinger, adjutant of Bataillon 201, also remembers:

> It was a senseless fight. In the days to follow, our battalion was left completely in the dark about its hopeless situation, and resupply was almost nonexistent, while the enemy bombarded us ceaselessly with artillery, mortars, tanks, and aircraft.

Five days earlier, on 26 October, confusion was the order of the day at German LXXXIX (89th) Corps headquarters at Dompaire. With communications to Gebirgsjäger Bataillon 202 completely broken off, it appeared as though the thousand-man unit had been swallowed by the forest. A flood of orders was issued, amended, and countermanded, while corps commander Gen. Werner Albrecht Freiherr von und zu Gilsa argued with his superior, Gen. Friedrich Wiese, over just how to stop the Americans. By then General Haeckel's 16th Volks-Grenadier Division had virtually ceased to exist as an infantry unit, and Panzer Brigade 106 (Feldherrnhalle) on his right had failed to stop the American 3d Division. Also, Gen. Edgar Feuchtinger's 21st Panzer Division was preparing to pull back from Baccarat. With a twenty-mile gap in the German main defense line, the only card left to play was that of Gebirgsjäger Bataillon 201.

After training at Garmisch, Mittenwald, and Sonthofen, Heeres Gebirgsjäger Bataillon 201 was formed only a month earlier, and placed under the direct command of OKH. Like its sister battalion from Salzburg, this battalion was made up of convalescent veterans of the Russian front—from the battle-hardened 1st and 4th Gebirgsjäger Divisions—and young recruits from Wehrkreis 7, which included Munich and the Bavarian Alps. Most of the men had volunteered when it became evident that the battalion was headed for the western front.

Bataillon 201 had three rifle companies, a weapons company with mortars and heavy machine guns, and an artillery platoon (equipped with three 7.5cm mountain howitzers for the battle at Haut Jacques). The 5th Company, reflecting the independent nature of the unit, was comprised of battalion staff, and one platoon each for communications, combat engineers, medical/veterinary, and a supply unit equipped with horses and mules. Like Bataillon 202, this unit also received brand-new weapons and uniforms. As fortune would have it, their weapons functioned very well.

The propaganda ministry didn't miss the opportunity to take newsreel footage of the mountain troops parading about Garmisch in dress uniform, an army band escorting one of the companies back from a training exercise, and the good-bye speech made by Gauleiter Wagner. But the glamour was short-lived. Battalion staff company, and Companies 1 and 2, left late on 23 October, followed by Companies 3 and 4 the following day. At first glance it appeared as though their fate had been sealed, like that of the battalion from Salzburg. When Companies 1 and 2 arrived at St.-Dié in the early hours of 26 October, they were assigned to General Haeckel's 16th Volks-Grenadier Division. By then rumors were already circulating about the demise of the Salzburg battalion.

It was still dark as the coal-gas-powered trucks hauled the men across the Col du Haut Jacques. In the gray hours of a new day, they were met by a gruesome sight—the bloodied and dismembered corpses from Bataillon 202, lined up on both sides of the road. As the trucks exchanged the living for the dead, Oberleutnant Karl Hiller collected his men of 1st Company and headed up into the steep, wooded hills east of les-Rouges-Eaux.

Oskar Abbold was digging his foxhole when he got his first taste of what was to come.

A fiery steam roller of American artillery telling us old-timers that we were in for a difficult fight. Robert Lechner, from Memmingen, was in my group when a piece of shrapnel killed him.

It was particularly tragic because he suffered from a severe throat infection and could have stayed behind in Garmisch. But he had convinced the staff physician to let him go with his platoon.

At dusk General Haeckel appeared and told us that no more German troops were to be expected from the west, and that American infantry was close. He was dead wrong. During the night we could hear tanks approaching, and had it not been for the tank commanders speaking German, we would have fired on them with our Panzerfaust.

We kept changing positions throughout the night, and at dawn fell into a French partisan ambush. We had many casualties, dead and wounded, most of them from shots that came from above. I remember one sergeant with a head wound, screaming for his mother before he died. None of our medics could get close on account of snipers. Finally, Oberleutnant Hiller and the rest of us shot into the trees with rifle grenades and machine guns. A number of snipers fell halfway down, still strapped to the trees, some dead, some wounded.

The ambush was followed by another artillery barrage, which once again underscored the deadly accuracy with which FFI pinpointed German targets.

When battalion commander Maj. Franz Seebacher and his staff arrived late on the twenty-sixth, he was confronted with the difficult task of finding his first two companies scattered throughout the woods. Seebacher insisted that his lead companies be pulled back so the battalion could fight as a cohesive unit. But it wasn't until his 3d and 4th Companies arrived on foot a day later that Seebacher was able to complete his defenses along the serpentine road leading to the top of the pass.

Seebacher, a graduate of the Austrian Military Academy at Wiener Neustadt, was a career soldier who had begun the war as a brand-new lieutenant. Five years of combat had taken him from Poland to Greece and finally Russia, where he participated in the Caucasus campaign and the skillfully executed withdrawal across the Kuban bridgehead. Along the way he had earned the Iron Cross and German Cross, and was still recovering from a serious back injury.

After collecting fresh stores of ammunition, Seebacher was to make his stand at Col du Haut Jacques where, outnumbered, outgunned, and poorly supplied, his mountain troops were to battle elements of the 3d and 36th Divisions for six days.

For eighteen-year-old Toni Stocker, this was to be his first combat. Stocker was born on his grandmother's farm only two miles from where Hitler was to build his Berghof on the Obersalzberg. He was a high school student at nearby Traunstein when his age group was called up for service. To escape muster by the Waffen SS, he and two dozen classmates volunteered for the mountain troops. Like Stocker, most were sent to Garmisch or the Luttensee Kaserne to undergo mountain training—in his case as a member of the engineer platoon.

"When we got to Haut Jacques there wasn't time to build fortifications. Each of us just dug a foxhole and waited. We had only three small artillery pieces and our mortars. We didn't know that we were up against two divisions," Stocker said.

After his Cotton Balers killed and captured most of Gebirgsjäger Bataillon 202, Col. Benjamin Harrell's 7th Regiment advanced toward the pass with the 1st Battalion on the left, 2d in the center, and the 3d on the far right near Hill 585, where his men linked up with the Japanese-Americans.

The first major contests between the Cotton Balers and the Gebirgsjäger Bataillon from Garmisch took place on 28 October. As the Americans moved on either side of the serpentine road leading up to the Col du Haut Jacques, Oberleutnant Hiller's 1st Company opened fire from well-camouflaged positions. One of the first to die was Pvt. Macario Gallardo, who tried to knock out a machine-gun position with hand grenades (a DSC was awarded posthumously). Soon after, Lt. Albert Tetreault was cut down while trying to fight off the first of many counterattacks.

One counterattack was led by Leutnant Jennerwein, twenty years old, just like Tetreault. Jennerwein was so far ahead of his men that he ran into his own machine-gun fire, taking three bullets in the back. Hunched over as though waiting for his men to catch up, he rose stiffly, refused all offers of help, and told his men to continue the attack. Then he slung his Schmeisser across his shoulder and staggered off toward the rear. Some time later Bernhard Weyerer saw the lieutenant slumped over his weapon, sitting alongside the path lead-ing up to the pass road. He was dead.

After engaging infiltrators during the night of 28–29 October, the 7th Regiment's battle patrol and Company K continued to fight pitched battles against scattered platoons from Bataillon 202 and the forward 1st Company of Bataillon 201. Companies I and L captured thirty-one mountain troops, bringing the week's total to more than six hundred.

1st Company of Bataillon 201 had entered the fight with one hun-dred and fifty men. When Major Seebacher was finally permitted to pull them back, only thirty-two remained. At one point, when Adju-tant Kolbinger made his way to the surrounded company, he found Oberleutnant Hiller on the edge of a small depression, firing his pis-tol at anything that moved. Physically and mentally exhausted after three days and nights of artillery and air bombardment and close combat, Hiller appeared as though in a trance. When Oberleutnant Hans Gessler of 5th (Headquarters) Company was sent to relieve Hiller, he was captured by the Americans, and soon after, Hiller was seriously wounded and taken out of the fight. The remaining *Jäger* of 1st Company, led by Corporal Frey, fought on until all were killed or captured.

Fair weather continued on 30 October, as the 7th Infantry moved through the morning with only light resistance. But by late after-noon, as the "Alamo" Regiment's 1st Battalion was relieved by the Japanese Americans five miles to the south, Companies A, E, and G were met by heavy machine-gun and mortar fire half a mile short of the Col du Haut Jacques. By now the remaining *Jäger* companies had dug in and carefully camouflaged their positions—3d Company north, and 2d Company south of the pass road. Backed by mortars and heavy machine guns from 4th Company, they were ready to do battle. Earlier, Leutnant Kolbinger had found a quartermaster eager to part with six boxcars full of mortar ammunition, and a truck and driver to haul it to the front. Major Seebacher, expert in the use of mortars, had carefully plotted his concentrations, and now used them to maximum advantage.

Major Glenn Rathbun of Great Falls, Montana, was used to end-running Germans, bypassing their positions during the night and, at dawn, attacking from behind. "This was my kind of country, just like the backwoods of Idaho—woods, brush, and streams; I was right at home, and so were my Blue Ridge boys; they began to shine."

But on this day his 3d Battalion found its match in the determined Alpine soldiers entrenched on Hill 491. Rathbun's battalion took casualties; one of the first being Capt. Ralph Yates of Company L. "Slammed in the head by a 20mm shell," recalls Rathbun. "He lived to go home and follow a career as a teacher in Texas. We kid him about losing half his brain and still becoming a teacher."

Major Seebacher didn't know that the 21st Panzer Division on his right had already withdrawn from Baccarat, and that his battalion stood virtually alone. With a break in the weather, Allied fighter-bombers resumed their ground support, adding to the already formidable firepower of the 3d and 36th Divisions.

Nineteenth Army daily log entry:

> Ht. Jacques is still in our hands. Main defense line between the pass and Marmonfosse must be reestablished. West of Ht. Jacques, the enemy is increasing attacks on either side of pass road. . . . two attacks repulsed, third attack with three tanks and two companies breached defenses.

But on Tuesday, 31 October, at Nineteenth Army headquarters, more attention was being paid to their distinguished visitor, General Feldmarschall Gerd von Rundstedt, than to the mountain troops at Col du Haut Jacques. Also, Gen. Ernst Haeckel was oblivious to the fate of Bataillon 201 just assigned to him. Only three days after receiving the Knight's Cross to the Iron Cross, the commander of the 16th Volks-Grenadier Division was standing before a court-martial, accused of refusing a direct order (Article 92). Charges read that he had failed to hold his line, and abandoned most of his heavy weaponry and equipment at Langres. He was acquitted of all charges, but the strain of the proceedings, which carried a potential death sentence, and weeks of grueling retreat and the loss of his division twice over, had begun to affect his health.

After another "fiery steam roller" passed over the German positions at Haut Jacques, the Cotton Balers' Company A and C again inched their way up the wooded slopes through mine fields, tree bursts, and withering machine-gun fire. Major Benjamin Boyd, commanding the 1st (red) Battalion, was one of the casualties that day, to be replaced by Capt. Ken Wallace.

Major Clayton Thobro's 2d (white) Battalion fared little better against the mountain men trained for this sort of warfare. By early afternoon Capt. George Ellis's "Easy" Company tried to make some headway with Lt. James Powell's 1st platoon on the left and Lt. Ralph Street's 3d platoon on the right—fighting at close quarters, crawling and blasting away at the mountain troops' first line of defense with hand grenades and bazookas. But after breaking through in a few spots, they found themselves facing another line on either side of the serpentine road, and another one behind that, well camouflaged and mutually supported by mortars and machine guns.

By late afternoon the platoons of "Easy" Company had gained a little ground, sacrificing one man for every two yards. Still, with ammunition nearly exhausted, Captain Ellis's men continued to struggle up Hill 652. Credit for capturing the hill late that day went to First Lieutenant Powell's platoon, which killed six and captured twelve *Jäger.*

Colonel Glenn Rathbun's 3d (blue) Battalion did somewhat better in the woods one mile south of Haut Jacques. But before long, Company K became embroiled in a "moving firefight" between Hills 491 and 699. Company L also encountered strong resistance near Marmonfosse, yet the Cotton Balers continued their relentless assault. Along the way, SSgt. George Grando single-handedly moved against two machine-gun nests, firing his tommy gun, and then the BAR of a fallen comrade, until both positions were silenced. For his valiant action Sergeant Grando received the Distinguished Service Cross posthumously.

# 9: Crossroads of Hell

The weather turned bad again on the third day of the attack, 1 November. As always, General O'Daniel was in the thick of it, watching his Cotton Balers wage their uphill battle. Fifty-year-old John Wilson O'Daniel had come up the ranks, from corporal in the Delaware National Guard, to company commander in the 25th Infantry Regiment, to division commander by February 1944. He had been wounded a quarter century earlier, fighting at the Meuse-Argonne, and since Americans set foot in North Africa he had made every landing from Sicily to southern France. Now, as he watched his young men die, he thought of their wives, mothers, and fathers who would receive the terrible news, just as he had received word of the death of his only son, John Junior, a paratrooper killed in action just a few months earlier.

Staff Sergeant George "Reb" Rebovich knew that his straight-trajectory antitank guns were of little use in the dense forest, but still his men did the best they could to aid their comrades. Rebovich's family, now living in Perth Amboy, New Jersey, had immigrated from the Carpathian Mountains of Eastern Europe, and his father had served in the Austrian Army. "We didn't make much headway; three hundred yards in three days. Ken Wallace was always up front, but there was little he could do against their mortars."

As Captain Wallace's 1st Battalion negotiated the narrow trails north of the pass road against Oberleutnant Franz Kapfer's 3d Company, Major Thobro's 2d Battalion headed northeast from Hill 552 toward the crossroads on top of the pass, defended by 2d Company under the command of Oberleutnant Höss. By now the Americans were anywhere from three hundred to one thousand yards short of their objective—lethal yards strewn with mines and covered by snipers, machine guns, rocket-propelled grenades, and mortar concentrations.

Difficult terrain and the unreliability of radios and telephones forced the German company commanders to use signal flares to announce each American attack. This, in turn, would trigger the prearranged mortar barrages. American casualties mounted, most of them from tree bursts. Medics and chaplains worked around the clock to attend to the wounded, the dying, and the dead. Among the dead was Capt. Roy Cook of Company C, who had commanded the unit for less than four hours. Capt. George Ellis of "Easy" Company was wounded in a barrage, and 1st Lt. James Powell had to assume command. American artillery retaliated with thousands of high-explosive and white phosphorous rounds, impact and delayed fuses.

Adjutant Kolbinger writes, "We knew that after the artillery fire had rolled over us, infantry would advance. Our aim was to shoot at the point men, knowing that this would usually stop the American attack. In Russia, Major Seebacher had learned how to use mortars to their maximum advantage. Unlike the Americans, we had little artillery and no tank support, and had to make the best of the terrain and equipment we had brought along. "We had no winter gear, and often went hungry, but ever since Russia we knew there was no turning back. We had to defend ourselves as best we could, and counterattack when necessary."

Major Seebacher agrees: "Luckily, the Americans never attempted a breakthrough on our flanks. They obliged us by bravely attacking from the front, day after day, which made it possible for us to hold out as long as we did."

After another American artillery barrage, Companies C, E, and G pressed on just to be met by yet another counterattack. All afternoon mountain hunters and Cotton Balers fought at close quarters—so close that each could see the smoke rising from their adversaries' red-hot barrels, and hear commands being shouted. American fighter-bombers managed to fly only two sorties, which proved ineffective, due to poor weather and the proximity of the troops. The fighting went on all afternoon, with all of "Charlie" Company's reserves committed by the time darkness brought a temporary halt.

According to Toni Stocker, one of the casualties was a mule belonging to the mountain troops' supply unit. "That wounded mule kept braying, giving away our positions. Finally the sergeant gave it the 'coup de grace.'"

The struggle continued unabated on a miserably cold and rainy 2 November. Their hands and feet stiff from cold, the riflemen of Companies A and B got out of their water-filled foxholes once again to push through minefields and barbed wire toward one of the road-blocks ahead. But the Germans had trained their automatic weapons on the obstacle. During the occasional lulls, soldiers could hear the church bells at St.-Dié, reminding the faithful that this was All Souls' Day. But Americans and Bavarians, regardless of their religion, had no time to reflect on that holy day, or on the dead. Using powerful loudspeakers, the Americans exhorted the mountain troops to surrender, but none did.

Just a few hundred yards to the south, Companies E and G were pinned down by mortar and machine-gun fire, and just before noon, "G" was counterattacked again. Then, following the usual artillery and mortar preparation, the 1st and 2d Battalions tried again at 1415 hours, but failed to make any appreciable gains. By now "Easy" Company's losses were so heavy that Lieutenant Powell had to call up his headquarters group to fill the ranks.

Seventh Army commander General Patch noted in his diary: "Two companies of the 1st Battalion, 7th U.S. Infantry Regiment decimated at Haut Jacques, west of St.-Dié."

Besides their dead and wounded, the Cotton Balers lost three tanks, and thirty men were taken prisoner.

Early that afternoon, in his command post, Maj. Franz Seebacher was bending over a map, when artillery shrapnel pierced the wooden logs and hit his spine—"The same spot where I got hit in Russia." He was evacuated, and replaced by his 3d Company commander, twenty-eight-year-old Oberleutnant Franz Kapfer from Heidenheim in Frankonia.

Regimental and division headquarters refused to pull us back, and by now Vitus (Kolbinger) and I knew that we had been written off. My main concerns were resupply and getting the wounded to the rear. Most had to be carried back. Through Vitus I let the battalion surgeon know that he should send as many as possible to the hospital. That way I knew that at least some of the men would be saved.

We were anything but heroes, and afraid. But most of us officers and noncoms had years of war experience. We were some of the last professionals the Wehrmacht could muster, and this was to be the worst test any of us would undergo.

The situation was far more difficult for the young soldiers who had not experienced anything like this. It was a very difficult task, also for the Americans. I salute them and their courage as they tried day after day to take the pass, sometimes four to five attacks per day. They were fine soldiers.

Meanwhile, south of the main event, Major Rathbun's 3d Battalion tried to keep in touch with the Nisei of Colonel Hanley's 2d Battalion 442, pushing east through another day of icy rain. "We didn't have too many problems with trench foot," Rathbun recalls. "My boys knew to massage their feet with Barbasol—shaving cream from a tube. It did the trick for most of us."

During the night of 2–3 November, the mountain troops continued to fire their mortars on Major Thobro's 2d Battalion. In two days of fighting his men had gained barely five hundred yards. Along the way Thobro had lost his battalion operations officer, intelligence officer, and forward observer, and was himself lightly wounded. But at daybreak his men, and those of the 1st Battalion, got up to again commence their uphill fight. As expected, they were met by a hail of mortar and automatic weapons fire. After twelve days of battling their way through the les-Rouges-Eaux valley, the men of the 7th were approaching the limit of their endurance. Of all the battles fought on French soil, this was the worst—man against man, moving from tree to tree, clawing their way up the steep slopes as friends were cut down left and right, wondering, "When is it going to be my turn?"

The riflemen of Company C pressed to within one hundred fifty yards of the crossroads, when they were again stopped by dug-in mountaineers. By noon "Charlie" Company found itself cut off from the rest of 1st Battalion, unable to get much-needed ammunition or evacuate their wounded. The few remaining Gebirgsjäger of 1st Company, now minus Leutnant Hiller, were surrounded, and intense firefights lasted all day. Finally, at dusk, the Americans managed to break out, taking twelve *Jäger* prisoner along the way.

Company B was still stuck short of the roadblock covered by German automatic weapons, and an attempt by Company A, 10th Engineers, to remove the obstacle was repulsed. At the same time SSgt. William Dezarn led two of Company A's anemic platoons in three separate attempts to break through the German defenses. Moving ahead of his men, he detonated several mines, directed artillery, and single-handedly destroyed a machine-gun emplacement with hand grenades. But when he tried to rush his men through the breach, he was disabled by shrapnel. For his valor Sergeant Dezarn was awarded the Distinguished Service Cross.

Company G made no headway at all, and its commander, Lt. William Maguire, was wounded and taken out of the battle while Lt. Bertram Trump's 1st platoon of "Easy" Company gained two hundred yards at a cost of eighteen men, including the lieutenant himself.

"I've got a bad feeling I'm not going to make it through another day," 2d Platoon leader Robert Beemer told Pvt. Wendell Erickson that evening. He then asked Erickson to take his wallet and other personal possessions and make sure they got to his family. Erickson assured him that nothing was going to happen to him, but the next day he had to add Staff Sergeant Beemer to Company G's list of the dead.

After Major Rathbun's 3d Battalion was relieved by the 2d Battalion of the "Alamo" Regiment, it too joined the fray at Haut Jacques. On Saturday, 4 November, the sixth day of battle, Col. Ben Harrell ordered every one of his companies (except "L" in reserve) to attack the top of the pass. American howitzers, antiaircraft guns, and mortars fired relentlessly on that small piece of real estate now known as the "Crossroads of Hell." But as tanks and infantry pressed ahead through fog and icy rain, German machine guns and mortars opened up again, firing at maximum elevation until the tubes glowed red-hot.

From a knoll north of the road, Sgt. "Reb" Rebovich was watching the German mortars in action when the cigar-chomping mortar platoon leader from Delta Company, known as "the Swede," joined him. Together they watched as the mountain troops fired another mission and then took cover under a rock overhang. "The Swede" was timing them. "Just about now," he said as the German mortar crews reappeared. A short time later the American's mortars fired back, catching the German crew in the open.

With the 3d Battalion pinned down by machine guns, and Company A reeling from a counterattack, it was "Easy" Company that once again took the lead. But as Lt. James Powell's men inched their way forward, firing at point-blank range, German mortars wiped out his 60mm mortar section. At the same time, one of his heavy machine-gunners, Pvt. Edgar Cosson, dueled with the machine-gun crew of Hugo Sommer and Aurelio Piai. Bullets ripped through Cosson's backpack and blanket, and his ammo bearers were unable to reach him, but he didn't quit. After a brief lull Cosson engaged another machine gun, and earned the DSC that day.

A short distance south, 2d Lt. James Crough led his platoon around the exposed left flank of Leutnant Höss's 2d Company and toward the crossroads. Only Lt. Günter Krebs from Dieringhausen, and his platoon, succeeded in breaking free of the American end-run, reaching the battalion command post at the eastern end of the pass. Krebs, who had lost his left hand in Russia, was no longer required to serve in combat, but nevertheless had volunteered for Bataillon 201. Some believed that underlying his extraordinary courage was a reckless disregard for life, and perhaps a death wish—which, if true, was to be realized six weeks later when his company took the heights at Sigolsheim from the 36th Division.

After more than two hours of bloodletting, "Easy" Company had come to within arm's reach of their objective. In a final effort, the 2d platoon overran the "Crossroads of Hell," and the MG position manned by eighteen-year-old Hugo Sommer and his friend Aurelio Piai, both of whom were captured. At the same time Americans John

Nutter and Tony Belletini blasted away with their heavy machine guns and the captured MG42, covering "Easy" Company's move toward the first of three buildings still held by the eleven remaining men of 2d Company. Oberleutnant Höss was a career officer who did not know the word *retreat*. But when he saw the Americans closing in, he knew that his situation was hopeless. Faced with the choice of being taken prisoner or pulling back, he shouted, "Let's make a run for it, boys. See you on the other side." Along the way the lieutenant from Munich was killed by a rifle bullet.

By now, as the men of "Easy" Company made their final run, machine gunner Belletini lay dead, and when the Cotton Balers burst into the building, they found the basement filled with communications gear and thirty-five German and American wounded. A short time later they reached the abandoned mortar positions three hundred meters east, with large stores of ammunition littering the ground.

In their final assault the men of the 7th had suffered 109 wounded and 16 killed, bringing the gruesome total to 148 dead and 822 wounded in three weeks' time. In other words, half of the regiment had been killed or wounded. "Easy" Company alone had lost 77 men in six days, while being credited for killing 37 and capturing 78 Germans. For their gallantry the men of "Easy" Company received a Presidential Unit Citation.

Heeres Gebirgsjäger Bataillon 201 had also suffered. By late afternoon only 180 men had found their way back to the command post. Of their number, 50 were so ill that Surgeon Segmüller sent them to the rear. During 9 days of continuous combat, Heeres Gebirgsjäger Bataillon 201 had suffered 167 dead, more than 100 captured, and 600 wounded, sick, and missing. Not until nightfall did the mountain battalion receive permission to pull back from Col du Haut Jacques toward Rougiville. On the way down the Gebirgsjäger were punished by a three-hour artillery barrage.

Toni Stocker remembers:

> It was horrible. My friend and I hid under a rock overhang and agreed that we'd let ourselves be taken prisoner as soon as the Americans attacked. But the attack never came. We lost a

lot of our fellows after we pulled off the pass: Berg, Berner, Salmansberger, Schobenhauser, all of them dead. I remember Fredl Berg running past me on the 5th of November. A short time later he took a bullet in the stomach and died.

Toni Stocker lost half of his classmates during the last six months of the war.

Adjutant Kolbinger, who hadn't slept in four days, finally reached for the Pervitin pills issued to frontline officers. But the strong stimulant did not have the desired effect. Instead of reenergizing him the pills brought about his collapse and a comalike sleep lasting for more than a day.

On that 5 November, the Cotton Balers, supported by fighter-bombers, continued their push east through sleet and mud, fighting small engagements with the Gebirgsjäger on the other side of the pass. During the night of 8 November, a combat patrol from the 3d Battalion overran a platoon of 4th Company. Oberleutnant Willi Scheuerecker and a handful of men rushed back to free their comrades. Covered by a machine gun, the German lieutenant crawled up to a nearby farmhouse and fired his "Panzerfaust" through the door. When he called on the Americans to surrender, they did. But only his platoon leader was freed. The twelve other mountain troops had already been sent to the rear.

On 9 November, the 7th Regiment was relieved by the 103d Division, and three days later Rougiville was taken. Vitus Kolbinger made a desperate effort to reach the command post of Infantry Regiment 225 to have Gebirgsjäger Bataillon 201 pulled back from its hopelessly exposed position. Adolf Hitler, who felt an odd sense of kinship with the mountain men from Austria and Bavaria, took a keen interest in their progress. But they were not spared his apocalyptic sense of destiny in which still thousands of his countrymen were to become fuel for his funeral pyre.

If the war is lost, the German people too are lost. Therefore it is no longer necessary to concern oneself with the foundations a nation needs to survive. On the contrary, it is better to destroy those foundations. Because the people have proven themselves to be weak, the future belongs to the stronger East. Those who survive the war are only the inferior, for all the superior ones have fallen." [Recorded by Albert Speer]

Lieutenant Kolbinger persuaded Colonel Röder to withdraw his battalion across the Meurthe River, but General Feldmarschall Wilhelm Keitel personally countermanded the order, conveying the Führer's message: "The mountain troops must hold their present positions to the last man!"

Kolbinger hung up and faced the regimental commander. "That's a death sentence for us. Why don't you just give us the order, honestly, to sacrifice ourselves!"

The colonel paused, and then answered. "Yes, I order you to sacrifice yourselves."

After Kolbinger communicated the fatal order to his battalion commander, Oberleutnant Kapfer, the battalion crossed the narrow valley at night, and the next morning Kolbinger returned once more to the regimental command post. There he blatantly lied that all he could find were a few stragglers. For whatever reason the lie was accepted, and after several more telephone calls, new Führer's orders came down. "Collect stragglers and establish defense line on east side of creek."

On that day the commander of the 16th Volks-Grenadier Division, Gen. Ernst Haeckel, diagnosed as suffering from high blood pressure, was sent on vacation. Nineteenth Army log, 11 November:

> General Haeckel's health has deteriorated to a point requiring a long vacation. Apparently his court-martial was the last blow. . . .

A week later Haeckel was assigned to the leader reserve, followed by medical leave. On 14 November, his decimated division was detached from the Army Corps and sent to Neuville-sur-Fave to regroup.

The remnants of Heeres Gebirgsjäger Bataillon 201 pulled back to the ridge east of La Bollé, where torrential floods aided them in holding the line a bit longer. The battalion, now down to company strength, was finally withdrawn on 14 November.

Adjutant Kolbinger recalls: "For the remainder of the month our unit became the 'Vosges Fire Brigade,' moving at night from one hot spot to another—Badonviller, Saales, Bertrambois, and Harzviller, to put out too many fires. Bataillon 201 was replenished several more times before it lost its independent status and was incorporated into the 2d Gebirgsjäger Division in February 1945."

After the "Fiasco of Épinal," General of Panzer Forces, Hermann Balck, took command of Army Group G from Colonel General Johannes Blaskowitz. *National Archives*

General der Infanterie Friedrich Wiese managed to save his Nineteenth Army, but could not save himself from Heinrich Himmler. *Bundesarchiv*

Major General Lucian K. Truscott led the 3d Division at Anzio, and later the VI Corps in France. *National Archives*

Generalleutnant Wilhelm Richter's 716th. Volks-Grenadier Division was decimated at Normandy, but he successfully delayed the Americans between Bruyères and St. Dié. *Bundesarchiv*

Major General John Ernest Dahlquist, commanding the 36th "Texas" Division; a controversial figure to subordinates and superiors. *Minneapolis Public Library*

Major General John W. "Iron Mike" O'Daniel, commanding the 3d Division, had lost his only son earlier that year. His 7th "Cotton Baler" Regiment battled valiantly against German mountain troops entrenched at le Haut Jacques. *National Archives*

Colonel Charles W. Pence,
Commanding Officer of
the 100/442d Regimental
Combat Team, had no use
for bigots in his unit.
*National Archives*

French Forces of the Interior (FFI), like Sgt. Paul Charpin and Paul
Gerard (in back of jeep) were invaluable assets to the Allies. *National
Archives*

Joe (Osamaru) Hattori and sister Yaeko who collected 1000 stitches for his senin-bari at Heart Mountain internment camp. *Yaeko Sakamoto*

The Nisei 522d Field Artillery Battalion provided continuous support during the attack on Bruyères and the push through the Forêt de Champ. *U.S. Army Military History Institute*

Nisei entering Bruyères, October 18, 1944. *National Archives*

German prisoners taken at Bruyères, October 18. Boy in foreground claimed to be 18 years old. *U.S. Army Military History Institute*

The 2d Battalion aid station in the Forêt de Champ, 29 October 1944, the day of the "Banzai" charge. *National Archives*

Technical Sergeant Charles H. Coolidge's men repulsed several German counterattacks in the hills east of Belmont. For his steadfast action Coolidge was awarded the Medal of Honor. *Charles Coolidge*

Hans-Paul Geiger, who enjoyed "the fruit of heaven," while surrounding the "Lost Battalion."
*Joseph Schwieters*

Staff Sergeant Shiro "Kash" Kashino won five Purple Hearts, two of them during the "Lost Battalion" push.
*Shiro Kashino*

Lieutenant Martin Higgins left, after the rescue of the "Lost Battalion." Note the stock of his carbine shattered by mortar shrapnel.
*National Archives*

Weary trooper grabs a bite to eat just after the relief.
*National Archives*

Members of the 1st Battalion, 141st "Alamo" Regiment just after the relief. *National Archives*

"Lost Battalion" survivors, Oct. 30, 1944: (1) Lieutenant Chester Hanes, Mt. Vernon, Washington (2) SSgt. Jack Wilson, Rockport, Indiana (3) Bert McQueen, Wind Cove, Kentucky (killed soon thereafter). *Jack Wilson*

Nisei light machine gunner holding the thin line, following the relief of the "Lost Battalion." *National Archives*

Virginia Spetz said goodbye to a New York modeling job to serve as a Red Cross volunteer in Europe. *Alvin Spetz*

A captured vehicle is the supply truck for these American Red Cross volunteers with the 36th Infantry Division From left to right: Dorothy Boschen, West Orange, NY, Virginia Spetz, Rochester, NY, Jane Cook, Scottsbluff, Nebraska, and Meredyth Gardiner, California. *Alvin Spetz*

Six-foot-tall mortar platoon leader, Lieutenant Joseph Kiyonaga of Company M, and "friend" in France. While he fought for the United States, his grandparents suffered through the inferno in Okinawa. *Alvin Spetz*

100/442d RCT memorial service on 11November 1944. From left to right: SSgt. Kaminishi, Sadaoka, Yamane and Sgt. Kokubun of Antitank Company.

Lieutenant Colonel James Hanley led his 2d Battalion, 442d RCT into Bruyères, and against the mountain troops from Salzburg and Garmisch. *Col. James Hanley*

Lone sentry after the first snowfall in November.
*National Archives*

Gerwin Eder climbing the Gosaukamm on his last furlough, September 1944, before being sent to the Vosges with the doomed Gebirgsjäger Bataillon 202.
*Gerwin Eder*

Eighteen-year-old Toni Stocker. Many of his classmates died during the last six months of war. *Anton Stocker*

Heres Gebirgsjäger Bataillon 201 Adjutant Vitus Kolbinger located the trainload of mortar ammunition which wreaked havoc among the "Cotton Balers." *Vitus Kolbinger*

German medical corpsman surrending to Nisei trooper. *National Archives*

Oberst (Colonel) Walter Rolin's Grenadier Regiment 933 surrounded the "Lost Battalion" and fiercely battled the 422d RCT. *Bundesarchiv*

Senior Lieutenant, Franz
Kapfer, assumed command of
Battalion 201 after Major
Seebacher was wounded.
*Franz Kapfer*

One of the 7th Regiment's new Shermans entering Brouvelieures, 21
October 1944. *National Archives*

The 7th Regimental command post at Mailleufaing before it received a direct hit. Colonel Benjamin Harrell flanked by Lt. Colonel Frank Izenhour left, and Major Duncan right. *7th Regimental History*

After his surrender, Field Marshal Hermann Göring chats with Major General John E. Dahlquist (left) and Brigadier Robert I. Stack (right) on the balcony of the Grand Hotel in Kitzbühl, Austria, May 17, 1945. *Minneapolis Public Library*

Glenn and Louise Rathbun were married one week before the attack on Pearl Harbor. During the next three years of war they would spend only six months together.
*Glenn & Louise Rathbun*

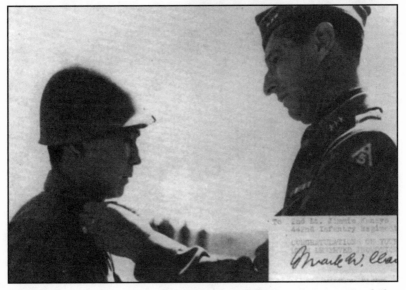

Jimmie Kanaya, who was taken prisoner at Biffontaine, survived the 300-mile death march from Poland to Germany. He received a battlefield commision from Lt. Gen. Mark Clark.

The first reunion of Heeres Gebirgsjäger Bataillon 201 in Breitenwang, Tyrol, 1986. Front row, second from left Toni Stocker who saw his first combat at Haut Jacques. Behind plaque, Franz Kapfer, who led the battalion after Franz Seebacher was wounded. Under arch (white hair), Adjutant Vitus Kolbinger. *Vitus Kolbinger*

Fifty years later, the rescuers of the "Lost Battalion" meet again. Front row, left to right: Allen Okamoto, George Miyashiro, George Oshita, Takashi Senzaki. Back: Sam Handa, Tadao Saito, Shig Doi, Suguru Takahashi, and Shiro "Kash" Kashino. *Shiro Kashino & Shig Doi*

# Part 2: Echoes of War

# 10: Beyond "Lost Battalions"

On 31 October, as a Signal Corps camera crew filmed the evacuation of the American "Lost Battalion," and General Haeckel stood before a court-martial, a somber General Dahlquist attended the funeral of his aide, Wells Lewis. After the burial, his new corps commander, General Brooks, challenged Dahlquist for having relieved three of his colonels and several battalion commanders. Dahlquist was curt: "My division is tired. You've got to pull it out!"

Brooks replied, "I can't. Sandy Patch is determined to finish this job now!"

Under General Truscott VI Corps had advanced 650 kilometers in six weeks, and only 25 kilometers within the month of October. Brooks, who had successfully led the 2d Armored Division across France, was not about to support his division commander's request.

A memorandum dated 24 October had called for the Nisei 442d to be attached to the newly arrived 103d Division, while the 36th Division received a ten-day rest period. But the "Lost Battalion" episode had voided the plan. By now the 36th from Texas had suffered more casualties than any other division in VI Corps.

After fifty years Henry Nakada, who along with "Mutt" Sakumoto had been first to reach the "Lost Battalion," still feels bitter. "We were kept up there taking hill after hill until nearly no one was left. If the Germans had known, they could easily have overrun us. It was those last two weeks for which I can never forgive General Dahlquist."

The days following the dramatic rescue of the "Lost Battalion" were anticlimactic, but no less lethal. Just above la Houssière the Nisei 100th and 3d Battalions consolidated their positions as best they could, while Colonel Hanley's 2d Battalion and the "Alamo" Regiment continued shielding the division's left flank, and the Cotton Balers faced their uphill fight at Haut Jacques.

On 1 November, General Dahlquist urged Lt. Col. Virgil Miller of the 442d, and the new commander of the "Alamo" Regiment, Col. Charles Owens, to push their men harder. At Marmonfosse the Nisei, Texans, and Cotton Balers fought bravely, side by side, but with line companies down to fifty or sixty men, exhausted and cold, little progress was made. Even the tankers supporting Maj. Walter Bruyere's 3d Battalion of the 141st had lost their drive, prompting an angry General Dahlquist to threaten court-martial if they did not resume the attack. As a spotter plane searched for German movement, Colonel Pursall's anemic 3d Battalion, with Major Bruyere's equally thin lines to his left, braced for counterattack. But other than some stiff firefights, the situation remained static.

Thursday, All Souls' Day, 2 November, was a terribly cold and gloomy day. A direct hit on the 100th Battalion command post killed two Americans and two German prisoners who were being interrogated.

French farmers brought the German dead through Biffontaine on horse-drawn wagons, and General Dahlquist sent the "Lost Battalion" back on the line. When Major Bruyere's 3d Battalion attacked at noon, German mortars and machine guns stopped his men in their tracks. General Dahlquist called Colonel Owens.

"Charlie, you've got to push your men!"

"General, I'll personally lead the 3d Battalion tomorrow to get around the Jerries. But if I fail, you've got to pull the men off the line. They're spent."

The planned attack never got off the ground. Bruyere's battalion was no longer combat effective, and had to be withdrawn early on 3 November. The Nisei carried on for them.

At twenty-two, Franz Alois Herrmann was the youngest officer in Gebirgsjäger Bataillon 201, but not the least experienced. He had already served three years on the eastern front, where he had earned the close combat badge in bronze, the wounded badge in silver (wounded three times), the Iron Cross 1st Class for conducting a raid behind the Russian lines, blowing up a command bunker, and then carrying his seriously wounded sergeant back to his own lines.

On this day he was sent out to make contact with any German unit he could find near Marmonfosse. Cloaked in fog, he moved from tree to tree and bush to bush, stopping frequently to listen. Finally, low-crawling through a depression, he heard a hiss. He carefully raised his head and, to his surprise, saw a group of Asians wearing American uniforms. He froze, lying in cold mud and covered with leaves while the Nisei heated their rations over a can of sterno. Finally, by evening, he made his way back to the battalion command post and gave his report. But Oberleutnant Kapfer doubted the sighting. Fifty years would pass before Herrmann learned that he had been correct, that he had come face-to-face with the Nisei of Colonel Hanley's 2d Battalion.

That same evening, at his Bruyères command post, General Dahlquist wrote to his wife, Ruth. His letters, normally well composed, for the first time revealed fatigue and a sense of despair:

*Dearest Ruth,*

*There isn't the slightest reason for my writing a letter tonight. Nothing has happened since last night when I wrote and there was not a letter tonight. But I was sitting here thinking of you and so I might as well talk to you.*

*I stayed in the CP all day, something which I have not done more than once or twice. This morning, about 5:30, Charlie [Colonel Charles Owens of the Alamo Regiment] telephoned and asked permission to come in. He arrived in about an hour, and I went over his problem with him—I do not know if he got breakfast or not. He certainly is a great soldier. He has stepped into a very tough situation for me, but I know he will come out on top. If he does, I certainly hope I can get a star for him.*

*This afternoon I did leave the CP for about 45 minutes to get a bath. I really do not remember when I had my last one. Lewis (Wells Lewis) used to politely urge me once in a while to get one. I also got a haircut. . . .*

*I wish I could say the same for my infantry. Those poor devils
have a terrible time. . . . It rained all day yesterday and last night,
but today it stopped, and so far it has not started again. Mountains,
woods, and rain are things I do not like anymore, at least in war.
But I will probably see a lot more of them before I am through, so I
had better get philosophical about them.*

One month later he would write to his predecessor, Gen. Fred L.
Walker.

*The 141st has been unlucky and is not in very good shape now.
Loss of Battalion Commanders and Executives have been very high.
Watson, Amick, Coyle, Bird, Simpson, Middleton, Bowden, Hough,
and Selkirk were all wounded. Of course the loss of Company Officers
and noncoms has been high.*

*The terrain we worked through was terrible, and the weather was
atrocious. Although casualties were generally light, the cumulative total for the Infantry is very large.*

The total was staggering indeed, ten thousand men—a 100 percent turnover of frontline troops within four months. By now
Dahlquist was smoking heavily, making him winded as he rushed
from one battalion to the next to spur them on. But inside he was
torn between the responsibility toward his men and loyalty toward
his new corps commander, General Brooks. According to Dahlquist,
"Brooks came over with very grandiose plans for the future. I argued
with him about the fact that the troops were now ineffective and had
to be retrained. He practically refused to listen. I stayed in the CP
all day, sending Albright out to check on 141st and 442."

By now Dahlquist's division was barely able to maintain its front,
running thirty-five kilometers from les-Rouges-Eaux along the high
ground to la Houssière, and southwest toward the French II Corps
near le Tholy. A strong counterattack might well have succeeded at
this point, but the German leadership was unwilling to commit its
reserves already earmarked for the upcoming Ardennes Offensive.

With Gebirgsjäger Bataillon 201 committed against the U.S. 7th
Regiment at le Haut Jacques, only General Richter's 716th Volks-

Grenadier Division made a feeble attempt to break through the Nisei lines running along the narrow valley north from la Houssière. But Companies I and L managed to repulse the attack.

On 4 November, as the French II Corps and German 198th and 269th Divisions suffered heavy losses in the forests of le Tholy, General Dahlquist again visited his regiments. Dahlquist wrote:

> Found 442nd had done practically nothing to clear its position and get a defensible position. Talked to Miller [Lt. Col. Virgil Miller], who started to faint. He is apparently in a very bad physical condition.

The only positive that day was that the Nisei finally received their winter issue—field jackets, wool sweaters, shoe pacs, and heavy shoes. Lieutenant Alvin "Bud" Spetz of Company M had not yet received his winter clothes when his weapons platoon was relieved by the "Alamo" Regiment. As one of the newly arrived officers handed him a cup of coffee, Spetz was trembling violently, so sick from cold that he threw up. Seeing this, the Good Samaritan took off his own overcoat and draped it around Spetz's shoulders—A gesture I will never forget!

On 5 November, in freezing rain, the 142d Regiment attacked east of Marmonfosse, and Lieutenant Colonel Pursall's 3d Battalion 442d descended toward the railroad line at Vanèmont. But as they came out of their foxholes, the Nisei fell victim to mines, artillery, mortar, and recoilless rifle fire, which had been scarce during the previous four days. The Company M command post took a direct mortar hit, and each of the companies, F, G, I, K, and L sustained casualties while gaining barely two hundred yards. Company I, which had fought so valiantly alongside K during the "banzai charge," lost ten more men, reducing its fighting strength to thirty-four. But by nightfall the objective was nowhere in sight, and company commanders had to pull their men back to their starting point.

On 6 November, Company E and combat engineers joined in the fray. Supported by mortar fire they moved down the slope and up toward Hill 688, but received a hot welcome from six machine guns, recoilless rifles, artillery, and mortars. Company E gained only one hundred fifty yards, at a cost of one officer and one enlisted man killed and fourteen wounded.

Every step along the way, the 232d and 111th Engineers had performed magnificently, keeping the single useful trail open day after day in icy rain to support the push for the "Lost Battalion," laying corduroy steel, repairing fills that had been torn open by their own tanks and the constant pounding of German artillery, and more than once performing as infantry.

At 1400 hours Lieutenant Colonel Pursall's 3d Battalion resumed the attack with Companies K, L, and G. But the "G-Men" soon ran into an unusual minefield, with wires running from each mine toward a German foxhole. Each time a Nisei got close, the opposing soldier would pull the wire to detonate a mine. One American tank was disabled and captured by the Germans before it was shot up by another Sherman's 75mm gun. A counterattack late in the afternoon, and an attempt to infiltrate Company L during the night, were repulsed, while Companies A and B of the 100th Battalion exchanged fire with Germans still holding la Houssière.

That evening General Patch answered the first letter his wife sent since the death of their son, Mac.

> I am so proud of you, Julia, just as proud as I am of our magnificent boy. You and I and our family and their progeny will not allow adversity to get us down. . . . There are thousands of mothers and fathers who are undergoing just what we are.
>
> Mac's personal belongings have been inventoried and are being prepared for shipment to Ginger. . . .
>
> Yesterday I received a package you had mailed Mac long ago. It contained cocoa, candy, coffee, and the like. I've turned it over to the Red Cross for the use of Infantry soldiers who are enduring such frightfully difficult conditions in prosecuting my orders. I don't know if it is understood that my Army is faced with the need to assault the precipitous, heavily wooded, rain-soaked Vosges mountains. But we are, and will continue to take attrition from the enemy that eventually he cannot stand.

On 7 November, heavy rains grounded aircraft all along the Seventh Army front, and made the ground soldier's life miserable. General Patch asked Gen. Jacob Devers to replace the First Airborne Task Force with the 442d RCT. "The climate in the south will be better for the Japanese, who are suffering from respiratory diseases and trench foot."

The Nisei knew nothing of this as they prepared once again to drive the Germans from la Houssière and Vanemont. The attack was preceded by a thousand-round mortar barrage, and Company G got as far as the railroad embankment at the base of the hill.

"Many of our men died, and some went crazy," reported one German prisoner from Grenadier Regiment 305.

As the Nisei dug in that evening, sleet turned to snow, and the southern sky glowed red as the town of Aumontzey burned—torched by General Richter's retreating troops.

General Patton's Third Army was launching a major offensive on 8 November, as the Nisei companies continued to clear the slopes at Langefosse. By now Company I had four riflemen left on the line, Company L had seventeen, and Company K was under the command of a sergeant.

Private First Class Joe M. Nishimoto, an acting squad leader in Company G, crawled through a heavily mined and booby-trapped area toward a German machine-gun position, and destroyed it with a hand grenade. Then he circled to the rear of another gun and killed its crew with a burst from his tommy gun. He went on, killing a rifleman and driving another machine-gun crew from its position. His actions broke the stalemate in his area, earning him the Distinguished Service Cross. Private First Class Nishimoto was later killed in action. Having thus driven a wedge through the German line, the companies spent most of the day clearing the hillside and farmhouses between Vanemont and Langefosse. Finally, late in the afternoon, the Nisei were relieved by the 142d Regiment, and the 100th Battalion was detached from the 36th Division. Major Bruyere's 3d Battalion of the "Alamo" Regiment was withdrawn for a much-needed rest at Lepanges.

Like the wake of a storm, relative calm now prevailed in the Forêt de Champ and Haut Jacques, while occasional thunder disturbed the air. But the worst was over for now.

Just before dusk Lt. James Jernigan and Sgt. Sherman Pratt of the Cotton Baler Regiment went ahead to scout toward St.-Dié. The day was cold and overcast, with patches of fog clinging to the hollows, as the two men carefully made their way through thick underbrush and up the reverse slope of a hill. Once on top, they could see the rain-swollen Meurthe river and beyond, the town of St.-Dié. The town, once populated by nearly ten thousand, was deserted.

"Like a ghost town," Pratt said as Jernigan surveyed the landscape with his binoculars.

"Spooky," the lieutenant answered quietly. It was getting dark, time to pull back, when Jernigan said, "Hold on, Pratt. There's movement down at the other end of the street. They're Germans."

Soldiers were entering the houses one by one, and soon smoke and flames leaped into the night sky. The faces of the two American observers glowed red as the holocaust below raged through the medieval town, its textile and lumber mills, and the eleventh-century cathedral. St.-Dié, a hub of French underground and German counterintelligence activity, was to burn on for days, reducing much of the town to ashes.

On 9 November, one month after the VI Corps had begun its push through the Vosges, the Cotton Balers near Rougiville were relieved by the newly arrived 409th Infantry Regiment of the 103d Division. "The new guys were clean and dry, with full field packs, and their expressions were those of men going to their execution," recalls Major Rathbun. "In contrast, my old, unshaven vets stood without a dry stitch on their dirty bodies, and with a bit of snow on their helmets and near empty field packs. Gaunt but hard as nails, they laughed and joked quietly among themselves. Next month they would spearhead the drive to the Rhine."

With the Americans again poised for attack, and his Nineteenth Army in tatters, General Wiese was again forced to withdraw. Of his remaining nine divisions, only three deserved the designation. All others had the fighting strength of reinforced regiments. Adding to his problems, General Gilsa and staff were sent north for the upcoming Ardennes Offensive, and the 21st Panzer Division was taken away, leaving him with fewer than twenty tanks and assault guns.

As General Richter's 716th Division continued its retreat to the Meurthe River Line, the Japanese Americans enjoyed hot food, showers, and clean clothes. The men of Alvin Spetz's heavy weapons

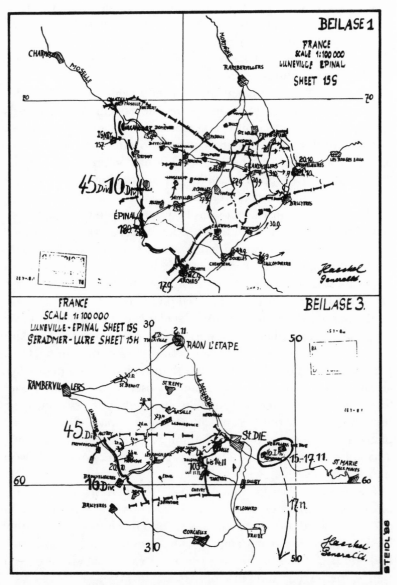

Two maps reconstructed by General Ernst Haeckel while a prisoner of war. Map 1 shows his 16th Division retreating from Épinal to Brouvelieures (24 September–20 October). Map 3 shows his area of operations between Brouvelieures and St.-Dié (20 October–14 November).

platoon got to sleep in a barn, and the next morning, in the farm's kitchen, they were surprised by a woman's voice calling out the lieutenant's name. Alvin Spetz immediately recognized his sister's voice. Virginia, a top New York fashion model before the war, was working as a Red Cross volunteer with the 36th Division. The men watched with a sense of wonder as she and her fellow volunteers proceeded to make donuts and coffee, played the latest Glenn Miller records, and danced with those GIs whose feet hadn't succumbed to trench foot. A month earlier, in Italy, Virginia's group, traveling in a captured truck, had passed the 442d convoy just before embarking for France. She had stopped to ask for her brother, just to be told that he had passed minutes before.

One of Spetz's close friends was Lt. Joseph Kiyonaga, who had received his battlefield commission in Italy. At six-foot-two, Kiyonaga was a target for jokes among fellow Nisei. But their attitude was to change dramatically when, a few months later, Okinawa became one of the most horrendous battlegrounds of the war. Kiyonaga's men knew that his grandparents still lived on the island.

Making use of the respite, the Nisei looked for friends and relatives, just to find that many were gone. The prize for breaking through the Vosges was high. After twenty-five days of fighting, Companies E, F, I, and K had lost more than four hundred men killed and wounded, and another two hundred lost to exposure and trench foot. Company K alone had gone through eight officers—one every three days, leaving only seventeen riflemen and part of the weapons platoon, commanded by Sgt. Tsutomu Yoshida (who later received a battlefield commission). The ranks of the other companies were similarly depleted.

Private First Class Joe Hattori finally rejoined his friends at the 522d Field Artillery, exhausted and ten pounds lighter than when he and the forward observer team had set out. In a letter to his brother Fred, at Heart Mountain Camp, he only alluded to the hardships they had endured. It would take years to absorb and deal with the experience, the tragedy and sense of personal loss.

Losses in the "Alamo" Regiment were also heavy. The 1st Battalion had begun October with 20 officers and 693 men. After the "Lost Battalion" was relieved, they joined 13 officers and 260 men who had not been cut off, plus 200 fresh replacements. In other words the 1st Battalion lost 425 officers and men killed, captured, or wounded in one month.

Colonel Lynch's 142d Regiment finally secured the towns of la Houssière and Vanemont on 10 November, and patrols pushed out to Mount Mours to the east. At VI Corps headquarters, General Dahlquist again asked to have his 36th Division pulled off the line for rest and training. He recorded the answer in his diary. "The infantry is becoming very poor. I have pleaded with Brooks to take some consideration of this in his plans, but he refuses to listen."

On Armistice Day, 11 November, Generals Patch, Dahlquist, de Lattre, and other dignitaries honored the war dead at Luxeul. As he reviewed American, French, and colonial troops, nothing in General Patch's demeanor betrayed that he had just lost his own son. But the day before, he had expressed his hurt in a letter to his wife, Julia.

> *My Jul, I see that you are devoting all your thoughts and energy toward keeping up my morale—because you, only you, know how deeply hurt I am.*
>
> *I remember well your premonition and fear that that good-bye in Palm Springs would be the last—and even I feared the same thing. But darling you reared a man, let there be no mistake about that. When I talked to the field artillery forward observer who was near him, that young man cried as he spoke of Mac's bravery and even felt ashamed in my presence. Yes darling, I had perhaps the most powerful urge I've ever known to go up there personally and turn myself loose with everything we possessed to atone for our Mac's loss, but I restrained myself and have resolved to face fate.*
>
> *You asked me to please not let him get back to his outfit too soon— and I can hardly stand it, knowing if I had done just that—I shall never quite be able to forgive myself. Had I waited three more days it never would have happened.*

A cold wind was blowing as Chaplains Yost, Yamada, and Higuchi held memorial services for the 442d RCT. At Fays the men of the 2d Battalion huddled together on a gentle sloping hill, listening to Lieutenant Colonel Hanley and Chaplain Higuchi deliver the memorial oration for the eighty-two friends and relatives killed in their battalion alone.

When General Dahlquist came to inspect the regiment on 12 November, he was surprised that so few stood muster. When he asked, "Where are the men?" Col. Virgil Miller replied, "That's all that's left."

Lieutenant Daniel Inouye, who had just received his battlefield commission, and who was to become a U.S. senator from Hawaii, remembers: "Company E, that day, was the largest company in the regiment; we had 42 men in formation. A company at full strength had 197 men . . . that shook me up. When you're in combat, all you see is your platoon, but when you line up like this and all of a sudden you realize your company of 42 men is the biggest . . . my God!"

The regiment had shrunk from thirty-five hundred to twenty-one hundred men. More than 1200 men lay in hospitals all over France and England, recovering from wounds and illness—some never to be whole again in body or spirit. The losses were taken particularly hard because the 100/442d was a segregated unit that had trained and fought together for more than eighteen months. Chaplain Masao Yamada, of the 3d Battalion, expressed his sorrow in a letter written to Col. Sherwood Dixon right after the costly "banzai charge."

> *I am spiritually low for once. My heart weeps for our men. . . . To me the price is too costly. When we complete this mission, we will have written with our own blood another chapter in the story of our adventures in democracy.*

As General Dahlquist pinned medals on the men a light snow began to fall, covering all like a shroud. Later that evening, in a letter to his wife, the general complained that his fingers had turned numb from pinning so many medals on the men.

The decision to hold back Nisei replacements, and send Colonel Hanley's and Colonel Pursall's battalions back into the Forêt de Champ on 13 November, rested on Seventh Army plans to have the 442d RCT relieve the 1st Airborne Task Force in southern France, and General Brooks's refusal to withdraw the decimated 36th Division. Keeping the Japanese Americans on the line for five more days was viewed merely as a stopgap.

But for those who had to go back into the snow-covered mountains, it was hell. During the night five mortar rounds hit Company M's command post, killing two and wounding four. Also, Company E at Vanemont took mortar rounds, and Antitank Company was shelled by self-propelled guns. Sergeant Shig Doi remembers going out into the snow during those last days. "A German machine gun was holding us up all morning. We couldn't see the guy until the snow around the gun barrel melted and the steam gave him away. He had dug his hole under a rock. That's when we got him—shot through the jaw."

When Sgt. Larry Tanimoto was killed, and his radioman wounded, Shig Doi and a medic tried to retrieve their fallen comrades. But a burst from a machine gun ripped through their Red Cross flag. "Then somebody yelled something in German, and the firing stopped. They let us take out the wounded."

On 14 November, Nisei patrols were sent east, and south toward Corcieux. At le Petit Paris, about fifteen Germans with machine guns hidden inside the buildings opened up on a Company L patrol. Of the seven Nisei wounded, two fell into German hands. Company E at Vanemont was shelled by more than one hundred mortar rounds, and Antitank Company and 522d Artillery dueled with German self-propelled guns and artillery.

The 141st and 143d Regiments met with little resistance on 15 November. More evidence of the German withdrawal and "scorched earth" policy was visible that night as Corcieux went up in flames. General Dahlquist wrote to his wife, Ruth:

> *The evening broadcast of news is just coming on. However, it is about the same as 8 o'clock. We always listen just the same to see what they say about us. You apparently did some good guessing with your clipping from New York. [Referring to the news articles about the "Lost Battalion," which had appeared on 5 November.]*
>
> *If the men and junior officers of the infantry did not weigh so heavily on my mind I really would feel carefree. The Germans do not bother me in the least when they shoot at me.*

But the shooting did bother the men of Antitank Company when, earlier that day, a direct hit on the 3d platoon command post killed

2d Lt. Ben Rogers and wounded Dave Kawagoye, Masao Haya shikawa, and Masao Aizawa.

On 16 November, General Dahlquist wrote in his notebook: "Spent most of the morning with the 141st. Owens [Col. Charles Owens] is struggling valiantly, but has a job. The regiment is rotten. Went to Corps headquarters to check on telephone conversation. Will attack on the 19th. Relieve Japs tomorrow."

A brief spell of fair weather set in as patrols from the 143d Regiment entered the burned-out towns of Corcieux, Barbey, and Seroux on 17 November. Relief of the 3d Battalion, 442d, by the 143d Regiment was completed in the morning, and that of the 2d Battalion in late afternoon. Company E, near la Côte, still under fire, was last to be withdrawn at 1915 hours.

Effective 1700 hours, 18 November, the 442d Regimental Combat Team was detached from the 36th Division and VI Corps, and ordered to move by truck to Nice, France. General Dahlquist sent a letter:

> *1. The 36th Division regrets that the 442d Combat Team must be detached and sent to other duties. The period during which you have served, 14 October to 18 November 1944, was one of hard, intense fighting through terrain as difficult as any army has ever encountered.*
>
> *2. The courage, steadfastness, and willingness of your officers and men were equal to any ever displayed by United States troops.*
>
> *3. Every officer and man of the Division joins me in sending our best personal regards and good wishes to every member of your command, and we hope that we may be honored again by having you as a member of our Division.*

On 18 November, VI Corps published Field Order No. 8, calling for the continued attack on St.-Dié—Strasbourg by the newly arrived 100th and 103d Infantry Divisions, alongside the battle weary 3d, 36th, and 45th. General O'Daniel's "Task Force Whirlwind" hastened toward the Saales Gap, and the 103d Division crossed the Meurthe River. But when they entered St.-Dié on 22 November, theirs was a Pyrrhic victory. Major General Charles G. Haffner's soldiers found much of the town burned to the ground, looted, and void of inhabitants. From a historic standpoint it was particularly sad, because St.-Dié was home to the printers who in 1507 published the *Cosmographiae Introductio*, which for the first time referred to the New World as "America."

The second day of clear weather found the U.S. Seventh and Third Armies, and French First Army, making good progress against the Germans, now in varying stages of retreat. XII TAC flew 45 missions and 392 sorties that day, and General Dahlquist's 36th Division gained considerable ground against light rear-guard action around the scorched town of Gérardmer. Two days later, as the Japanese Americans headed toward the Riviera, Belfort fell, and French forces reached the Rhine. After a two-month respite in Nice and the French Maritime Alps, the so-called "Champagne Campaign," the men of the 442d RCT were sent back to Italy to fight their way north through the Gothic Line and the Po Valley. The 522d Field Artillery was detached, and participated in the push through the Siegfried Line into Germany. On 29 April 1945 members of this Nisei unit took part in the liberation of the Dachau concentration camp.

The "Lost Battalion" continued to battle its way across the Meurthe River, into Clefcy, through St. Marie Pass, and into what was to become the "Colmar Pocket." There, at Sigolsheim, Company A of the "Alamo" Regiment was once again cut off. After two days of fierce house-to-house fighting Lt. Marty Higgins was wounded and taken prisoner along with his men.

Technical Sergeant Charles Coolidge, whose Medal of Honor was pending, received the worst pounding since the Rapido River campaign. Within five days his twenty-eight-man machine-gun section was cut down to eight.

After Bataillon 201's commander, Major Seebacher, was wounded at le Haut Jacques, he was taken to a hospital in Strasbourg. There, at the end of November, as General Leclerc's 2d French Armored Division and the U.S. 7th Regiment battled their way into town, Seebacher made his escape by train, eventually reaching his native Graz. He was still convalescing when he received orders to organize Heeres Gebirgsjäger Regiment 1, which saw action during the final days of the war near Rothenburg ob der Tauber. His unit was overrun near Werishofen, and Seebacher, along with a handful of men, made his escape through the woods. He once again reached Graz without being taken prisoner. After the war Major Seebacher pursued a career in law.

Also his successor, Oberleutnant Franz Kapfer, made it home to the Algäu in southern Bavaria. He was still recovering from wounds to both thighs when the French occupied his hometown of Bühl. Two years later he completed his studies and became a master forester.

On Christmas Day, 1944, Gen. Wilhelm Richter was sent to the "leader reserve," and by 14 February 1945 the remnants of the 716th Volks-Grenadier Division were absorbed by the decimated 708th Volks-Grenadier Division. Ten weeks later the war in Europe was over.

On 4 December, with most of Strasbourg in American hands, Maj. Glenn Rathbun, commanding the Cotton Balers' 3d Battalion, was reconnoitering the banks of the Rhine with the new regimental commander, Lt. Col. Frank Izenhour, when a German artillery round exploded near them. Izenhour was wounded, and Major Rathbun blinded for life.

# 11: Life, Death, and Honor

**Glenn E. Rathbun**

After four hundred days of combat, a German mortar shell ended Maj. Glenn Rathbun's career on 4 December, at Strasbourg. At the time, the 26-year-old ex-football player (right tackle for the University of Idaho) commanding the Cotton Balers' 3d Battalion was on a reconnaissance on the west shore of the Rhine with his new regimental commander, Lt. Col. Frank Izenhour.

I heard the whisper of the shell far overhead when suddenly the alarm bells went off in my head. There was just enough time to bend my knees when the round hit and the light of day turned black. I continued to the ground, and slid sideways into the ditch between road and railroad track, and automatically checked my body for wounds. No sign of any . . . but my eyes. I knew I had been hit across the eyes but knew better than to put my hands up and find out.

The lieutenant grabbed my arm and ran with me to a house where he lay me down on my right side to keep the blood from drowning me. I knew I was blind, yet my whole life was in focus—my military career over, my wife Louise and the load she would have to carry, and the fact that if I killed myself, she wouldn't get my insurance. It was then that I got sick from shock. I couldn't get my .45 out from under my hip.

There was nothing Doc Sladeck could do for me at the aid station. At the evacuation hospital I was stripped naked, but when the nurse tried to remove my wristwatch, I came up flying. I had heard how many wounded men lost everything they had. But she assured me that my watch, buckled around my billfold, would be put under my pillow. I threw up and, semiconscious, experienced how they put me on a stretcher, covered me with a wool blanket, and put me into an ambulance. Later I learned that the ambulance was heading for the station hospital more than 100 miles away through the Vosges. It must have started snowing pretty hard because we slid around the road a lot. The road was rough, and my head felt as big as a washtub and hurt like hell. They never give a head wound a hypo, so I had to grin and bear it. Sometime during the night we went into a ditch, and I almost ended up in the driver's lap. We must have been there for hours, but I didn't care, and even dozed off a bit. In the middle of that cold night another ambulance arrived and we resumed our treacherous journey.

During the wee hours the ambulance came to a halt and I was taken inside a warm building, dressed in pajamas, and put into a bed. I slept off and on for a week. I would come to and moan, and the nurse would shove a tube into my mouth; I'd sip some water and lapse back into oblivion. It was my hottest battle to date, just hanging on to my life. My bed must have been next to an angel of mercy, because every time I moaned she was there. Finally, after a week or more, I was x-rayed and put into another ward. When the doctor examined me he noticed that the top of my left ear had been cut, and upon closer examination found a cut in my skull. Taking a scalpel from his coat pocket, he flipped out a piece of steel. He also told me that another piece of steel had gone through my left eye, under my nose, through the right cheekbone, and lodged above my back teeth in the upper cheek muscle. The broken right cheek had been jammed up against the right eye, causing the retina to rupture, filling the eye cavity with blood. The contusion was beginning to clear a bit, and I was able to see some light, but not enough for the doctor to tell how much damage had been done to the retina. That's when the doctor gave me the bad news—there wasn't much of a chance to get my sight back in the other eye.

I was eating very little, so the doctor prescribed a shot of whiskey before each meal. It was terrible stuff—the worst bourbon money could buy. I put up with it for three days, and then passed it on to the fellow next to me—an oil driller from Texas. Those guys usually drink anything. But in a couple of days he also gave it up. Also, I hadn't had a bowel movement for days. We called the big bedpans B-17, and the smaller urinal a P-38, and I didn't like either one. I finally persuaded the nurse to help me to the bathroom, and for half an hour dug the hardened stuff out with my fingers. I felt human again, and managed to follow the wall back to my bed.

A Red Cross volunteer stopped by the second week, and I dictated a letter to my wife in Milwaukie, Oregon. I told her the facts, and left it up to her to tell Mother when she went home to Bonners Ferry for Christmas—our third Christmas apart.

We heard about the fighting at the Colmar Pocket and the Battle of the Bulge, and after New Year's it was safe enough for the trains to take us south to Marseilles. But my wound wouldn't heal, and it began to affect my right eye. Finally my attending physician set out with tweezers to pull steel fragments, rocks, and pieces of bone from my oozing socket. He got half of Strasbourg out of there. On top of that I had scabies from sleeping in the dirt all that time in the Vosges.

It was decided that Major Rathbun needed a specialist back in the States, and along with another patient, he was put on the train to Paris.

When I got there, two Majors, medical officers, wanted to operate on me, but I told them no! When they insisted I said, "I'm a combat soldier with more than 400 days on the line. I'll kill you before you get to operate on me." That same night I was on a C-54, heading back to the States—first the Azores, Newfoundland, and when we got to Maine the ceiling was zero. The copilot let me sit up front and told me that we didn't have enough fuel to make it to New York. It was Groundhog's Day, February 2; I'll never forget it. Finally, Presque Isle called in, "ceiling 200 feet, but come quick." Twenty minutes later we landed in driving snow and stayed snowed in for a week. From there I called home, but both my mother and my in-laws were out. The only thing going on at that time was the movies, so the Bonners Ferry operator called the theater, and sure enough all of them were there.

When it was safe to fly again we headed for Montreal, Detroit, Chicago, dropping off patients along the way. Then St. Louis, Colorado Springs, Denver, Salt Lake City, Modesto, and finally Moffett Field near Palo Alto. That's where Louise came to see me, at the hospital in Menlo Park. I had a high fever, sweating profusely when she walked in the door.

After spending two-and-a-half of their three-year marriage apart, Glenn and Louise were together once again. Says Louise:

I knew how severely he had been wounded. First I got the telegram, and then a letter from a Red Cross volunteer. As the daughter of a country doctor I had no illusions. I hadn't seen Glenn since he shipped out of Norfolk on October 3, 1942, and now it was February 1945.

In retrospect I would say there were three things that helped us keep our sanity during the war years. First, the Depression had taught us to tighten our belts and be thankful for what we had. Second, in World War II everyone was in some way affected. This made the situation more bearable. And third, one took one's marriage vows seriously in those days.

With the encouragement of his physical therapist, Glenn Rathbun enrolled in the MBA program at Stanford University in the fall of 1945.

Louise read everything to me. For nine weeks all she did was read, days, nights, and weekends. It was difficult for me to learn by listening. In between, I had seven operations, usually performed on a Friday, and by Monday I'd come to class with my head all bandaged up and my glasses askew. It all went very well until the next year when Louise was pregnant with our first child.

### Wells Lewis

Wells Lewis might well have stepped out of his father's shadow, Nobel prize winning author Sinclair Lewis, had not a German bullet ended his life in the afternoon of 29 October, 1944. First Lieutenant Lewis, aide de camp to Gen. John Dahlquist, was twenty-seven years old.

Wells, named in admiration of H. G. Wells, was born by cesarean section to Grace Hegger Lewis on 26 July 1917. Sinclair—married to his craft and booze his mistress—was not much of a father. To satisfy the popular writer's wanderlust and his mother's eagerness to mingle with high society, the Lewises lived all over the United States and Europe, which meant one boarding school after another for young Wells. It wasn't until Wells's sixth birthday that Sinclair (called Hal by his wife) "discovered" his son. On that day, near Fontainebleau, Sinclair gave Wells a magnificent French cuirassier's uniform, complete with metal breastplate, plumed helmet, sword, and scabbard— the love of Wells's life. He strapped it on for breakfast and at night placed it beside his bed. Once back in England, the Lewises moved into a large house in Chelsea where young Wells was given his own room, and where he spent many a night alone while his parents mingled with the cream of European society. His mother wrote in 1923:

*And how brave Wells is, dear lamb, about sleeping on the third floor all alone. This house is an open cozy sort of house so he is not as remote as he was in the huge French one, but I know how he feels. Each evening he asks me with such circumlocution if we are going to be home for dinner, and the relief in his face when I say we are.*

*[January 1924] I was worried about Wells, who was making no progress in school, and had remained a grownup's child, frequently behaving like an arrogant little beast with his contemporaries. We were again, as we had been in 1921, thinking seriously of adopting*

*a child. It would have to be an American child, and not younger than four, I thought, since a child smaller than that would be no help to Wells, and even so, I was afraid he might patronize an adopted brother or sister. The plan of adoption arose out of Hal's fear of another cesarean operation for me—an unnecessary fear—but, as nothing ever came of it, he probably regarded it as something to talk about but not act upon.*

A year later, in Switzerland, away from his parents at Christmas, precocious seven-year-old Wells wrote a poem reflecting his gloom and, in a way, foreshadowing his untimely end twenty years later.

> There is a great big French window
> That lets in all the winter breezes.
> Through it I can see everlasting winter.
> No matter where I turn, all that I can see is large
> mountains covered with snow
> And with black pines through which the snow mocks me.
> The mountains tell me, flatly, finally,
> That spring will never come again.

A week earlier Wells had sent his father a delicately carved wooden horse, and a bear to his mother. Upon receiving the gifts in Paris, his mother reflected:

*He must have saved up for this out of his small allowance. Our dear little son. Never again must we let him spend Christmas with strangers. We put our arms around each other and smiled tearfully.*

Unlike his father, a Yale alumnus, Wells chose Harvard. But when news reporters tried to buttonhole the son of the Nobel prize-winner, he gave each a drink and kindly asked them to leave him alone. In spite of Sinclair's marginal parenting skills, Wells loved his father. In 1936, while spending the summer at their Vermont farm, Wells wrote to his now divorced mother, "Father's a bit difficult at times, but I love the old bastard." And at Christmas he followed up with a letter sent to her in Mexico.

*After eleven months of complete sobriety Father has returned with a whoosh to the bottle. . . . I have always felt that Father's drinking was not my business but this spell of sobriety resulted in so much happiness for everybody, especially himself, that I decided, as he treats me like a pretty responsible person, that a word from me in this new crisis might be valuable. So yesterday I approached him to perform my duty, feeling impertinent and priggish but somehow justified. But, by God, the angel of righteousness had got there first and I found Pappy drinking a milkshake!!!*

His friends described Wells as a young man of great charm, intelligence, and even rarer willpower. While a senior at Harvard he published a small novel, *They Still Say No,* and after graduating *magna cum laude* in 1939, he went to work as a news editor in Greenville, Mississippi, and then as a reporter for a New Brunswick, New Jersey, paper. In August 1940 he enlisted in the 7th Regiment, New York National Guard, "to practice what I am preaching." He served in Africa and Italy, earning both the Bronze and Silver Stars. Because he was fluent in French, Wells was chosen to work with the French underground before becoming General Dahlquist's aide. On 29 October, two days before reaching the "Lost Battalion," Wells and General Dahlquist were visiting the front lines in the Forêt de Champ. Dahlquist, who had written the manual on machine guns, did not heed the warnings of the Japanese Americans. He continued to walk upright, with Wells by his side, when a machine-gun bullet pierced the aide's helmet.

Two days later General Dahlquist wrote to Sinclair Lewis:

*I was near enough to him to catch his body as it fell. He was dead before I laid him on the ground. I was present at his funeral, and it was as though my own son was being buried. I had known Wells only since July of this year, but in this short period he had endeared himself to me as a real man. His constant good nature, his keen mind, and his everlasting willingness to perform every task given him marked him as a real soldier. He was dependable and courageous.*

Sinclair Lewis replied on 27 November:

> *Dear General Dahlquist. Your letter of October 31, regarding the
> death of my son Wells, has just come in. It was so clear and sincere
> and brave a letter that I want to go beyond all formalities and thank
> you for it personally. It could not have been more fine and solacing if
> it had come from a very old personal friend. I am proud to know that
> you, like myself, are a son of Minnesota.*

Wells's mother, Grace Hegger Telesforo Casanova de Ojea, replied
to the general:

> *For a soldier to die in his General's arms is in the great tradition,
> a literary symbol which I know Wells himself would appreciate.*
>   *At first I was sorry that you had sent me the photographs of the
> funeral—it seemed so agonizingly final—but after looking long and
> often at all those tall brave men, standing bowed and bare of head
> before that flag-draped box, I was proud and grateful.*

Sinclair Lewis, author of *Main Street, Arrowsmith, Elmer Gantry,* and
*Babbitt,* outlived his son by six years.

### John E. Dahlquist

Monday, 14 May 1945: General Patch called me about one o'clock
and read me a very bitter and stinging reprimand from General
Eisenhower concerning what he calls "fraternizing with high ranking German Officers." It was apparently the result of distorted state-
ments in London and New York papers.

May 1945 marked both the high and low points in Gen. John
Ernest Dahlquist's career. Under his leadership the 36th Infantry Division had fought its way from southern France through Germany
and Austria, capturing thousands of Axis soldiers and scores of high-
ranking officials—Hermann Göring among them. But it was the cavalier attitude with which the general received the Reichsmarschall
that culminated in scandal and General Eisenhower's rebuke and for-
mal investigation, which almost led to his undoing.

After the war ended on 8 May, Göring had sent word to the Americans that he was ready to surrender. Coming from Brucht Castle in

Austria, he arrived at General Dahlquist's headquarters at noon, wearing his uniform and regalia. As the number two Nazi stepped out of the staff car, General Dahlquist saluted and shook his hand. A cordial interview and lunch followed—chicken, potatoes, and green peas. This cavalier treatment, as reported by the press, brought about a flurry of furious articles, editorials, political cartoons, letters, and finally, General Eisenhower's stinging reprimand.

Following the "Göring Affair," Dahlquist wrote several letters admitting to the salute but denying the handshake. Nevertheless he went on to explain why "a handshake is such an automatic proposition which in no way implies fraternizing with the enemy." The affair obviously bothered the general, who kept a scrapbook full of articles and letters, including the drawing of a bloody handshake.

John Ernest Dahlquist was the last of four children born to Swedish immigrants Eric and Charlotte Dahlquist on 12 March 1896, in Minneapolis, Minnesota. He grew up in the two-room house his father had built, and, along with brothers Carl and Harry, and sister Elizabeth, was raised Lutheran, regularly attending Sunday school at the Swedish Augustana Church. John was twelve when his father was crushed to death by a steel girder at the American Bridge Company. Like other boys his age, he was to enter a trade, but he insisted on continuing his education, working small jobs on the side.

"I was perfectly capable of paddling my own canoe," he told a reporter many years later. John played football at old East High School, and as a freshman at the University of Minnesota, he took an interest in Swedish literature. Young Dahlquist got good grades and focused on debate, forensics, and drama, playing a leading role in *Rika Morbror (Rich Uncle)* staged by the Swedish Literary Society. But his greatest honor was his being chosen as editor of the university annual, *The Gopher.* "A position which usually went to a fraternity member, not a 'Barbarian' like me who had to work his way through school and couldn't afford joining a fraternity."

Even though ROTC training was obligatory at the university, Dahlquist at first had no particular love for the military. But with America's entry into the world war, he applied to both the army and the navy for a commission. The army bit first, and he joined the service as a Second Lieutenant on 15 August 1917. But the war ended before his unit was shipped overseas. The assignment which was to shape his thinking and career came in September 1919, when he was transferred to Germany to join the Army of Occupation. During that three-year stint he got to know the provinces along the Rhine that were to become his area of operations some twenty years later. He traveled throughout Germany and Austria, and briefly served as the appointed mayor of the medieval town of Mayen, near Koblenz.

*The American Swedish Monthly* of September 1942 quotes Dahlquist:

> Great tact and firmness were essential to a successful filling of the office, for the Germans were naturally antagonistic and suspicious of all foreigners, especially of the Army of Occupation, whose presence they resented.
>
> They soon found out that their new mayor was a humane and just man, and his experience as head of this German community is remembered by him as very pleasant. He did, in fact, discover, as so many others have done, that the Germans in general are a good-natured and friendly people as long as they are not dominated by evil-minded and tyrannical leaders.

When the American contingent was withdrawn in 1922, he considered leaving the service to take up law. But finances and a love interest from his student days prompted him to postpone his plans—permanently, as it turned out. John Dahlquist married Miss Ruth Dampier of St. Paul in September 1923. His superior officers, recognizing his ability and integrity, encouraged him to remain in the army, and paved his way for further promotion. His career eventually took him to Fort Benning, Georgia, where he remained from 1925 to 1930 as a student and then teacher at the Infantry School. His specialty was the use of automatic weapons, which led to his writing the army manual on machine guns.

The year 1931 saw him at the Command and General Staff College at Fort Leavenworth, followed by a three-year posting to the Philippines, where he assisted in developing the defenses of the islands. On his way back to the States, he took his wife and young son on a three-week tour of China and Japan. His assignment to the Army War College was followed by the Air Corps Tactical School at Maxwell Field and the Planning Branch, Personnel Division of the War Department General Staff.

Six months before the United States entered World War II, Lieutenant Colonel Dahlquist's "good judgment and integrity" landed him a job in England as assistant chief of staff, Personnel, Special Army Observers Group, and then assistant chief of staff for Personnel of U.S. Forces in the British Isles. During the "Blitz" he was promoted to colonel, and four months later to brigadier. By August 1942 he rose to lieutenant general, Eisenhower's deputy chief of staff, responsible for the planning and construction of bases in Northern Ireland designed for U.S. troops headed for North Africa.

In an interview conducted by the London correspondent of the Swedish *Dagens Nyheter,* Dahlquist declared, "My hobby now is to win the war!" In February 1943 he got what he wanted—command of a division. To the correspondent from his hometown, Minneapolis, he boasted, "The 70th is the best damn infantry division in the world. When this division goes into combat against the Nazis or the Japs it's going to be a headache for Hitler or a toothache for Tojo."

But Dahlquist was to see combat with the 36th Division, which had already fought up and down the Italian peninsula by the summer of 1944. Typical of his style of leadership, Dahlquist was the first division commander to go ashore in southern France on 15 August, during Operation Dragoon. After the battles of Montélimar and the crossing of the Moselle, the 36th reached the Vosges by mid-September. Well aware that no invading army had ever crossed the Vosges successfully, Dahlquist was determined to be the first to do so, and the first to reach the Rhine. For the former mayor of Mayen, it was to be a homecoming of sorts, but the Vosges and a tenacious foe did not oblige.

Six feet tall, dour, and sometimes brooding, John E. Dahlquist was the opposite of his assistant division commander, Gen. Robert Stack, who frequently joked and sent Bill Mauldin cartoons to his brother Jack. Whatever his faults, Dahlquist was no coward. He personally led riflemen in the Vosges, which earned him a Silver Star and later the DSC. It was his habit to show up at the front lines, often to the dismay of his commanders, whom he sidestepped and chastised as a matter of course. Dahlquist liked to eat well, saving menus from military banquets, and describing fetes in great detail.

Under his leadership the 36th Division spent 121 days on the line without relief (15 August to 14 December 1944) from southern France to Colmar, sustaining 12,201 casualties. Among Nisei veterans, who have little regard for the general, the question persists, "Did Dahlquist use us up because we were Japanese?" The answer is a qualified no. With his 142d and 143d Regiments committed along a thirty-five-mile front, the "Alamo" Regiment spent and its 1st Battalion trapped, the general had no choice but to commit the 442d resting at Belmont. The ferocity with which German reinforcements fought caught him and his superiors by surprise. And, with nearly three hundred men trapped, it was his duty to rescue them. Responsibility for the high casualty rate sustained by the Niseis certainly rests on the general's shoulders, but war is an inexact science. Judging from casualty reports and regimental records, he drove his own regiments no less. In his defense it must be said that his repeated requests to Generals Patch, Truscott, and Brooks to have the 36th relieved were not heeded until Christmas of 1944.

At their 1947 division reunion, the general approached Marty Higgins of the "Lost Battalion," seated with a group of fellow officers and wives, and apologized for having driven the men too hard.

It wasn't until 2 December 1944 that General Dahlquist got to cross the Rhine at Selestad. On 23 March the T-Patchers breached the Siegfried Line, and by war's end reached Tyrol. Along the way General Dahlquist took the surrender of Feldmarschall Karl Rudolf Gerd von Rundstedt; Admiral Horthy, the Regent of Hungary; Feldmarschalls List and von Leeb; Gen. Ritter von Epp; and Feldmarschall Ritter von Greim, who had succeeded Göring as head of the Luftwaffe. Among other notables captured were Reichsminister Frank and filmmaker Leni Riefenstahl. Also liberated were French Generals Weygand and Gamelin, and Premiers Daladier and Reynaud.

By 1955 Dahlquist had risen to four-star general, head of the Continental Army Command, and retired one year later. Back in his hometown, Minneapolis, he became department head for the New York investment firm of Harris Upham & Company, and after retiring a second time traveled to Russia, Austria, and Germany. There he went fishing and in Munich visited the Bavarian State. General Dahlquist died on Independence Day, 1975, at Ft. Lauderdale, Florida.

# 12: Prisoners of War

**Marty Higgins**

Congenial, unassuming, and speaking fast with a slight Jersey accent, Martin J. Higgins doesn't fit the stereotype of the war hero. But a hero he is, not only because of his sterling combat record and having survived the ordeal of the "Lost Battalion" and German POW camps, but because he had the moral courage to personally involve himself in the effort to obtain citizenship for Issei immigrants at a time when anti-Japanese sentiment still ran high.

Born in Jersey City, Marty Higgins graduated from Dickinson High School and St. Peter's College before going to work for the All American Cable Company. He enlisted in New York's 101st Cavalry (horse), and after Pearl Harbor attended Officer Candidate School.

In May of 1944, Lieutenant Higgins was assigned to the 36th Infantry Division in Italy, and on 15 August 1944 he took part in the Allied landings in southern France. Leading his men, he hit Blue Beach near the French Riviera towns of Fréjus and St.-Raphaël, "stepping into a shell hole and going down." After the German garrison surrendered to Company A, led by Capt. James McNeil, they came under sniper fire.

My platoon took the brunt of it. I lost several men killed or wounded. At one point, diving for cover, I felt a whack in my butt. When I checked my fanny the "whack" was from a bullet that went through my back pocket, creased a notebook, and emerged the other side without wounding me. The first of many close calls. Marge's prayers, saying the rosary, and making the stations brought me home. Luck helped as well.

Eventually the Germans surrendered—the only time in combat I almost lost my cool. I came close to shooting them. My platoon sergeant, thank God, restrained me.

Higgins's platoon took part in the race north and then west to cut off German forces retreating alongside the Rhône River. As the Americans got to a hilltop outside Montélimar, they saw the battle unfold between the 36th Infantry and 11th Panzer Divisions.

With a ringside seat to one of the most spectacular events of the war. A German panzer division came through, and we watched them attack another unit in a classic battle pattern. They were beyond the range of our weapons, and we had no forward observers to fire artillery.

In the push to the Vosges Mountains, both Captain McNeil and his successor, Lieutenant Daugherty, were killed in action. A new and reluctant company commander was relieved by Colonel Steele near the village of St. Amé, and Lieutenant Higgins was put in charge. He successfully led his company through dense woods, surprising and routing the defenders, part of the German 198th Infantry Division, in a pitched battle.

After the fall of Bruyères came the "Alamo" Regiment's push through the Forêt de Champ and the ordeal of being cut off for five long days and nights.

Ernest Hemingway's wife, Mary, came to interview us afterward, but her piece was never published. Not good for the morale of the home folk. I had bitched about the 36th being on the line so long; we really had taken a pounding.

[Ernest Hemingway was serving as a war correspondent at the time. On 21 August, on the outskirts of Paris, he and OSS Col. David Bruce were waiting for the Allies to arrive.]

By Marty Higgins's own account, being part of the "Lost Battalion" was not the worst experience of the war. Three days after being relieved by the Nisei 442d Regimental Combat Team, he was back on the line. A month later, on 11 December, Companies A and B were approaching Sigolsheim just north of Colmar, when friendly tank-destroyer fire hit Harry Huberth's Company B. Huberth, who had been cut off with the "Lost Battalion," lost twenty-five men. Higgins's Company A continued down the hill toward Sigolsheim. Arctic conditions and self-propelled artillery fire made life miserable as his men struggled down the forward slope and fought their way into town. Later that afternoon Higgins's first platoon fired on three tanks, disabling one, and a half-track sent to guard it was blasted by a bazooka and set on fire.

Unable to establish wire communications, Higgins sent an urgent radio message to the 1st Battalion, giving his positions and requesting reinforcements. The night was relatively quiet, but the next day, 10 December, German armor and infantry approached town from the south. An attempt to ambush them failed, and the tanks attacked. Higgins believed he could hold out inside the houses until reinforcements arrived, but none came.

> About one o'clock a tank opened up on my CP, and I heard a man scream. I went into the downstairs room, thinking I might be able to get the Jerry with a rifle grenade. Evidently they saw me first. There was a loud explosion; my pipe fell out of my mouth, my helmet went flying, and I spun around a couple of times. My right leg went numb and I thought it was missing. . . . Just then two men came and helped me upstairs and laid me on the bed. I told Lieutenant Crown that I was wounded and temporarily out of action, but that he should go on fighting.
>
> Backed by tanks the Jerries attacked the houses one by one, using smoke—the first time I'd seen them use it. And that is how they got most of the company.
>
> At about 2:30 I tried my 300 radio which hadn't worked, and got through to the Charley Company radioman. . . . I didn't dare tell him how badly off we were, for fear the Jerries would know. After seeing all our positions overrun I asked my eight

men if they wanted to fight or give up. They told me whatever I did would be all right with them. No help was coming, most of my men had already been captured, and we had fired all our ammo, including that taken from our seventeen prisoners.

Still dazed from the shell concussion, I finally walked out. It was the most miserable feeling I've ever had in my life. I felt let down by the regiment, shaken up, and expected to be shot for holding out so long. We found out later that we had been attacked by a regiment.

Lieutenant Higgins surrendered his carbine and grenade launcher, and a German sergeant removed the .45 he carried under his parka in a shoulder holster. A few days later Higgins's wife, Marjorie, received a copy of an Internews wire:

> . . . Higgins Jersey City NJ . . . soft-spoken wiry little officer loved by his men . . . commanded Company A, First Battalion One-four-first Regiment, Thirty-sixth Infantry Division . . . listed missing in action since December twelfth . . . stop . . . December twenty-first, papers arrived promoting him to captain . . . stop . . . Night December eleventh, twelfth company under Higgins was surrounded and cut off while spearheading attack Kaysersberg northwest Colmar . . . stop . . . Nobody knows exactly what happened to Higgins and his company . . . stop . . . During action, battalion pushed on to Sigolsheim . . . Later a French priest said about eighteen soldiers and some civilians barricaded inside Sigolsheim building battled heavy enemy . . . still later artillery observation pilot reported building flaming . . . stop . . . Officers who knew him say Higgins men "idolized" him because, while born leader, he was one of them, always looked after them, went to endless pains to make sure they had dry blankets . . . Regimental commander considered Higgins one of regiment's best company commanders . . . stop

General Dahlquist's diary entry, 11 December:

> The counterattacks started again, but were repulsed. We have given Company A, 141st, up as being lost.

December 12: The enemy attacked on three fronts today. All attacks were strong and were made with units brought from other fronts and from Germany. On my right flank a penetration was almost made. Infiltrators got into a position to cut the Ribeauville–St. Marie Road. The pressure on me to commit troops was heavy. Actually, by nightfall I had committed everything except one company.

The penetration occurred in the 141st Regiment's sector holding the heights west of Sigolsheim. It was made by the 2d Company of Gebirgsjäger Bataillon 201, which a month earlier had battled Cotton Balers, Nisei, and the "Alamo" Regiment at le Haut Jacques. Led by Lt. Günter Krebs, who had lost one hand in Russia, the company infiltrated behind the American lines and destroyed an artillery battery with rocket-propelled grenades. Then they set an ambush along the road to Ribeauville (Rappoldsweiler) and destroyed four ammunition trucks and two half-tracks.

A military study, prepared by General Helmut Thumm, corroborates the account of what the Germans called "Unternehmen 'Habicht'" (Operation Hawk).

Only a company of mountain troops met with success. This company advanced to protect the western (left) flank in the woods north of Kaysersberg. Its mission was to block the valley about 2½ kilometers northwest of Reichenweier (Riquewihr). It reached its goal, running into a heavy artillery battery, engaging it with rocket propelled grenades (Faustpatronen).

On 12 December, after wreaking havoc in the 36th Division's rear, Leutnant Krebs's company attacked the Alamo Regiment's 1st Battalion from the north at Riquewihr (Reichenweir) while Battle Groups Reimer and Ayrer attacked from the south. Every cook, clerk, and mechanic in the 141st used a rifle that day, defending the heights at Sigolsheim. But two days later, as elements of the 142d and 143d Regiments counterattacked, Krebs was killed in action. For his valor Leutnant Günter Krebs received the Knight's Cross posthumously.

Soon after he was taken prisoner, Lieutenant Higgins met one of history's most notorious characters.

> We were treated well by our captors, and after a couple of days the officers Loomis, Crown, Hancock, and I were taken away from our troops and put up in a very quaint hotel. There Lieutenant Crown was summoned to an interview, and when it came to be my turn, he told me in passing, 'Heinrich Himmler.'
>
> I was brought into a large room where a general and another man were waiting. I recognized Himmler. The general interviewed me. He didn't believe that our few men had caused so many of their casualties. He was quite belligerent and went on to castigate President Roosevelt, calling him an evil Jew. Finally Himmler spoke to me in German. The general interpreted. "You are lucky. You will survive the war!"

By this time Reichsführer SS Heinrich Himmler, commander of Army Group "Oberrhein," had already sent out peace feelers to Allied master spy Allen Dulles. But as he betrayed his own Führer in an effort to save his own neck, he continued to issue a stream of suicidal orders to his command.

> 1. The commanding general of 64 Army Corps personally vouches for the fact that Colmar will remain in our hands.
> 2. Every village and every house is to be converted into a fortress and defended; not a single foot of ground will be relinquished to the enemy. I forbid the movement of supply and train units to the right side of the Rhine.
> 3. In the Upper Rhine a crisis situation must be surmounted for three more weeks, at which time a favorable and decisive change is to be expected (Ardennes Offensive).

According to Marty Higgins:

> En route to our final destination we rode the Berlin subway where people secretly gave us thumbs-up. We reached Oflag 64 in Schubin, Poland, just before Christmas. We got a very cold welcome. The prisoners suspected all new arrivals to be German

plants. Luckily I met a friend from my hometown, Frank Maxwell, who identified me, and I was able to vouch for the others. The camp was well organized, and I received a Red Cross parcel every week. But it was too good to last.

After four weeks, during sub-zero weather, Oflag 64 was evacuated from the oncoming Russians. At night we'd get watery soup, and they'd pile us in barns where we slept on top of each other. One evening we stole some raw potatoes from the pigs, and got dysentery. I hung my soiled long johns on a tree limb, and the next morning they were gone. To this day I can't conceive of someone stealing them like that.

When I collapsed from vomiting and diarrhea, I was put in a boxcar with other unfortunate comrades. Our next stop was Stalag III-A at Luckenwalde*, 35 miles southwest of Berlin. We were cheering as high-altitude bombers unloaded on that city.

We slept on two-tiered bunks with wooden slats. In order to keep warm, everyone contributed whatever slats they could for firewood—leaving just enough to support the body—one for the feet, knees, maybe two for the fanny, and one for the head and shoulders. The highlight of the day was splitting a loaf of bread—eight to a loaf. Whoever got the biggest slice had it made, worth a prayer of thanks. Soup—very, very thin; bugs in it, good protein.

The Russians eventually overran Luckenwalde and the German guards took off. Townspeople came in and begged us to stay with them, fearing rape and pillage from the invaders. When some deuce-and-a-half sent by our forces were sent back empty by the Russians we made our escape. I put on a French beret and a British uniform, and six of us reached a truck which

---

*Stalag III-A at Luckenwalde held about 17,000 prisoners of war, officers, and men from the Soviet Union, France, Italy, Poland, Norway, Serbia, Rumania, Greece, Great Britain and its Commonwealth, and the United States.

In January 1945 an additional 600 Americans arrived from their forced march originating at Oflag 64 in Poland, followed in February by some 4,000 enlisted men from Stalag II-B located at Hammerstein, Poland. Most were quartered in circus tents and slept on the ice-cold ground. The camp was liberated by Soviet forces on 22 April 1945. (Source, *Ex-POW Bulletin,* May 1992.)

took us back to the American lines. We were flown to "Lucky Strike," had a physical, and ate a full-course steak dinner. Then all threw up.

One thing I must add. The march helped me overcome the feelings I had about being captured. When I collapsed, a German guard prodded me with his rifle butt, but I didn't care if I died. One of my buddies lifted me up and supported me to the next stop at a barn, and the following day to a boxcar. I think that episode affected my quality of life. Material things meant and still mean little to me.

After his return Marty Higgins received the captain's bars that had been approved just days before his capture. On 1 July 1945 he was awarded the Silver Star.

For gallantry in action from 23 to 31 October 1944 in France. When the 1st Battalion was completely surrounded by hostile troops and isolated from other friendly units, Lieutenant Higgins assumed command of the organization, and despite heavy artillery and mortar fire, skillfully directed his men in establishing a perimeter for defense. Although the troops were without food and water, and were subjected to a series of strong German attacks, Lieutenant Higgins worked tirelessly and courageously to maintain the morale of his men, and bravely exposing himself to hostile fire, directed elements of the battalion in repelling the attacks with heavy losses to the enemy.

[Note: After Company A was captured, the unit was rebuilt and participated in the drive through southern Germany and Tyrol, Austria. In April 1945, at the small Bavarian town of Bad Tölz, Lt. Joseph Burke and a detachment from Company A captured General Feldmarschall Karl Rudolf Gerd von Rundstedt, who had been one of Germany's top strategists until relieved by Hitler on March 1.]

### Eddie Guy

Eddie Guy was on the "Lost Battalion" perimeter, next to a light machine-gun crew manned by Jake Mason and Sergeant Stevens, when he recognized a GI in the trees ahead. He jumped up and, shouting, ran down the slope toward the 442d trooper. That's when Mutt Sakumoto, in way of greeting asked, "Need any cigarettes?"

"It was one of the happiest days in my life," said Guy, father of six and grandfather of sixteen. "I knew the Japanese Americans from Italy. When I was in the hospital in Naples, after the Rapido River, the fellow next to me was Freddie Sawada from the 100th Battalion. Fine soldiers!"

Sergeant Eddie Guy knows about soldiering, fighting with the 36th Division from North Africa to Italy and France. "One of my rocks," Marty Higgins calls his weapons platoon leader and acting first sergeant. When asked what he thought when his battalion was cut off by the Germans, he says, "We just dug in and got ready. I figured we'd get relieved sooner or later. We were dug in good, with machine guns spread out between riflemen."

What about the patrol that went out to reestablish contact with the regiment?

"There were forty to fifty men, some from each company. I believe four made it back, one of them from Company A, a fellow named Cunningham. The rest got killed or captured."

What about Sigolsheim? What happened there?

"Lieutenant Higgins did his job. We went in, expecting rein-forcements. But nobody came. After beating the Germans off for a day, we finally ran out of ammunition. We had to give up. My men and I were treated well. All of us noncoms were sent to Stalag III-A at Fürstenberg. But when the Russians advanced they marched us out. We covered 150 kilometers in three days. We ended up at Luck-enwalde, a disaster. They put us in large tents and we slept on straw. There were a lot of lice, and only one faucet, and many of us came down with diarrhea."

After fighting their way through France, being cut off in the Forêt de Champ, captured at Sigolsheim, separated, imprisoned, and marched through ice-cold weather, destiny brought Marty Higgins and Eddie Guy back together again.

"That's where I met Lieutenant Higgins again, after his group of officers came in from another camp. We could just talk through the fence because the officers were segregated from us noncoms. But I was happy to see him.

"Finally, at the end of the war, the German guards all disappeared. Six of us took off and walked to the Elbe River. But the Russians wouldn't let us cross. So one of the fellows, John Baumhausen, who was originally from Germany, persuaded a local fellow to take us across in his rowboat. We finally ran into the Americans, and they shipped us to Halle and finally Lucky Strike at Le Havre."

[Author's Note: When I told Eddie Guy that I was about to meet the Nisei from Company I who had first made contact with the "Lost Battalion," he said, "Please thank them for me. Tell them, 'Thanks from the red-haired kid from the 36th.'"]

### Jimmie Kanaya

If there had only been one litter case, my team could have gotten out of there that night, but there were at least three seriously wounded, and one barely alive. He had a piece of shrapnel protruding from his stomach. The entry wound was in his back. I had two litter bearers from the 3d Battalion, Sueo Fuji from Hawaii and Mas Uchimura from Seattle, and a medic from the collecting company we only knew as "Tex" because of his Texas drawl.

Lieutenant Jimmie Kanaya, a senior medic, stayed up all night in Madame Josephine Voirin's cottage at Biffontaine to attend to the wounded, especially the soldier with the shrapnel wound who required constant attention and morphine to ease his pain.

I remember the French lady providing us with hot soup that night; one bowl had an egg in it. I don't recall who got the egg, but I'm sure that it was worth its weight in gold to those people who suffered through years of German occupation.

I had just started smoking cigarettes a couple of months earlier, and went through two packs that night, ending up with a sore throat and a nicotine hangover.

At first light, 23 October, Kanaya, his three assistants, and medics from the 100th Battalion prepared the wounded for the trek back to friendly lines. But the encircled battalion could spare no men to carry the litters, and it was decided to use German prisoners instead. But to do this required armed guards. "There was a conflict of interest, having a Red Cross flag up front and POWs with armed guards carrying the wounded, but to this day I don't know of another way we could have done it. We didn't have helicopters in those days."

With medic Richard Chinen and walking wounded Lt. Sam Sakamoto up front, the party left Biffontaine mid-morning. German POWs, guarded by a handful of riflemen, carried the litters, followed by the walking wounded and medics. The line stretched for more than a hundred yards when, halfway through the woods, they were stopped.

Word got back to us that a German unit had intercepted us, and that they were discussing whether or not to let us through. Just about that time Captain Kim, one of the litter cases, walked past us, followed by the medic from the 100th Battalion. It wasn't long before German riflemen came over the knoll and started disarming our guards. But our infantrymen thought that they should be taking the weapons away from the Germans. A tug of war ensued over whose rifle should be removed from whom.

The German patrol made up of some forty men won out, and as the tables were turned, Kanaya heard the German POWs grumbling.

They weren't happy. The war wasn't about to end for them yet; no chance of going to the "Land of the Big PX." Our weapons were being distributed among our ex-POWs, and a German noncom took my wristwatch. Finally, our medics and guards had to carry the litters with our captors following behind.

Along the way the German officer kept reading his compass, and coming over the crest of a steep hill, we met a French farmer leading a mule toward Bruyères. When the officer asked for directions, the farmer pointed the other way, indicating that we had been heading for the American lines. After about an hour of carrying the litters across mountain trails we heard a rifle shot and a GI's cussing. Our captors whispered to us to remain quiet, and the German noncom who had earlier taken my watch now gave it back. Maybe he thought it was their turn to be captured. Later, I found out that the fire had come from the direction of the 1/141 lines. We went right past them, and a short while later entered a village. There the noncom took my watch for good.

As the Germans got organized I had the chance to escape, but decided against it because of the wounded and medics in my charge. Then the wounded were turned over to German medics while we were marched off to the rear. Later, Sam Sakamoto told me that the soldier with the severe internal injuries died at a German medical facility [Victor Akimoto was buried at the Lorraine American cemetery near St.-Avold. Next to him lies his younger brother, Johnny. After the war their mother had asked that Johnny, who had been killed earlier in Italy, be laid to rest next to his brother.]

"Tex" was interrogated first because the Germans thought that he, a Caucasian, was a 442d officer. I remember our interrogator, an officer with spit-shined riding boots and an immaculate uniform who spoke perfect English, the first of many interrogators as we were sent farther and farther to the rear.

Our train was strafed several times before our group of eight officers arrived in Berlin on Thanksgiving Day. On December 4, we got to Oflag 64 in Poland. There an American major interrogated all new arrivals to make sure we weren't plants. Luckily, Joe Shimatsu, who had been captured in Italy, identified me. I had never been issued winter clothing, which made the bitter cold even more severe.

On 21 January 1945, with the Russians approaching Oflag 64, all 1,400 POWs (including Marty Higgins) were evacuated. In 45 days we walked more than 360 miles through ice and snow across northern Poland and Germany. About 500 men, among them Joe Shimatsu and Sam Sakamoto, escaped by hiding in barns and allowing the Russians to catch up with them. Many others, too sick and malnourished to survive the forced march, died along the way. Our guards didn't even bother to shoot them. When we got to Hammelburg on the 9th of March, only 400 of us were left, including General Patton's son-in-law, Lt. Col. John K. Waters, who had been prison camp executive officer at Oflag 64.

At Hammelburg we joined some 1,000 Americans captured during the Battle of the Bulge. On March 27, a task force of twenty-five tanks, armored personnel carriers, and jeeps broke through the German lines in an effort to rescue us. When Colonel Waters walked to the main gate with an American flag to take command of the camp, he was shot in the hip by a German guard. He survived. The rescue team expected 400 prisoners but got 1,500—too many to carry back. Prisoners piled on the vehicles while others escaped on foot to make the fifty-mile dash back to the Allied lines. But at night the column was ambushed. Many of the prisoners, and even the wounded, fought back, but the rescue team got annihilated. I was in a group which covered about four miles before we were recaptured by a German antitank patrol.

General George Patton was reprimanded for authorizing the raid led by Capt. Abraham Baum. Equipped with ten Shermans, six light tanks, three assault guns, twenty-seven half-tracks, seven Jeeps, and one ambulance, the three hundred men of "Task Force Baum" had set out from the Aschaffenburg bridgehead just before midnight on 26 March. Along the way the task force shot up a dozen trains, including a flak-train near the town of Lohr, and lost one tank to a recoilless rocket (Panzerfaust). At dawn they reached Kleingemünden and shot up four Main river barges and a train leaving the station— causing a fiery inferno of exploding ammunition. At nearby Gemünden, birthplace of Gen. Ernst Haeckel of the 16th Volks-Grenadier Division, the citizens had no idea that the Americans were racing toward their small town. The previous day's bombing raid had destroyed the post office, along with the town's telephone net.

The townspeople were roused from their sleep when Captain Baum's Shermans roared past and captured the Saale bridge at Kleingemünden. As ordered by Gen. Karl Bornemann, the bridge had already been prepared for demolition by the 46th Pioneer Training Battalion, most of them raw recruits led by veterans from the Russian front. An explosion from an ammunition car, and the clatter of approaching tanks, alerted German soldiers who now, some of them only half dressed, rushed to the Saale bridge and pushed the detonator as the first Sherman approached. Then a wounded German soldier stopped the tank with a Panzerfaust, while its crew sought cover in a nearby house. A firefight ensued in the narrow streets, and another Sherman was knocked out. Some civilians had sought shelter in the basement of the old gendarmerie. One of the women remembers:

> Suddenly a young SS-man stormed into the cellar, bleeding on his left side, crying for help. When I laid him down to bandage him, I saw that his liver and spleen were hanging out. I cradled his head and tried to calm him, and, because he thought I was a nurse, he told me that today was his 18th birthday. He told me that he had fired his Panzerfaust in the narrow passage between our house and the tank, and probably got injured that way.

As white flags appeared in some windows, American medics cared for the wounded, including Germans, and Father Gehrlich gave absolution to the dying. Captain Baum ordered his task force to pull out, leaving four burning Shermans behind. The retreating tanks fired on Kleingemünden, setting several houses on fire. Moving past Rieneck, Burgsinn, and Gräfendorf, the task force finally reached Hammelburg. On the way back Task Force Baum and hundreds of liberated POWs were surrounded and captured east of Höllrich.

On the following day proclamations appeared throughout the district, signed by Nazi chief Röss:

The tank unit, which yesterday rolled through our district, was almost totally destroyed by 3 A.M. Its decimated remnants were surrounded and destroyed near Hammelburg by superior German forces.

Fellow citizens, now is not the time for idleness and rumor, but to act and work. Therefore, all of you must return to your work and fulfill your duty. But those who spread dissent through the telling of horror stories will find themselves before a military court.

Sueo Fuji, one of the medics with Kanaya's party at Biffontaine, was interrogated by a German-Japanese woman in Stuttgart. "She knew all about the 442d, and even the island I came from, and all about the training problems we had at Camp Shelby."

Fuji was sent to Stalag V-A for enlisted men, where he cared for American prisoners. All were caucasian amputees who couldn't believe that I was an American. I worked twelve to fourteen hours a day, and didn't eat till late at night. All we got to eat was barley soup, tea, and bread. I lost twenty pounds and ended up with hepatitis.

In January 1945 Fuji was sent to Stalag VII-A, where he continued to work as a medic. Occasionally he managed to sneak out with a work detail to barter for food in Munich. On 29 April, Fuji was liberated at a quarry outside Munich. His first meal in freedom was creamed rice.

Jimmie Kanaya was eventually shipped to Oflag 13-D near Nuremberg, and managed to escape one more time before being liberated by the Allies. Like Marty Higgins of the "Lost Battalion," he was sent to Lucky Strike at Le Havre, repatriated, and in Chicago joined his family, who had just recently been released from the Minidoka Internment Camp. There he received orders to attend the Army School of Military Government at the University of Virginia. As part of a military government team he was sent to Korea where he was with the administration overseeing Japanese prisoners of war.

Today, as he speaks of his capture, there is a note of regret in Colonel Kanaya's speech. In Japanese culture, a soldier's lot is to win or die. Capture is not considered a viable option, even among some Japanese Americans. According to Colonel Kanaya, many former prisoners at Oflag 64 do not want to be included on mailing lists or attend reunions. "For them it is too painful. They just want to forget."

After his escape from the death march, Sam Sakamoto made his way through the Soviet Union to Yalta. An American freighter took him aboard, and he reached the United States two weeks after Jimmie Kanaya.

# 13: Go for Broke

**Young Oak Kim**

Korean American Capt. Young Oak Kim was Operations Officer for the 100th Battalion when his right hand was severely wounded in Biffontaine. He had just completed his inspection of the perimeter, when he and Bill Pye of Company C observed the tank from inside the village church. Neither of them saw the German soldier exiting the basement of a horse stable and aiming his submachine gun. Captain Kim said, "At dusk, Bill Pye and I were watching a German tank, when this fellow fired his Schmeisser. I believe he was aiming at Pye but hit me instead."

Kim, like the other wounded, had to remain in the village as General Richter's infantry and armor counterattacked during the night. When the litter train was captured the following day, Kim narrowly escaped, reaching his beleaguered comrades in Biffontaine and eventually a field hospital. The episode interrupted Captain Kim's remarkable combat record, which had begun a year earlier at Oran, North Africa. There, while attached to the 34th (Red Bull) Division, the 100th had fought at Kasserine Pass, Hill 609, and near Tunis before being sent to Italy.

Kim earned his first Silver Star near Cassino while leading a twenty-man reconnaissance patrol. At Hill 600, he and his men were credited for destroying one machine-gun nest and capturing the crew of another. The next morning, as a German company counterattacked the Americans at the foot of the mountain, Captain Kim's patrol struck from above, capturing fifty-eight men. Kim said, "When Gen. Mark Clark pinned the medal on me, he whispered, 'I think there was a mistake; it should have been a DSC.' Naturally, I dismissed it as the kind of compliment a general might make."

But not long after that, Kim got his Distinguished Service Cross with best regards from General Clark—after earning it on another mission.

It happened at the Anzio beachhead, surrounded by Feldmarschall Kesselring's armor, infantry, and siege guns. American intelligence was desperate to find the Hermann Göring Panzer Division. Kim volunteered for the mission, which called for snatching a German soldier from behind their lines. The terrain around the Mussolini Canal was flat as a pool table, the same area where, some weeks earlier, American Rangers had been decimated. Kim and Irving Akohashi set out at noon. "Suicidal," some called it, but Kim and Akohashi managed to low-crawl seven hundred yards across no-man's-land, past mines and sentries, to "persuade" two men from a headquarters unit to accompany them back. Low-crawling and periodically watching behind and in front of them through a periscope, they and their prisoners finally reached their own lines after dark. Kim recalled: "We were debriefed until midnight, and when we were done, Colonel Singles came up to me and shook my hand. 'Congratulations, you got the DSC!' I didn't believe it at first. After all, we had just come back, and it takes a lot of paperwork. . . . Well, to make a long story short, there was a note attached and signed by General Clark: 'I didn't forget my promise.'"

When Kim was wounded at Biffontaine, Capt. Sakae Takahashi, monitoring the radio, mistakenly believed that his friend had been hit in the head. His assumption was based on the fact that Kim never wore a helmet. After being himself wounded in the right arm, Takahashi caught up with Kim at the evacuation hospital. He recognized Kim's name on the chart and pulled back the blanket. To his surprise and relief, Takahashi found that his friend had been hit in the hand and not the head.

Captain Kim remained in the service and was sent to Korea. As commander of the 1st Battalion, 31st Infantry Regiment, from March 1951 to September 1952, he fought up and down his ancestral land,

winning yet another Silver Star. After a distinguished military career
on four continents, Colonel Kim retired in 1972. He was a strong
force in the effort to erect a monument to Japanese-American soldiers, and continues to be active on behalf of veterans in his native
Los Angeles.

### Sergeant Senzaki's Patrol

When Pfc. Matsui "Mutt" Sakumoto from Hawaii asked Sgt. Eddie Guy from New York, "Need any cigarettes?" the relief of the "Lost
Battalion" was complete. But the war was far from over. Earlier that
day, just after the death of Capt. Joseph Byrne, TSgt. Takashi Senzaki had picked his men: "Sakumoto and Nakada—scouts; Ishikawa,
Saito, Takahashi, Handa, Shiroyama, Ugai. . . . There weren't many
left to choose from. Company I was down to thirty men on the line."

Henry Nakada remembers: "Fred Ugai was really mad. 'Why do
they always pick on 1st platoon to do these nasty jobs? I ain't going!'"
But, like the others, Ugai finally went, toting his trusty BAR, mum-
bling how 1st platoon was always getting the short end of the stick.

"The patrol moved along carefully from tree to tree. We were
scared because of what happened before," says Henry Nakada, who
was on point with Sakumoto. "But there were no Germans. When the
fellows from the 'Lost Battalion' recognized us, they were very happy,
and they gathered around."

For Sergeant Senzaki and the others, the historic moment was
anti-climactic. After three days of continuous and bitter fighting
through the densely forested mountains, the 442d had sustained
more than three times the number killed and wounded than they
had rescued.

When I caught up with Mutt Sakumoto and Henry Nakada,
they were in a foxhole, smoking cigarettes and having a good
time with the boys from the "Lost Battalion." I chewed them out
and said, "We got to keep going or the same thing is going to
happen to us. We'll be surrounded and stuck in a foxhole like
they are." So we walked to our objective—at the end of the
ridge. There we dug in for the night, but we didn't sleep.

The next morning we advanced, and right away they opened
up on us with machine guns. They had that place surrounded

real good. We knocked out one machine-gun nest and captured a second one. Then the Signal Corps came up with their cameras. "Can you reenact the rescue?" We were up ahead already, so I said, "We can't do that."

Fifty years after the event, his men still look up to Sergeant Senzaki, a soldier's soldier who had led them through hell in France and Italy. In the spring of 1942, Senzaki was only twenty, working with his father in the retail produce trade in Los Angeles, when Executive Order 9066 went into effect. After being rounded up and sent to the Santa Anita racetrack, he and his family were shipped to the relocation camp at Rohwer, Arkansas. But when a recruiting team came to camp one day, Takashi volunteered.

> Dad said, "This is your country. Don't bring shame on your country or your family. Go!"
> I remember, on the way to Little Rock, there were some black soldiers sitting at the back of the bus. I, as an Oriental, was told to sit in front. There they were, in uniform, ready to fight for our country. It didn't sit too well with me.

After fighting in Italy, Sergeant Senzaki and his platoon were shipped to France.

> There was house-to-house fighting until Bruyères was freed, but we didn't get to sleep in any houses. As the attack company, we had to push on to the next hill. The ones who came behind us got to meet the townspeople.

For Sergeant Senzaki, as for most of the men in Company I, the push toward the "Lost Battalion" is a blur of slogging through dark woods, rain, mud, machine-gun fire, and tree bursts. Still, each man has his particular recollections of intense moments; when a friend was hit, or a hill scaled; and the final push to the men of the "Alamo" Regiment. And all remember Captain Byrne.

> I knew Captain Byrne still from Camp Shelby when he was first platoon leader. He could tell his men from the back of their

heads. "Nakada, get a haircut," he would yell—just by looking at the back of a man's head . . . and we all looked pretty much the same. He was a straight-shooter, called it like it is. After Captain Graham he became our company commander. "Senzaki, take out a patrol!" he'd say. He liked to send me out.

Suguru Takahashi recalls: The Germans had pulled back, and everything was quiet that morning. When we got to the "Lost Battalion," they were in deep holes with logs on top. Some had tears in their eyes when they saw us. We left them some rations and moved on. For us things weren't over yet. The Germans kept shelling us and we had to hold the line. Imagine, two PFCs way out there, so close to the Germans that we could hear them digging across the ravine.

As Suguru Takahashi spoke, Tadao Saito joined us. Together they reminisced about how Sgt. Larry Tanimoto and Lloyd Onaya got killed—a bullet through the neck as Tanimoto threw a grenade, and the final yards to the "trapped," not "lost" battalion.

Takahashi, who calls the island of Maui home, had been with the 100th Battalion before being reassigned to Company I. He vividly remembers moving out in the middle of the night, holding on to the backpack of the man ahead until the front lines were reached at dawn. He also recalls General Dahlquist coming out to see what was holding up the troops.

I was in a foxhole right next to one of our tanks, when I saw the General talking to Colonel Pursall. His aide was right next to him as they looked at a map. Right after that the colonel told us to charge. But the German machine guns were well dug in and camouflaged, and we didn't get very far. The next day the general came out again, and that's when a sniper killed his aide, Sinclair Lewis's son, as I later found out. I remember the general running past me and the tank.

When the Germans brought up a self-propelled gun, we hollered "Bazooka man up!" and after that we charged. The Germans were firing at us, holding their guns over their heads, usually two men to a hole. After it was over we counted eighty

German dead on the forward slope. It was a real infantry charge.

We were dug in for the night when General Dahlquist told us to get going. We were only a few feet from the Germans. At one point two of them tried to surrender, and one of them was shot in the back by his own men. I tried to bandage him.

Sergeant Senzaki [remembers the general asking him], "'Have you been doing any fighting, soldier?' That's when the German machine guns opened up and the general's aide got killed, and Akira Ito got hit by a burst."

George Miyashiro was a squad leader in third platoon during the big push, and later first sergeant of Company I.

When we made the charge, it was up this steep hill—"suicide hill" some called it. German tracers were coming straight down at us. That's when I got hit in the foot. Captain Byrne asked me if I needed a litter, but I told him, "No, I'm just going to take a hand grenade with me," and hobbled back to the aid station.

Sergeant Miyashiro's brother, Tasuku, was wounded on the same day. "When I got to the field hospital, the doctors and nurses were 'slap-happy' on account of so many casualties. Our men were in hospitals all over France. One of them, Ike Ito, was sent straight into the Battle of the Bulge before he could rejoin the 442d in southern France."

Sergeant Senzaki was lucky. He got away with a dent in his helmet and a bullet hole in his trouser leg. Private Junji Shiroyama was assistant BAR-man in Sergeant Senzaki's patrol. A farm boy from California's San Joaquin Valley, he was inducted in Fresno, California, and trained at Fort Leonard Wood before joining the 442d. When he and BAR-man Fred Ugai from North Platt, Nebraska, reached the trapped battalion, "The fellows came out of their holes, but we had orders to push on. We didn't have time to celebrate."

Platoon Sergeant Kazuo Takekawa, and the remainder of 4th platoon, got there soon after the initial contact. Takekawa, who came from Hawaii, was the first of ten children, and probably the only

Nisei who hit the beach in southern France on a stretcher, "shivering with malaria." But he was not about to quit his unit.

Takekawa said: "Weather was bad for Hawaii people. No winter clothing. Hawaii boys casual on rank; everybody same level. But we trust each other, respect elders and superiors.

"We lose a lot of our friends. 'Hey, Kaz, got me a million-dollar wound. See you back in the States.' A lot of them die. I see my mother in my dreams, standing on back porch, and I yell in Japanese. . . .

When I come home, leave ship, they pile us in trucks. A lot of people there to welcome us. Suddenly I hear my father calling out my name."

At age seventy-eight Kazuo Takekawa fights back his tears. "My father calling me. And then at home, brothers and sisters there . . ."

Soon after Sergeant Senzaki's patrol made contact with the surrounded Texas battalion, the main body of the 3d and 100th Battalions arrived. Their impressions are much like those just described, and their contributions no less valuable. The esprit de corps of Sergeant Senzaki and his men is typical of the 100/442d Regimental Combat Team. By honoring them, all are honored.

Unlike the fictitious regiment in James Michener's novel *Hawaii*, in which the battle of the "Lost Battalion" was carried live on radio, and heatedly debated by Congress, the 100/442d RCT remained anonymous when news of the rescue was revealed a full five days after the event. Newspaper correspondents were incensed when ABC News beat them to the punch, airing the story at 1730 hours, 4 November. Newspaper correspondents promptly lodged a protest with Seventh Army, and General Patch ordered an investigation which determined "that the matter had been withheld from the press until it was reasonably certain that this information, reaching the enemy through press or radio channels, would no longer be of advantage to him or disadvantage to the command concerned."

Once clearance was given, the story appeared in most of the major papers, identifying units and individuals by name—except for the 442d. Some papers even printed photos of the artillery projectiles being loaded with candy bars, alongside shots of Lieutenant Higgins shaking hands with "Lieutenant C. O. Barry, Williamstown, Pa., of the relief unit." (Barry was not a member of the 442d Regimental

Combat Team.) Of ten newspapers surveyed, including The *Stars and Stripes* of 6 November 1944, none mentioned the 442d RCT, or the fact that the rescuers were of Japanese descent. Instead, terms like "the relief unit," "another unit," or "other doughboys" were used. Even in descriptions of the episode in which Sergeant Guy met Mutt Sakumoto, the latter is referred to as "a private who wasn't a Jerry." None of the reports described the horrendous effort involved in reaching the trapped battalion, and not until late November did American newsreels and papers* disclose that the relief had been effected by the Japanese-American Combat Team, suggesting that the selective release of information had been a high-level decision.

Many Nisei veterans believe that politics also played a hand in downgrading Barney Hajiro's recommendation for the Medal of Honor. Like other recipients, Hajiro, who "went for broke" on "Banzai Hill," would have been thrust into the limelight at a time when Japanese Americans still languished in internment camps and the war with Japan was going at full throttle. Potential embarrassment to the government may have influenced the decision to deny Hajiro the Medal of Honor.

Eventually the 442d Regimental Combat Team did receive the recognition it deserved, collecting honors in Italy, France, and Washington D.C. In 1946, President Truman personally presented a unit citation, and commended the valiant men. "You fought not only the enemy, but you fought prejudice—and you won!"

But even the sterling achievements of the Nisei and their Caucasian officers, and the president's words, could not erase anti-Japanese sentiment still strong after the war. For Henry Nakada, who along with Mutt Sakumoto was first to reach the "Lost Battalion," the prejudice he experienced was more an irritant. The fifth of twelve children, Nakada was one of seven brothers in uniform. Using his GI benefits, Henry went on to earn a Ph.D. in biochemistry, and had a successful seventeen-year teaching career at the University of California, Santa Barbara, before retiring to Alaska.

* Listed in chapter notes.

Others, like 1st Sgt. George Miyashiro, had more poignant experiences. On their way home to Hawaii, he and other Nisei had a one month stopover in Marysville, California. There, the veterans of Cassino and liberators of Bruyères, the "Lost Battalion," and Dachau found that "Japs" weren't welcome. Most of the town shut down rather than serve them. Only the Chinese restaurant remained open.

When Sergeant Senzaki joined his family in General Dahlquist's hometown, Minneapolis, there were no jobs for him. Drawing from his 52/20 government allotment (52 weeks at $20 per week), he eventually accepted his sister's offer and moved to Chicago. There he applied to school under the GI Bill, but his transcripts from Belmont High in Los Angeles never arrived. He eventually went to work in a pinball machine factory before making his way back to California.

Sam Ahnda, from Salinas, who served as a BAR-man with 3d Platoon, was drafted before his family was evacuated to an internment camp. While on a three-day pass to visit them, he was refused service at the Denver railroad station. He angrily slapped a sugar bowl off the counter, and refused to move. When the military police were about to arrest him, he was fortunate that one of them, a friend from Salinas, recognized him and let him go. Like many other Nisei, Ahnda found no one willing to employ him after the war, and he eventually joined one of his brothers in San Diego and became a commercial fisherman.

At seventy-eight, Kazuo Takekawa still is angry at those who called him a "Jap," including a soldier from the "Lost Battalion." "Maybe he didn't mean it to be bad, saying, 'Here come the Japs,' but it hurt." Takekawa points to his heart.

The most virulent form of race hatred was experienced by Shig Doi's family. At the time he was fighting in the Vosges, his oldest brother, Sumio, and their parents, having obtained an early release from Colorado's Grenada internment camp, were struggling to reestablish their fruit-growing business in California's gold country. Two months after the rescue of the "Lost Battalion," the packing shed of the Doi farm was firebombed, and shots were fired at their house. When Shig came home, "No Japs Wanted" signs greeted him at Newcastle.

### Dear Charlie

Perhaps the most eloquent statement on behalf of Nisei soldiers was made by Lt. Col. James Hanley, commanding the 2d Battalion. In January 1945, Charles Pierce, the editor of his North Dakota hometown newspaper, the Mandan *Daily Pioneer*, had written in his column: "A squib in a paper makes the statement that there are some good Jap-Americans in this country, but it didn't say where they are buried."

Pierce was a close personal friend of Hanley's, the more reason to send this scathing rebuttal:

> *Dear Charlie,*                  *10 March 1945*
>
> *Just received the Pioneer of Jan 20, and noted the paragraph enclosed.*
>
> *Yes, Charlie, I know where some good Japanese Americans are—there are some 5,000 of them in this unit. They are American soldiers—and I know where some of them are buried. I wish I could show you some of them, Charlie. I remember one Japanese American, he was walking ahead of me in a forest in France. A German shell took the right side of his face off. I recall another boy, an 88 had been trying to get us for some time—finally got him. When they carried him out, the bloody meat from the middle of his thighs hung down over the end of the stretcher and dragged in the dirt—the bone parts were gone.*
>
> *I recall a sergeant—a Japanese American, if you will—who had his back blown in two. What was he doing? Why, he was only lying on top of an officer who had been wounded, to protect him from shell fragments during a barrage.*
>
> *I recall one of my boys who stopped a German counterattack single-handed. He fired his BAR ammunition, picked up a German rifle, emptied that, used a Luger pistol he had taken from a prisoner.*
>
> *I wish I could tell you the number of Japanese Americans who have died in this unit alone. I wish I could tell you the number of wounded we have had, the sightless eyes, missing limbs, broken minds.*
>
> *I wish I could tell you the decorations we have won.*
>
> *I wish the boys in the "Lost Battalion" could tell you what they*

*think of Japanese Americans. I wish that all the troops we have fought beside could tell you what they know.*

*The marvel is, Charlie, that these boys fight at all—they are good soldiers in spite of the type of racial prejudice shown by your paragraph.*

*I know it makes a good joke—the kind of joke that prejudice thrives on. It shows a lack of faith in the American ideal. Our system is supposed to make good Americans out of anyone—it certainly has done so in this case of these boys.*

*You, the Hood River Legion Post, Hearst, and a few others make one wonder just what we are fighting for. I hope it isn't racial prejudice.*

*Come over here, Charlie, I'll show you where "some good Japanese Americans" are buried.*

### Joe Hattori

After the battles in the Vosges and a respite in southern France, the 522d Artillery Battalion was detached from the 442d RCT and sent north for the push through the Siegfried Line. When interviewed after the Combat Team's reunion in Hawaii in spring of 1993, Joe Hattori produced the following piece, which had first appeared in the battalion newsletter:

I remember you, Joe, when you first came into the Battery. You seemed bewildered, lost and alone. Disillusioned, too. I didn't blame you; after all you had just left behind unhappy experiences within barbed wire fences only to see once more drab and ugly barracks. But you got over it. Hutment 6 became your home too. Remember?

Remember basic and unit training? Regimentation, discipline, uniformity—as if we were a bunch of regulated automatons. Remember maneuvers, and the wilds of Louisiana, and our first taste of C-rations?

Italy, our first glimpse of war-torn Europe . . . hungry, ill-clothed, and homeless. Italy and our baptismal fire at Grosseto. But all wasn't the grim business of fighting. Remember our first unpleasant taste of raw, red vino? And the pass to the Eternal

City of Rome, and Via Roma in gay Napoli? I can still hear the city's cry of "Hey Joe . . ."

Remember France and the rain, the mud, the snow, and the cold? The bitter fighting up in the Vosges Mountains. Then Sospel and Menton and the Riviera and Nice. Nice, naughty but delightful. Nice and champagne and cognac, très jolies mademoiselles and jitterbug. Au revoir to fascinating France was pretty painful, huh?

And, at last, to Germany . . . The Siegfried Line and the maddening, unrelenting drive across the vaunted defenses of the Rhine, across the Danube, up to the foot of the Bavarian Alps. The V-E and cease fire . . . Remember our last drink together with the boys at Cafe Engel?

Joe said, "He lives in Japan now—can't find him—Sam 'Sad Sack' Sakamoto."

"Where's Cafe Engel?"

"Donauwörth," Joe answered. "Had a good time there after the war. We went all over the place—Munich, Berchtesgaden when the 101st was still there. We saw Hitler's house, the Eagle's Nest. Went to Brussels too. Nobody bothered us."

Joe was with A Battery of the 522d Field Artillery Battalion all the way into Germany. As the war neared its end, the artillery battalion, at that time attached to the 45th Infantry Division, approached the small town of Dachau, north of Munich. On 29 April 1945, Joe and a group of his fellow Nisei came upon what looked like a work camp—one of several comprising the large prison complex. A short time before, Tadashi Tojo and Robert Sugai had shot the lock off the gate and, along with Capt. Billy Taylor, saw what none of them would ever forget—the crematoria of the infamous concentration camp, with emaciated bodies stacked like cordwood.

George Oiye's voice was trembling with emotion when he recounted his experiences on 13 June 1993 at San Francisco's Temple Emanuel.

There wasn't much we could do. Dachau was a surprise, not a military objective. Later, when I had time to reflect on it, I felt guilty. I don't know why. I guess I felt guilty for mankind degenerating this far—and I am part of the human race.

The experience was particularly painful for the Japanese Americans, because most still had families interned back in the United States.

When the Roosevelt High School Class of '43 held its fiftieth reunion in Los Angeles, Joe was one of fifty Japanese Americans who finally received his diploma. The event, held at the Universal Sheraton, attracted more than four hundred alumni and family members, and considerable media attention.

In May of 1995 the 522d Field Artillery Battalion held its reunion, also in Los Angeles. Joe, who at the time was undergoing chemotherapy, did not attend. Instead, fifty A Battery veterans and their wives came to his house with food and presents to honor their friend. After a three-year battle against stomach cancer, Joe Osamaru Hattori died on 14 August 1995.

# 14: Enemies and Friends

### The French Spirit

Contributions made to the war effort by French men and women, although invaluable, are generally neglected by historians. While the actions of regular French divisions were recorded, information about the underground, maquis, and later FFI is spotty because many of the clandestine groups operating in German-held territory did not record their actions, for obvious reasons. Much of what we know today comes from verbal histories and notebooks, which surfaced from time to time. Pierre Moulin of Bruyères knew virtually nothing about his father's wartime activities until after the death of Max Henri Moulin. At that time his mother produced the hitherto hidden records of the elder Moulin, outlining his day-to-day activities in the underground.

Men like Colonel Berger of the Alsace-Lorraine Independent Brigade, who pursued retreating Wehrmacht units from Bordeaux to Vesoul, were the eyes and ears for the Allies, including the Free French serving in regular units like General Jean de Lattre de Tassigny's First French Army, and Jacques-Philippe Leclerc's 2d French Armored Division. Although their politics varied widely from pro–de Gaulle FFI to numerous Communist organizations and other splinter groups, their common hatred toward Fascism united them, at least for the duration of the war. Some of their exploits are recorded at the French military museum, Les Invalides, in Paris, and the Centre d'histoire de la Résistance et de la Déportation in Lyon. But there are many unsung heroes, like Capt. Marcel Vichard, the

Corieux maquis commander who regularly transmitted radio messages about German positions; Albert Mercier, commander of the Bruyères FFI, and his secretary, Max Henri Moulin, who, years after the war, still carried a certificate of merit, signed by OSS Gen. William Donovan, in his wallet.

OSS operatives Helene and Jacqueline Deschamps risked their lives daily, gathering intelligence on German troop movements and passing it on to the Allies advancing along the Rhône. Both were nearly shot by their own countrymen when the fake German passes they carried made them out to be collaborators. Luckily an OSS member arrived just ahead of the execution squad and set matters straight. But a day later, as their car headed north, Jacqueline was killed by a stray machine-gun bullet. She died in her sister Helene's arms and was buried by her alongside the road. Today a commemorative column marks the spot.

Guides Henri Grandjean and Pierre Poirat risked their lives to lead the 1st Battalion, 141st, through the Forêt Dominale de Champ and were almost annihilated with the "Lost Battalion." Sergeant Paul Charpin and Paul Gerard guided the 2d Battalion, and Marcel Bello and Jean Drahon the 100th Battalion of the 442d Regimental Combat Team. Civilians also performed many acts of heroism and kindness, a fact that must not be forgotten.

### Josephine Voirin

Madame Josephine Voirin clearly remembers that night in Biffontaine when six wounded Nisei soldiers lay on her bed. "One of the soldiers lifted his cover to show me that his intestines were exposed. He took my hand and I embraced him as though he were my own son. I can see them lying on that bed. Every day there were six more, with the blood streaming out. Many were seriously wounded. They made me understand that they were thirsty. So I went out to the well, quite a distance away, during the shelling. I was afraid. But they were so young, and I did what I had to do."

Madame Voirin and her husband, Paul, did their best alongside the medics—providing shelter, water, nourishment, and comfort. When the German counterattack came to within a few hundred feet of their home, Paul kissed Josephine good-bye, and they began to pray for the soldiers and their own young son.

After the war some members of the 100th Battalion returned to Biffontaine and found that Mme. Voirin, now widowed, had saved the bloodstained mattress from those difficult and cold nights in 1944. She simply could not bring herself to dispose of the relic encrusted with the precious blood of those young men.

"I remember the soldiers who liberated Biffontaine—kind and sympathetic men who gave their own rations and candy to my son, cigarettes to my husband, and who paid me for the cabbages they took out of my garden when the battle stopped. After they left, my husband and I noticed that nothing had been taken. Instead, they left a large sum of French francs on my kitchen table," Voirin said.

Forty-five years after the battle for that small French village of questionable tactical value, Mme. Voirin died. But in the hearts of those who fought and bled, and their descendants, Josephine Voirin lives.

Similar is the story told by German Airman Joseph Schwieters, of the farm woman who tucked a down pillow under his bloodied head when he was wounded on 29 October. He never forgot her act of kindness, and in 1994 went back to search for her. But by then the family was gone, and the new Dutch owners knew nothing of her.

Also the innkeeper at Haut Jacques, who had been a prisoner of war in Austria, cared for the wounded Gebirgsjäger of Bataillon 201 and later buried their dead. His daughter ran the inn after the war and told the story to her former enemies.

### Georges Henry

With the thunder of artillery fire coming ever closer to Biffontaine, Georges Henry prayed that his village might be spared the ravages of war. But his prayers, and those of the others, went unanswered. On 23 October 1944, the men of the 100th Battalion rushed down from the forest, catching the German 716th Division signal unit by surprise. The fighting left its mark on this young man, son of a French veteran who had fought at Verdun.

After the war Georges Henry erected a monument to the 100th Battalion at the edge of the forest. A simple construction of wood, Henry decorated the shrine with wildflowers on appropriate holidays and hoped that someday he might replace it with enduring granite.

Georges Henry was elected mayor of Biffontaine, and in October 1984 his hope for a permanent marker was realized. In a circuitous way, Jean Bianchetti, a businessman from nearby Varigny, had met some Nisei veterans while vacationing in Hawaii. A friendship developed, which finally led to Mr. Bianchetti donating the granite monument near Milestone No. 6 outside Biffontaine.

In March 1993 both Bianchetti and Georges Henry were honored guests at the 100th/442d reunion in Honolulu, Hawaii.

### Madame and Suzanne Finnay

A week after the battle at le Haut Jacques, Sgt. George Murphy of the Cotton Balers' Company L was waiting for dawn, his clothes stiff from frozen rain, shaking uncontrollably. His buddy, Paul Kaniewski, fared little better under the overhang where they had found shelter. At the edge of the woods, near the village of Xainfaing, they could see smoke curling from a farmhouse chimney. A recon patrol was sent out, and, when the men didn't return, Murphy guessed that they hadn't fallen into a trap but surrendered to the comforts of home.

> So Paul and I went down to join them. I'll never forget standing inside that warm kitchen with the water sizzling in the stove's reservoir, looking out the window at the huge snowflakes falling. I could have spent the rest of the war right there.

In a small way Sergeant Murphy's wish did come true. He got a lucky turn when ordered to break in the new arrivals from the 103d Division fresh from the United States. He did his duty, and in his off-time he also helped Mme. Finnay by chopping wood, cleaning house, and doing odd jobs: four wonderful days of home-cooked meals, including chicken soup and an occasional shot of cognac from Mme.'s special reserve in the woodpile. On 12 November, he rejoined his unit and eight days later, near Colmar, was hit by shrapnel. On 25 January, a bullet went through his wrist—a million-dollar wound—ending Sergeant Murphy's war for good.

### It Would Have Been Nice to Be a Hero

It was late afternoon or evening when we heard the screams coming from down below in the ravine. "Help me, please!" He was one of ours. The screaming went on for a very long time, but nobody went down to help him. I guess we all rationalized that he was going to die. Maybe I should have gone down there, or asked for volunteers or asked the captain to send somebody. It would have been nice to be a hero. But the fact is that nobody went.

Sergeant George P. Murphy,
Company L, 3d Battalion, 7th Infantry Regiment

I remember at le Haut Jacques, in the draw on the east side of the pass, an American crying and moaning in pain. Our Oberjäger asked if one of us would go down to help or give him the coup de grace—to put him out of his misery. But nobody went. It was a failure of humanity.

Gebirgsjäger Anton Stocker,
4. Kompanie, Heeres Gebirgsjäger Bataillon 201

The same incident left an indelible impression on both Murphy and Stocker. Amid all the bloodletting, two men, enemies, felt for a soldier whose voice cried out in the night. As they reflected on the incident some fifty years later, and an ocean apart, both shared a sense of regret. But war, by its very definition, is inhumane, a time when empathy, ethics, and the commandments are suspended in favor of killing as many of "the enemy" as possible.

Sergeant Murphy was nineteen, and Toni Stocker eighteen, both of them Catholics who had grown up in middle-class families—Murphy on Cleveland's East Side, and Stocker in Berchtesgaden and nearby Teisendorf.

"They were afraid just as we were," said Stocker. "We didn't know where the Americans were. It's easy to say afterward what might have been, but the fact is that nobody was a hero that day."

"It would have been nice if our men or theirs had walked out with a white flag and done something for this man," says Murphy. "But it didn't happen. Ten weeks later, near Colmar, I pulled one of my men out under fire. 'Murphy, I'm hit, please help me.' I couldn't ignore his screams even though we were on the attack. I picked him up and ran to the rear—dropped him into a machine-gun emplacement. Soon after that I got hit."

For Toni Stocker, war also ended in January 1945, when he and 250 Gebirgsjäger with four assault guns attacked General Leclerc's Moroccans near Mülhausen (Mulhouse). Amid the carnage, Stocker was taken prisoner and spent the next four years as a POW in France. When he came home in November 1948, the idea of sharing a bench with seventeen-year-old high school students seemed somehow awkward, and he decided to became a brick mason, a profession that eventually led to a contractor's license and his own business.

George Murphy experienced VE day at a hospital in Birmingham, England, and after returning to Ohio, enrolled under the GI Bill at John Carroll University. Murphy later became partner in a mail order business providing tools for the Plexiglas industry.

### Joseph Schwieters

After a Nisei bullet shattered Airman Joseph Schwieters's lower jaw and left shoulder socket on the day of the "Banzai" charge, he eventually reached Colmar. By the end of November a hospital train brought him and other critical patients to the town of Würzburg, a jewel on the "Romantic Road," resplendent with churches, fountains, and palaces bearing the imprint of such renowned masters as Balthasar Neumann and Giovanni Battista Tiepolo.

It was just before Christmas when I awoke to an unusual brightness. At first I didn't know where I was, and then I saw the sunrise, glowing red above the Marienburg on the other side of the Main River. I was overcome with joy to witness this spectacle after weeks of gloom. But, by the end of January, my condition worsened once again, requiring yet another operation. When I awoke, I was back in the air raid shelter, wrapped from neck to waist in plaster, and with my arm braced. A nurse named Marianne tended to my every need, just as she did for the forty other patients on the ward, even spending her free time with us in the shelter. There was also a Catholic nun who cared for me, her 'little boy,' admonishing me to eat. "If you don't eat then you won't get on your feet again. And if you can't get on your feet, you won't get furlough to go into town to eat Meenfischli and drink Bocksbeutel."

What are Meenfischli and Bocksbeutel? Judging from the tone of her voice it had to be something good. My curiosity had been aroused, and, in my fevered dreams, I saw the restaurant on the riverbank, fish on my plate, and the oval-shaped bottle of wine.

I recovered to boredom and ever more bombing alerts that brought other patients to our basement shelter—not an unwelcome diversion. Rumors abounded that Würzburg would be declared a hospital town, and thus be spared the ravages of Allied bombs. When we found out that nurse Marianne's birthday was 21 March, we chipped in to buy her a small present and collected our scarce wine rations for the occasion. Little did we realize that all of our plans would be drastically altered. On the evening of 16 March, air raid sirens blared, and soon our basement ward was filled with patients. This gave us the chance to catch up on the news, and play chess, cards, and other games. The atmosphere was relaxed until the lights began to flicker. Internal alarms went off, and the intercom announced, "Enemy aircraft approaching Würzburg." Some shouted in disbelief, others jumped up as a steady thunder rolled closer. For eighteen minutes the ground trembled, eighteen minutes of terror that seemed to last an eternity. Nothing was said. We just looked at each other, alone with our thoughts. Some shook and flinched with each explosion. Others prayed, and others still pretended to be calm, cursing once or twice. The whine of bombs, an explosion—very close. Lights out. Suddenly our steel door blew off its hinges. Immobilized by my plaster corset, I realized that I was going nowhere. My comrades and I were trapped. After some time the trembling ceased, but outside the whole town was engulfed in flames. Fortunately the hospital did not receive a direct hit, but all of its windows were smashed, and doors blown off their hinges. Victims of the air raid were admitted and stories circulated that the other hospitals fared far worse than ours; patients being burned alive in their beds.

Suddenly, nurse Marianne came rushing in, pale, disheveled, distraught. The sister house had been destroyed by a bomb, burying several nuns in the air raid shelter.

A sense of normalcy returned during the next few days, even amid the chaos, with 1,500 patients now filling a hospital built for 400. We even managed to have a birthday party for nurse Marianne, which, thanks to the wine, ended on a cheerful note.

A few evenings later a bus took some of us to a railroad station outside town. A full moon illuminated the burned-out facades of a ghost town, with wisps of smoke rising from the ruins. The train brought my fellow patients and me to Bad Kissingen, the Palace Hotel, which had been converted to a military hospital. A spacious lobby, with red velvet upholstery and marble baths, reminded one of its former splendor. From the second-story room where I was quartered, a balcony opened up to a splendid view of the Saale River and the municipal park.

With physical therapy, the strength in my left arm returned slowly. On Good Friday I finally received permission to go into town. Some acquaintances and I went to an inn located in the old part of Bad Kissingen, where we ordered the specialty of the house—at that time a simple soup. When it was served, a gaunt, elderly gentleman carefully placed an egg next to my plate and said, 'Drop that into your soup.' In those days an egg, just like a cigarette, was a rare commodity, which the old gent had obviously saved from his own rations—a quiet gesture to show his appreciation to a wounded boy. It was the most beautiful Easter egg of my life.

There wasn't going to be another pass for me. Air raid sirens blared day and night, and we watched as huge bomber formations flew overhead. Artillery fire grew ever nearer, punctuated by the blasting of bridges. As German soldiers and civilians retreated in disarray, stores opened their doors to sell food, clothing, shoes, and other commodities that had been impossible to find a fortnight ago. During the night of April 7–8, several bridges and an ammunition dump outside town blew up, and the next morning fighter aircraft strafed town. It was a sunny afternoon, with a mild wind carrying the sound of tank tracks

churning closer on the other side of the river. The tanks
stopped alongside the park hedges, and several trucks pulled
up. From my balcony I watched as perhaps thirty soldiers, black
soldiers, disembarked. Would they attack the hospital? But before I could react, I saw one of them throw a football to one of
his comrades, and others piling on top of him. Within minutes
a spirited game was being played, and no heed was being paid
to the German soldiers watching from their balcony. Then it
dawned on me that soldiers who play ball don't shoot—not with
rifles at any rate, and all of us sighed with relief.

Still today, football symbolizes the end of the war for me, and
a sign of hope for a better future. And yes, I did eventually get
to eat Meenfischli and drink Bocksbeutel. It took me thirty years
before I returned to a rebuilt Würzburg. As I saw the lighted
town across the Main River, my thoughts went back to the Forêt
de Champ and the shot that had changed my life so dramatically. And I thought of the nun who tempted me with promises
of a fish delicacy and wine so I wouldn't give up.

Written from memory by Joseph Schwieters, Münster, Germany,
2–5 February 1995

Joseph Schwieters was fourteen when his brother Klemens was
killed in Russia. The oldest brother, Anton, survived the war. His parents and two sisters did not see Joseph again until he was released
from a POW camp in August 1945. Earlier, when his sisters wanted
to visit him in the hospital, their parents had denied permission
because the four-hundred-kilometer train trip from Heek near
the Dutch border to Würzburg was too dangerous on account of air
attacks.

After the war Schwieters and his surviving brother ran the family store, and he later studied law at the Universities of Münster and
Freiburg. In 1962 Schwieters accepted a government position with
the "Versorgungsamt," which cares for war victims by providing
pensions and medical care. He eventually became office director
in charge of 350 employees, including twelve doctors and seven
lawyers.

His friend and fellow soldier Hans-Paul Geiger, suffering from frostbite, was taken off the line in late November 1944. After being hospitalized for three weeks, he received a furlough, which brought him home to his beloved Edenhausen in the Black Forest and Christmas with his family. He was wounded toward the end of the war and died of tuberculosis in 1948 before he could realize his dream of becoming an interior architect.

After the death of his first wife, Schwieters married Hans-Paul's sister, Hannerose, who still had her brother's small diary recording his experiences in the Vosges.

In autumn of 1994, Joseph Schwieters attended the fiftieth anniversary of the liberation of Bruyères, where he met his former adversaries. Subsequently he appeared in Wendy Hanamura's documentary *Honor Bound,* the personal odyssey of the reporter's father while a member of Company L, 442d RCT. In October 1995, a meeting was arranged between Dr. and Mrs. Schwieters, Colonel Young Oak Kim, and ten members of the 442d Regimental Combat Team in Los Angeles. The Nisei veterans presented Dr. Schwieters with photos they had taken from German POWs, with the faint hope that their families might still be found.

### Alois Herrmann

Soon after the battle at le Haut Jacques, Lt. Alois Herrmann, who had spied "Japanese soldiers" in the Forêt de Champ, received an urgent letter from his mother. "Please take emergency leave. Your father is in grave danger."

It is only eighty miles from St.-Dié to the small town of Bühl in the Black Forest, where Franz Herrmann worked as a nurse practitioner. Exhausted from one straight week of duty, he walked home, when along the way he passed a line of old men and boys, some in uniform, and the local Nazi official, Kreisleiter Rothacker, barking commands. Warily Herrmann searched for familiar faces, veterans from his Baden Regiment who had served with him in World War I, when Rothacker called out, "Herrmann, you too. You belong to the Volkssturm! Time to pay your dues for the Vaterland."

"No time for jokes. I'm tired," Herrmann answered, walking on.

"You will report this instant. Führer's orders!"

At this older Herrmann lost his temper. "I paid my dues in the first war. I got shot at and gassed, which is more than a sack of shit like you can say!"

For that reply Franz Herrmann was charged with "refusal to serve and activities detrimental to the German state and the war effort."

Two of Franz Herrmann's sons were serving at the time—eighteen-year-old Gerhard as a radio operator on the eastern front, and twenty-one-year-old Alois with Gebirgsjäger Bataillon 201.

When Alois arrived in Bühl, he put on his best field grays, and all the medals he had won in three years of service. Before a panel of Nazi officials, including Kreisleiter Rothacker, he told of his own military service, that of his brother, and then pleaded for his father's release.

There was no trial, and it wasn't until after the war that someone found a tattered file in the city hall's bathroom. The label read, "Franz Herrmann," with a notation inside, "Recommended for forced labor on the eastern front. Has two sons who serve with distinction."

Apparently Alois's pleas had saved his father's life, and both brothers returned home. After the war rumors persisted that Kreisleiter Rothacker had been apprehended by the French and hung in St.-Dié for mistreating French laborers forced to dig defenses in the Alsace.

### Vitus Kolbinger

Vitus Kolbinger served as adjutant and briefly as commander of Heeres Gebirgsjäger Bataillon 201 from Garmisch. After the battle at le Haut Jacques, the company-size remnant of the unit was to be absorbed into the SS as part of Himmler's Armeegruppe Oberrhein. Eager to prevent this, Leutnants Kapfer and Kolbinger personally drove to Berlin during a lull in the fighting. They arrived at OKH still wearing battle gear and pleaded their case. General Jodl interceded on their behalf, and the Gebirgsjäger Bataillon retained its autonomous status.

During the attack on the heights at Sigolsheim, Kolbinger was wounded and out of the fight for three weeks. Eventually, Gebirgsjäger Bataillon 201 was integrated into the 2d Gebirgsjäger Division, which fought to war's end.

Why did the mountain troops go on fighting even though the war was already lost?

Kolbinger reflects: "It was a patriotic concern, love for one's homeland, particularly among the mountain troops; also sober pragmatism. Until that time, none of us soldiers had ever run away. And mountain troops never leave their friends behind."

Remnants of Gebirgsjäger Bataillon 201 continued to battle their way from Trier to Kaiserslautern when Kolbinger found the woods ahead already occupied by Americans. "At that point fighting would have been senseless. After fighting for five years and six months, I performed my last and most painful duty as a German officer. On 21 March, I surrendered."

Kolbinger said, "One felt lost and forgotten. All of us prisoners were assembled on a large open field outside Kaiserslautern. From there I was transferred to Baumholder, the officers' camp at Chartres, and finally to Cherbourg in early June. The camp was run by the French, and we suffered from malnutrition and disease. I contracted pneumonia, which for me turned out to be a blessing because it brought about my release in September 1945. I weighed eighty-nine pounds."

Vitus Kolbinger was born on 14 June 1915, during "the war to end all wars," which three years later took his father's life. At age sixteen, during the Great Depression, tuberculosis forced him to discontinue his high school studies until he recovered in 1934. Then the twenty-year-old began to study music, the love of his life, and performed with the Bavarian Landesbühne. Being of draft age he was first conscripted to the paramilitary Arbeitsdienst, and finally drafted into the army. Kolbinger saw action in Poland, France, Yugoslavia, and Russia, where a sniper's bullet pierced his neck and jaw on 23 March 1944. After convalescing he was assigned to Heeres Gebirgsjäger Bataillon 201 and sent to the Vosges.

"From August 1944 onward the continuation of the war was useless and senseless against the overwhelming Allied onslaught." Kolbinger recalled. "Resistance by Bataillon 201 could only be made in small measure. Bataillons 202 and 201 were essentially sent to the front lines to 'die heroically.' I lost many of my friends, especially during the last few months on the western front."

After release from prison camp, Vitus Kolbinger continued his studies, both academic and as an opera singer, successfully completing his examinations in 1952. He sang, among others, the role of the duke in Mozart's *Marriage of Figaro*, Papageno in the *Magic Flute*, and various parts in Verdi and Rossini operas. At the height of his career Kolbinger knew 250 Schubert lieder by heart and also performed and lectured at local high schools. His career was cut short, however, by recurring sinus infections, the result of severe freezing on the Russian front. A pensioner since 1978, he dedicated much of his time to chronicling the fate of Heeres Gebirgsjäger Bataillon 201 and 202. He has been married to his wife Franziska since 1943.

# Epilogue

In the annals of World War II the battles in the Vosges appear as a footnote, a brutish slugging match that cost the Seventh Army the race to the Rhine and into Germany. In its epitaph to General Patch, the New York *Herald Tribune* of 22 November 1945 described the Vosges campaign as "comparatively unspectacular though arduous." But for those who fought and died, it was the main event. Had General Patch heeded General de Lattre's warning and attacked at Gérardmer, his Army might have reached Strasbourg and crossed the Rhine before Hitler could set in motion his Ardennes Offensive. But war is an inexact science, and speculation not worth the paper it is written on.

What kept the Nisei soldiers going? *"Hattori no namae wo haji kake na!*—Don't disgrace the Hattori family name and reputation." Not to bring shame to the family and to one's friends was vital for the success of the "Go for Broke" regiment and accounts for its extraordinary "esprit de corps."

It is said that after the war Col. Gordon Singles, the 100th Battalion commander, refused to shake General Dahlquist's hand at a full-dress review at Fort Bragg, North Carolina. At the time Dahlquist was a visiting four-star general. Years after retirement the former commander of the 442d, General Pence, could not bring himself to mention Dahlquist's name without his voice trembling with anger. While it may never be known how General Dahlquist felt about the Nisei, it is what he did not say that speaks volumes.

When asked if the Nisei soldiers were "sacrificed" for the Texans, Marty Higgins of the "Lost Battalion" takes exception.

According to Higgins, "They were used because they were damned good. Also very few of us were Texans; I'm from New Jersey. They did suffer heavy casualties; we all did. But the rescue gave them more credibility . . . their men did not die in vain."

There is little doubt that the record of the Nisei soldiers played a significant part in gaining redress under President Ronald Reagan, and also repeal of Executive Order 9066, which had been signed almost fifty years earlier by President Franklin D. Roosevelt. No acts of treason or sabotage were committed by Japanese Americans during the war.

The first Nisei to be killed in the Battle for Bruyères, twenty-one-year-old SSgt. Tomosu Hirahara, still lies in a carefully tended grave at Épinal. After the war, when the remains of fallen soldiers were shipped back to the United States for reburial, the people of Bruyères wanted to keep one grave in memory of the Japanese Americans who freed their town. They petitioned the Hirahara family to leave him buried at their military cemetery. After much soul-searching, the family decided to honor the request.

When the German Grenadier Regiment 933 was withdrawn after surrounding the "Lost Battalion" and fighting the 442d RCT, only eighty men remained of a force that had counted nearly three thousand men three months earlier. The survivors were then attached to General Haeckel's 16th Division and rebuilt as Volks-Grenadier Regiment 221. In his study compiled after the war, Colonel Rolin accounts for his regiment's demise: "We received the so-called 'ear battalion,' about 400 men whose physical and mental abilities were insufficient to withstand the rigors of front-line soldiers. This circumstance, and the demand to hold a front of eight to ten kilometers with the men, led to the complete disintegration through bloody losses and prisoners taken. The survivors were detailed to other regiments. I myself was assigned to the Leader Reserve of OKH."

On 18 December, Adolf Hitler relieved General der Infanterie Friedrich Wiese, an ardent Nazi, from command of the Nineteenth Army because, as Heinrich Himmler put it, "He doesn't know how to instill the spirit of National Socialism in his troops." But before war's end, Wiese was again called up to lead an army corps in the east. After the surrender, wearing civilian clothes, he made his way on foot back to Bad Kissingen, where he was taken prisoner by the Americans. His incarceration and isolation at Dachau was so thorough that he did not learn of his wife's nearly fatal car accident until one year after the fact.

Both Gen. Ernst Haeckel and Gen. Wilhelm Richter were taken prisoner on 8 May 1945, and were released three years later. Haeckel died on 26 September 1967, while vacationing at the Mediterranean. Richter died after a serious illness on 4 February 1971 in Rendsburg.

General Alexander Patch outlived his son Mac by only one year. He succumbed to pneumonia on 22 November 1945, at San Antonio's Brooke General Hospital, and was buried at West Point. General Dahlquist retired to Ft. Lauderdale, Florida, where he died on Independence Day 1975.

At the end of the war, just before reaching Salzburg, the 7th "Cotton Baler" Regiment fought a brief skirmish near Toni Stocker's home at Teisendorf. Some SS men had barricaded themselves in a barn, which was quickly set ablaze by an American tank. Colonel John Heintges's men reached the Mozart City in the early hours of 4 May 1945, against only minor resistance. When scouts discovered two bridges still intact near the village of Piding, General O'Daniel decided to send the Cotton Balers across the Saalach toward Hitler's mountain redoubt in Berchtesgaden. Heintges's 1st and 3d Battalions arrived by mid-afternoon, just ahead of the U.S. 101st Airborne and French 2d Armored Divisions, which had been designated to take the town. Next day Heintges, himself a German-American whose father had fought in the Imperial Army, saluted the American flag being raised on the Obersalzburg. Berchtesgaden and Salzburg had given many of their sons to Gebirgsjäger Bataillons 201 and 202 which had fought the Cotton Balers, at Haut Jacques and in the Forêt de Champ, alongside the 141st and 442d Regiments.

Near Marseilles, Gerwin Eder and fellow prisoners from Gebirgsjäger Bataillon 202 spent their days digging up mines. Later they were distributed among French farmers to make good some of the damage done during the war. Eder was released in March 1946, and reached his native Gemünden ahead of his father, still a POW near Prague.

Machine gunners Hugo Sommer and Aurelio Piai, who had been inducted at the same time and captured at le Haut Jacques, remained friends for life.

Today memorials mark the trails of carnage through the Vosges. Each year veterans from both sides return to retrace their steps—fewer now as time takes its toll. Charles Coolidge, who won the Medal of Honor there, went back in 1987 with his wife and son and found his old foxholes and a marker reading "141st."

Like Vitus Kolbinger, his former adversary, Glenn Rathbun of the Cotton Balers still dreams about those battles. Wars don't end when the shooting stops. They leave scars on the land, the bodies, and souls of those who fought and those left behind—fathers, brothers, husbands, and the women who loved them. It is for them I give this account.

Perhaps the most fitting epitaph is written at Jebsheim near Colmar. At the site of the heavily contested mill now stands La Croix du Moulin with the inscription in French, English, and German. *They are united in death. May we also be united in peace.*

# Appendix

The 141st "Alamo" Regiment suffered 1,216 battle deaths from September 1943 to 8 May 1945. Among them were three lieutenant colonels, one major, fifteen captains, and forty-eight lieutenants.

At the beginning of October 1944, as they closed on Bruyères, the regiment had 103 officers and 2,724 enlisted men. By the end of the month, after "Lost Battalion," 84 officers and 1,372 men were left. During that period replacements accounted for 33 officers and 623 men, and there were 14 battlefield commissions.

The final tally of combat and noncombat losses for October was 33 officers and 1,338 enlisted men, or one-third of the officers and one-half of the men. When considering that headquarters and support units suffered fewer casualties, this makes the attrition rate on the line even more severe.

During the period from 15 October, when the Japanese-American 100/442d RCT arrived near Bruyères, to 17 November 1944, when it was detached from the 36th Division, casualties were the highest during the unit's history:

Throughout their 19 months of combat in World War II, the 100th Battalion, followed in June of 1944 by the remainder of the 442nd

|  | October | November | Total |
|---|---|---|---|
| KIA | 117 | 44 | 161 |
| WIA | 639* | 217 | 856 |
| MIA | 40 | 8 | 48** |
| Injured | 18 | 8 | 26 |

* In October alone 188 clusters to the Purple Heart were presented. In addition, there was a high number of serious trench foot cases and respiratory illnesses because the men did not receive their winter issue until 7 November. Losses from these (as many as 500 cases) depleted the ranks even further.
** Includes those taken prisoner.
Figures do not reflect losses sustained by attached units.

---

**100/442d Regimental Strength, October–November 1944**

| Date | Officers | Warrant Off | Enlisted Men |
|------|----------|-------------|--------------|
| 1 October | 186 | 7 | 3313 |
| 31 October | 117 | 6 | 2245 |
| 20 November | 114 | 8 | 2484* |

* Includes 23 new officers and 382 Japanese-American replacements from the United States, as well as 62 hospital returnees. According to War Department figures, replacement calls for 1944–45 were as follows: 234 men for 7 December; 400 men for 25 December; 600 for January 1945, 400 for February, and 250 for March 1945.

---

Regiment, lost 650 men killed in action, 3,536 wounded, 67 missing in action, and 177 noncombat injuries. Of the 28 Caucasian officers killed, 12 came from the 100th Battalion and 16 from the 442nd RCT.

Company I, for example, lost 28 killed and 205 wounded in action throughout the war. Forty-two men earned the oak leaf cluster for being wounded a second time, ten more earned two clusters, and Staff Sergeant Shiro "Kash" Kashino from Seattle, recipient of both the Silver and Bronze Stars for gallantry, had five oak leaf clusters on his Purple Heart.

Company I was fortunate to have a number of outstanding officers, like First Lieutenant Mike Kreskowsky, who was always up front with his trusty Tommy gun, calling out to the Germans, "Come out, come out, wherever you are!" There were Captains Joseph Graham, wounded on Hill 140 in Italy, and the 6-foot, 4-inch Joseph David Byrne, killed in action on the day the "Lost Battalion" was relieved. First Lieutenant James D. Wheatley Jr., who took over after Byrne's death, had three clusters on his Purple Heart when he was killed near Carrara, just days before the war ended.

Throughout its combat involvement from Salerno, on 27 September 1943, (100th Battalion only) until the end of the war with Germany, 8 May 1945, the 442nd accrued an impressive array of decorations:

| | |
|---|---|
| 1 | Medal of Honor |
| 52 | Distinguished Service Crosses |
| 1 | Distinguished Service Medal |
| 12 | Oak Leaf Clusters to Silver Star |
| 560 | Silver Stars |
| 22 | Legions of Merit |
| 15 | Soldier's Medals |
| 38+ | Oak Leaf Clusters to Bronze Star* |
| 810+ | Bronze Stars* |
| 1 | Air Medal |
| 500+ | Oak Leaf Clusters to Purple Heart* |
| 4,200+ | Purple Hearts* |
| 36 | Army Commendations |
| 87 | Division Commendations |
| 12 | Croix de Guerre (France) |
| 2 | Palms to Croix de Guerre |
| 2 | Croce al Merito di Guerra (Italy) |
| 2 | Medaglia di Bronzo al Valor Militare (Italy) |
| 7 | Presidential Unit Citations |
| 2 | Meritorious Service Unit Plaques |

* Note: Numbers of Bronze Stars and clusters may be as high as 3,000, and Purple Hearts and clusters 5,000, but could not be verified. Most often cited figures are by Shirey, 1946, and Tanaka, 1982. In June 2000, twenty more members of the 100/442d RCT were awarded the Medal of Honor from President Clinton.


### Excerpt from Gen. Alexander Patch's Calendar, 16 November 1944

In view of the inability to meet combat losses for the 442d RCT, Sixth Army Group has requested ETOUSA to hold all replacements for this unit in the replacement system until the entire 442d RCT has moved to the Southern Front, at which time it is desired that replacements move with them. Distribution of these replacements will be made by the Commanding Officer, 442d RCT, on the basis of greatest need and employment of units. All other replacement shipments of Japanese Americans should be held at Ports of Embarkation until move of the 442d RCT has been completed.

### U.S. Units Supporting 100/442d RCT During Attack on Bruyères
522d Field Artillery Battalion (organic)
83d Chemical Mortar Battalion (4.2 inch)
Company B, 752d Tank Battalion
Company C, 636th Tank Destroyer Battalion
Company D, 36th Cavalry Reconnaissance Troop
886 Medical Collection Company

### U.S. Units Supporting 100/442d RCT During Push Toward "Lost Battalion"
Companies B and D, 752d Tank Battalion
Company C, 3d Chemical Weapons Battalion (4.2 mortars)
Company C, 636th Tank Destroyer Battalion
Company D, 83d Chemical Weapons Battalion
522d and 133d Field Artillery Battalions

Among their extraordinary achievements, Japanese-American soldiers are also credited for capturing two submarines—the first, a Japanese midget sub beached off the coast of Oahu (Waimanalo) on 8 December 1941. Its pilot, Ens. Kazuo Sakamaki, became the first Japanese POW when he was taken by Sgt. David Akui and the men of the 298th Regiment (Federalized Hawaii National Guard). The midget sub was later displayed for public viewing on the mainland.

The second incident occurred during the so-called "Champagne Campaign" in southern France. Sighting a German two-man sub in the Bay of Menton, members of the 442d Antitank Company engaged it with machine-gun and mortar fire. The small craft, which apparently had engine trouble, came to shore and its pilot surrendered. He was surprised to find that his captors were Japanese.

### John Ernest Dahlquist
#### Awards
Distinguished Service Cross, Distinguished Service Medal, Silver Star, Legion of Merit with Oak Leaf Cluster, Bronze Star with two Oak Leaf Clusters, French Legion of Honor and Croix de Guerre, and the British Honorary Companion of the Military Division of the Order of the Bath.

## Promotions and Appointments

- 9 February 1918, 1st Lt.
- 1 July 1920, Capt.
- 1 August 1935, Maj.
- 18 August 1940, Lt. Col.
- 24 December 1941, Col.
- 19 April 1942, Brig. Gen.
- 23 June 1943, Maj. Gen.
- Reverted to Brig. Gen., 1 June 1946
- 24 January 1948, Maj. Gen.
- 1 May 1953, Lt. Gen.
- 18 August 1954, Gen. (4 star)
- November 1945, appointed a member of Secretary of War's Personnel Board
- 1 June 1947, Deputy Director of Personnel and Administration
- July 1949, European Command, 1st Infantry Division at Grafenwöhr, Germany
- August 1952, Corps Commander, V Corps, Bad Nauheim
- March 1953, CG, Fourth Army, Ft. Sam Houston, Texas
- 1 July 1953, Acting Chief, Army Field Forces, Ft. Monroe, Virginia; Chief in August
- 1 February 1955, Commanding General, Continental Army Command
- 29 February 1956, retired as four-star general after nearly forty years of service

The 36th "Texas" Division served 33 months overseas, 20 of them in combat, breaking the record with 132 consecutive days of combat. The unit sustained 3,717 killed, 12,685 wounded, and 3,066 missing in action. For their service the T-Patchers were awarded 12 Presidential Unit Citations, 15 Medals of Honor, 80 Distinguished Service Crosses, and 2,354 Silver Stars.

In the European theater, the 3d Infantry Division ranks first in battle casualties: 5,558 killed, 18,766 wounded*. The regiment

---

* The 7th Infantry chronicle, *From Fedala to Berchtesgaden*, published by Nathan W. White in 1947, lists 6,240 KIA, 24,793 WIA, and 3,191 MIA.

with the highest number of casualties was the 7th Infantry, of which 2,131 men gave their lives and 6,965 were wounded. While the name "Cotton Balers" evokes images of the South, most of its casualties were from the East: 243 from New York, 210 from Pennsylvania, 135 from Ohio, and 132 from Illinois; every state in the Union lost some of its sons.

### Units Supporting the 7th Regiment at le Haut Jacques:
10th Field Artillery
Reconnaissance Company, 601st Tank Destroyer Battalion
Company A, 601st Tank Destroyer Battalion
Company D, 3d Chemical Battalion (4.2 mortars)
Battery B, 441st Antiaircraft Battalion

### German Armored Units Defending Bruyères Sector (detached from 21st Panzer Division)
Staff of Panzer Regiment 22
1st Battalion, Pz. Regiment 22 equipped with 12 Panzer IV
1st Battalion, Pz. Regiment 192
reinforced by 7th Company, 192, and 1st and 6th Company, Regiment 125,
with 2 Panzer Werfer (rocket launchers) and one multiple rocket launcher (Screaming Meemie)

### 21st Panzer Division Strength in October 1944
The 21st Panzer Division had lost most of its men and equipment during the bloodletting at Caen and inside the Falaise pocket. By October 1944 it was woefully understrength. Depending on deliveries of new equipment and spare parts, the numbers of tanks fluctuated.
    8 to 19 self-propelled assault guns
    12 to 19 Panzer IV
    9 to 14 Panzer V (Panther)
    55 to 77 antitank guns (among them six to eight 88mm)

### 16th Volks-Grenadier Division Strength, October–November 1944
#### (excluding Gebirgsjäger Bn. 201 & 202)

| 1 October | 11 October | 21 October | 31 October | 14 November |
|-----------|------------|------------|------------|-------------|
| 3,000     | 2,200      | 2,400      | 900        | 600         |

### 716th Volks-Grenadier Division Strength, October 1944
#### (excluding attachments)

| 1 October | 11 October | 21 October | 31 October | 14 November |
|-----------|------------|------------|------------|-------------|
| 1,600     | 1,500      | 1,250      | 1,000      | 900         |

# Notes

## CHAPTER NOTES

Sources cited here are listed in order of appearance. Notes are numbered for ease of reference. Whenever possible, documents were reviewed in their language of origin to assure accuracy in translation.

### 1: Operations Meadow-Saffron and Dragoon

1. Quotations and information from and about Gen. Ernst Haeckel in this and subsequent chapters are from the following sources provided by the German Bundesarchiv/Militärarchiv, Freiburg, and the Suitland Branch of the U.S. National Archives:

Military Study B-452; "Die 16. Infanterie-Division (Im Frühjahr 1944 aus der 158. Reserve Division gebildet)"; II Teil "Der Einsatz im Feldzug im Rheinland (15.9.–Anfang Dez. 44)" by Generalleutnant Ernst Haeckel. Record Group 242 H6/26; Personnel record of Generalleutnant Ernst Haeckel (National Archives, NNG-94-145).

2. Disposition of the U.S. Seventh Army and German Nineteenth Army are based in large part on material provided by the U.S. Army History Institute, U.S. Army War College, at Carlisle Barracks, Pennsylvania. Assistance provided by Dr. Richard Sommers and his staff; in particular Pam Chaney has been invaluable. From the William Quinn Papers, the Seventh Army Intelligence Summaries spanning the period 15 August to 30 November 1944.

Military Study B-781; "Die 19. Armee in der burgundischen Pforte, in den Vogesen und im Elsass, von mitte September bis 18 Dezember 1944," by General der Infanterie Friedrich Wiese, 8 März 1948.

3. Military Study A-999, "Die Heeresgruppe G in der Zeit von September bis Anfang Dezember 1944," General von Mellenthin, 11. 3. 1946 (Bundesarchiv).

4. Material about Gen. Alexander Patch, including his recently released letters, was provided by the U.S. Military Academy at West Point, thanks to the research done by Carol J. Koenig of the Special Collections Division.

Daily journal of General Patch, pp. 222 to 389; Letters dated Nov. 6th, Nov. 10th, Nov. 14th; Article from the New York *Herald Tribune,* Thursday, 22 November 1945, "General Patch Dies."

5. Bundesarchiv MSg 1/2018; a brief autobiography of General Wiese dated November 1972.

6. Material about Operation Meadow-Saffron and Gen. Botho Elster is based on Seventh Army G-2 Summaries (and French reports).

7. Quotes from Oberst Hans von Luck, 21st Panzer Division, are based on a telephone interview and a letter of inquiry.

8. Entries about the 141st "Alamo" Regiment in this and subsequent chapters are in part based on the monthly reports of the "141st Regimental History," generously loaned by Carl Strom. Throughout my research, Carl Strom has been an invaluable resource.

9. Letter by Gen. Hermann Balck, courtesy of Werner Kortenhaus, who also provided copies of German maps for October 1944. Balck's reference to his twelve thousand combat troops is only slightly lower than Seventh Army G-2 estimates.

10. Report about the military situation in the west from microfilm series T175, San Jose State University Library; "Kurze Aktennotiz über Frontbesuch im Westen in der Zeit vom 22.9.–3.10.1944," der Chef des NS-Führungsstabes, signed von Hengl, dated 5.10.1944.

## 2: The Vosges

1. Nineteenth Army Log, German Bundesarchiv, Freiburg.

2. References to General Jean de Lattre de Tassigny and his recommendations against attacking at Bruyères are based on the daily journal of General Patch, and General de Lattre's book, *The History of the French First Army,* Allan & Unwin, London, 1952.

3. Details about the 36th "Texas" Division, and about his own life, come from the notebook carried by Gen. John E. Dahlquist. The notebook is part of the Dahlquist collection at the U.S. Army History Institute at Carlisle Barracks, Pennsylvania

4. "The Story of the 36th Infantry Division," booklet published by the division in 1945, and provided by Carl Strom.

5. References to 1st Lt. Marty Higgins in this and subsequent chapters are based on oral and written interviews conducted between

1994 and 1995, his own notes, copies of letters and telegrams, and copies of newspaper clippings graciously provided by Mr. Higgins and *Ex-POW Bulletin,* May 1992.

6. General Wilhelm Richter: Military Study A-875 (U.S. Army History Institute Library); brief military data provided by Bundesarchiv/Militärarchiv; National Archives Microfiche Publications Mi035, Foreign Military Studies B-Series, "Kampf der 716. Division in der Normandie vom 6. 6–23.6.1944, Generalleutnant Wilhelm Richter"; and Mi035, Foreign Military Studies, A Series, "Süd-Frankreich, 15. 8. 44–15.9.44, Generalleutnant Wilhelm Richter."

[Note: German "Datenschutz" law prohibits the release of personnel records for other than official business. Usually only a brief biography of pertinent dates, commands, and awards is provided. Through the tireless efforts of Joseph Schwieters, however, we were able to obtain permission from some German officers to review parts of their records.]

7. Werner Kortenhaus was first among German contributors. The author of *The History of the 21st Panzer Division* provided valuable data about tank units dispatched to the Bruyères sector, maps, and insights into the military situation and made the connection with Col. Hans von Luck.

8. The 100/442d Regimental Combat Team: Opening scenes are based on documentary film footage from the National Archives. Seventy minutes of film footage were reviewed to gain insights into the actions of soldiers, terrain, and weather conditions; filed under Japanese-American Combat Team, ADC2436; ADC2475; ADC2579; ADC2568-1; ADC2570; ADC 2606-1; ADC2423-1; ADC2618; ADC 2697-2; ADC 2675.

9. The 100/442d RCT Monthly Historical Reports (Record Group 407) gave strength and casualty figures, award citations, and summary of combat actions; filed under INRG 442-0.2.(23434) 38PP.

10. *The Story of the 442nd Combat Team,* published by Information-Education Section, MTOUSA, 1945.

11. Daniel Inouye's reflections are part of a speech the senator made before fellow 100/442d veterans at the fiftieth reunion in Hon-

olulu, Hawaii, 23 March 1993, and an interview conducted by Lt. Col. Hiroaki Morita, 25 November 1991 (U.S. Army War College).

12. Sergeant Peter Kawahara's letters are part of the 100/442d collection at the U.S. Army History Institute.

13. Joe Hattori and Yaeko Sakamoto are part of the author's family—Yaeko is the author's mother-in-law, and Joe is her youngest brother; both have been extensively interviewed.

### 3: The Battle for Bruyères

1. Background information about Bruyères comes from an interview with Pierre Moulin conducted in San Francisco in the spring of 1995, and from his two books on the subject, with the author's permission.

2. Brigadier General Charles Wilbur Pence, Department of Defense Office of Public Information, Press Branch (National Archives).

3. Eyewitness reports, like those of Capt. Sakae Takahashi, are based on interviews. A list of those interviewed appears at the end of the chapter notes.

4. SS Polizei Regiment 19: Fragments of records provided by the Bundesarchiv in Berlin-Zehlendorf deal with the replenishing of the regiment in February 1944, assigned weapons and equipment, and transfer from Yugoslavia to France.

Background information about the Ordnungspolizei and listing of regiments from the book *Zur Geschichte der Ordnungspolizei 1936–1945,* Hans Joachim Neufeldt, Jürgen Huck, and Georg Tessin, published in Koblenz, 1957.

5. Descriptions of the German situation in this and subsequent chapters are in part based on Military Study B-468, General der Infanterie Helmut Thumm "Kämpfe in den Mittleren Vogesen," (28 February 1947), and Military Study B-482, "Einsatz des LXIV Armee Korps vom 1. bis 16. November 1944," by Maj. Kurt Schuster (17 April 1947), and Military Study A-999, "Die Heeresgruppe G in der Zeit von September bis Anfang Dezember 1944" (11 March 1946), and A-1000, "Die Schlacht in Lothringen und in den Vogesen im November 1944" (10 April 1946), both by General von Mellenthin, supplied by

the German Bundesarchiv, with special assistance from Colonel Diefenbach.

6. From the book *Zwischen Kattegat und Kaukasus,* the history of the 198th Infanterie Division, excerpts provided by Richard Schwegler; chapter "Kämpfe in Burgund und in den Vogesen, 31. August bis 20. November 1944." The 198th Füsilier Bataillon, plus other "fire brigade" reinforcements were sent from the 198th Division to the south.

7. Lieutenant Colonel James Hanley granted an interview in 1994, and contributed excerpts from his memoir *A Matter of Honor,* which was published by Vantage Press in 1995.

8. Colonels Chris Keegan and Young Oak Kim have both been active in 100/442d veterans affairs in Los Angeles and have been valuable assets in obtaining accurate information through interviews and written contributions.

9. Dr. Joseph Schwieters has been an enthusiastic supporter of this project ever since I contacted him through Pierre Moulin. Along with his wife he attended the fiftieth reunion in Bruyères in the fall of 1994, and one year later met with me and 100/442d veterans in Los Angeles. As a former employee of the German "veterans administration," he has been a valuable assistant, locating personnel files wherever they could be legally obtained (segments of Walter Rolin and Otto Ottenbacher's military careers), and asking permission to review others, like that of Maj. Walter Eschrich, who battled the Americans at Biffontaine.

During Dr. and Mrs. Schwieters's 1995 visit, I was able to examine Hans-Paul Geiger's small and fragile diary written in pencil, which tracks their retreat through the Forêt de Champ. Dr. Schwieters also supplied the Secret Daily Summary of the German Wehrmacht, which corroborates American accounts with remarkable detail and accuracy, and gave his own vivid account of the ordeal in the Vosges and his hospital stay until the end of the war.

### 4: Biffontaine

1. Rev. Hiro Higuchi's service and good-bye to the men of the 2d Battalion, 442d, was recorded on film, now in the National Archives.

2. Staff conference minutes from 22 October, are part of the Dahlquist file at the U.S. Army Military History Institute.

3. Detailed assessments of the Biffontaine fighting and their own personal stories were collected from Chris Keegan, Young Oak Kim, Sakae Takahashi, and Jimmie Kanaya.

4. Information from Major Walter Eschrich's personnel file (Bundesarchiv, Zentralnachweisstelle, Aachen). When interviewed by Dr. Joseph Schwieters, recollections of the eighty-four-year-old Eschrich were feeble and were mostly confined to his Russian experience.

5. At General Dahlquist's 22 October conference, the buoyant mood and rationale for pushing through the Forêt de Champ (Operation Dog Face) clearly show that American intelligence was not aware of German determination to hold that area.

6. U.S. Seventh Army Intelligence Summary provides an overview of clandestine operations in its area.

Also, the German Reichssicherheitshauptamt was well informed about Allied maneuvers. Some of this information, mostly from SS and police records, is stored on microfilm at San Jose State University: Microfilm Publication T175, "Records of the Reich Leader of the SS and Chief of the German Police." List of collaborators executed by French; Reichssicherheitshauptamt VI B 2, 30 Oct. 1944, "Personelle und organisatorische Mitteilungen, 1. Fortgang der Sauberungsaktion."

**5: Lost Battalions**

1. Captured American plans and German response: See Military Study B-781, Gen. Friedrich Wiese (listed under Chapter One).

2. Colonel Walter Rolin, "Grenadier Regiment 933: Südfrankreich bis in die Vogesen;" Military Study A-953 (U.S. Army History Institute Reference Library) and personnel records (Bundesarchiv).

3. Technical Sergeant Charles H. Coolidge: *Chattanooga Times* and *Chattanooga News–Free Press* articles, courtesy of the Chattanooga-Hamilton County Bicentennial Library. Telephone interview with Sergeant Coolidge, 3 May 1995. Medal of Honor citation and photo provided by Mr. Coolidge.

4. Little written information exists about Heeres Gebirgsjäger

Bataillon 201 and 202. Fragmentary orders can be found at the Bundesarchiv/Militärarchiv, specifically the Nineteenth Army collection. Nearly all of what we know now about the two ill-fated battalions was preserved due to the tireless effort of one man—Vitus Kolbinger. The former adjutant of Bataillon 201 was instrumental in reuniting the survivors, and meticulously piecing together eyewitness accounts, which were sworn to and notarized. Smitten with stomach cancer and the ravages of old age, Kolbinger nevertheless managed to complete the history of the two mountain battalions by Christmas 1995. Since my letter of inquiry found its way to him two years earlier, Vitus and I became friends, and I was able to meet him and his wife Franziska for the first time in January 1996 at Toni Stocker's home in Teisendorf.

Since January 1996, "Sammlung authentischer Erinnerungen an Einsätze der Heeres-Gebirgsjäger-Bataillone 201 und 202 im zweiten Weltkrieg," has been stored at the Bundesarchiv/Militärarchiv Freiburg i. Br., Call Number MSG 2/5728.

5. Additional information about Heeres Gebirgsjäger Bataillon 202 was collected during follow-up interviews with Gerwin Eder and Joseph Breiteneder.

6. The U.S. 7th Regimental History, *From Fedala to Berchtesgaden,* by Nathan W. White (1947) was an invaluable guide in charting the progress of the "Cotton Balers." This information also proved to be of value to Mr. Kolbinger, and was instrumental in bringing about the first known postwar contact between Cotton Baler and Gebirgsjäger veterans.

7. Henry Nakada and fellow veterans of Company I gave me many hours of their time during and after their 1994 reunion in Las Vegas and at Shig Doi's home.

8. Additional information reviewed: "The Japs Who Saved World War II's Lost Battalion," by Paul Ditzel, published in "The Fighting 36th" newsletter (date unknown). "The Rescue of the Lost Battalion," by Chris T. Shigenaga-Massey, Honolulu, 1985.

## 6: The "Alamo" Regiment

1. Monthly history reports of the 141st Regimental History (declassified September 1958).

2. History of the regiment in part based on *Five Years, Five Countries, Five Campaigns,* edited by Clifford H. Peek Jr. (1945).

3. Company E background information thanks to Ed Moreno, who also provided newspaper clippings. "The Fighting Men of Company E," the *El Paso Citizen,* December 4, 1992. "El Paso's 'Fighting Machine' Takes the Limelight," *El Paso Herald-Post,* October 21, 1993. "Soldierboy: Many Lost Their Lives in Ill-fated Battle," *San Antonio Light* (supplement) March 4, 1988.

4. Henri Grandjean interview from unmarked videotape provided by Shig Doi.

5. The Seventh Army G-2 Summary mentions the downing of an American rescue aircraft due to friendly fire.

### 7: Banzai Hill

1. Most of this material is based on previously listed documents and eyewitness reports, and General Dahlquist's diary entries and letters.

2. The death of Capt. Joe Byrne was witnessed by one man, Sgt. Bert Akiyama, who contacted me to ensure accurate reporting.

3. By far the most difficult man to corner for an interview was Sgt. Tak Senzaki. But when I finally did, with the help of his wife, he gave a thoughtful, detailed, and unimpassioned account.

4. General Robert Stack's letters are part of the U.S. Army History Institute's collection.

### 8: Mountain Hunters and Cotton Balers

1. Both Majors Clayton Thobro and Glenn Rathbun offered much valuable information during their interviews, to which Rathbun added his autobiographical sketches. Additional information is based on the 7th Regimental History and Seventh Army G-2 Summaries.

2. Confusion at German headquarters based on communications fragments located at the Bundesarchiv (Kolbinger). Other material based on Vitus Kolbinger's history and interviews conducted with members from both German battalions, notably Franz Seebacher, Franz Kapfer, and Toni Stocker.

3. George Murphy diary.

4. General Haeckel's court-martial, from his personnel file and Nineteenth Army log.

### 9: Crossroads of Hell

1. Composite created from both American and German sources previously listed.

2. Wendell E. Erickson diary and casualty lists.

### 10: Beyond "Lost Battalions"

1. Newsreel: Trapped Battalion, United News, November 1944.

2. Dahlquist diary.

3. Seventh Army G-2 Summary and daily journal of General Patch.

4. Details about German dead (All Souls' Day) from Pierre Moulin.

5. Leutnant Alois Herrmann's contact with the Nisei was described by him during a series of telephone and written interviews.

6. Military Study B-781; "Die 19. Armee in der burgundischen Pforte, in den Vogesen und im Elsass, von mitte September bis 18. Dezember 1944," by General der Infanterie Friedrich Wiese, 8. März 1948.

7. Casualty reports: Alphabetical Listing, Battle Deaths of the 36th Infantry Division by Organization as of 30 June 1947 (CFN-161, Record Group 407); Monthly History Reports of the 141st Regiment and Monthly History Reports of the 442d Infantry (Record Group 407) at the National Archives.

8. Alexander Patch and 442d documentary footage from the National Archives; Patch letters from the U.S. Military Academy at West Point.

### 11: Life, Death, and Honor

1. Major Glenn Rathbun's account comes from interviews conducted with him and his wife in 1995, and his autobiographical sketches. It was truly a pleasure to get to know the Rathbuns, who were most generous throughout the interview process, and I was amazed by the photographic memory the major had half a century after the events.

2. I am grateful to the Harvard University Archives (Pusey Library) for providing background information about Wells Lewis, his photo, and a sample chapter from his novel *They Still Say No*. Segments about the younger years of Wells Lewis are from letters written by his mother, Grace Hegger Lewis (Telesforo Casanova), and the book

*With Love from Gracie, Sinclair Lewis 1912–1925,* by Gracie Livingstone Hegger Lewis, Harcourt Brace & Co., New York, 1953. Sinclair Lewis's letter to General Dahlquist is part of the U.S. Army History Institute collection, the Dahlquist papers.

3. Material about Gen. John E. Dahlquist is part of the U.S. Army History Institute's collection, U.S. Army War College, Carlisle Barracks, Pennsylvania; from Marty Higgins; and from the Department of Defense Office of Public Information, News Branch, 1956 (National Archives). Included are a letter to Gen. Fred L. Walker, 21 December 1944; from Minneapolis, Minnesota, Public Library: American Swedish Monthly, 7 September 1942; and assorted clippings from the *Minneapolis Sun Tribune.*

### 12: Prisoners of War

1. Marty Higgins's collection: personal papers, letters, telegrams (Internews wire), interviews, Silver Star citation, and newspaper clippings (listed in Chapter 13 notes); additional information from 141st Regimental Monthly History Summary, *Ex-POW Bulletin,* May 1992, and notations from Vitus Kolbinger, and Military Study B-468 by Gen. Helmut Thumm. A detailed report written by Captain Higgins, after his release from POW camp, was found among General Dahlquist's papers.

2. Interviews of Eddie Guy.

3. Interviews with Jimmie Kanaya, his diary, interviews with Young Oak Kim, and *Eine Stadt Stirbt* (the demise of Gemünden at the end of World War II), published by the Historic Club of Gemünden am Main, 1988.

### 13: Go for Broke

1. Interviews with Young Oak Kim.

2. Interview with Takashi Senzaki at the Company I fiftieth reunion in Las Vegas; other members interviewed: Henry Nakada, Suguru Takahashi, Tadao Saito, George Miyashiro, Junji Shiroyama, Kazuo Takekawa; Office of War Information, United News newsreel, November 1944 (Part 4, "Japanese-American soldiers rescue soldiers of the 36th Division surrounded in France"); New York *Herald Tribune,* November 6, 1944; New York *World-Telegram,* Monday, November 6, 1944; The *New York Times,* Monday, November 6, 1944; The

*Stars and Stripes,* Mediterranean, Monday, November 6, 1944; *Chicago Sun* (date unknown); two New Jersey newspapers (names and dates unknown); other clippings from same period (AP delayed).

3. Joe Hattori, interviews; "522d Field Artillery Battalion Newsletter," Donauwörth, Germany, 1945.

### 14: Enemies and Friends

1. Interview with Pierre Moulin.

2. Josephine Voirin composite from "100/442d Newsletter," and Company I interview videotape, courtesy of Shig Doi. Georges Henry from same tape.

4. Mme. Suzanne Finnay, from George Murphy interviews.

5. George Murphy and Toni Stocker interviews.

6. Joseph Schwieters: personal writings and interviews (Schwieters appears in the KPIX, Channel 5, San Francisco, video production *Honor Bound,* by Wendy Hanamura).

7. Vitus Kolbinger interviews and audio tapes.

### Epilogue

1. Epitaph to General Patch, New York *Herald Tribune,* November 22, 1945.

2. Military Study A-953, Walter Rolin

3. Military Study B-781, General Wiese.

4. Bundesarchiv biographic sketches, Generals Haeckel and Richter.

5. Toni Stocker, 7th Regimental History.

### Appendix

From previously cited sources.

### INTERVIEWS

Bert Akiyama, John Blaikie, Josef Breiteneder, Charles H. Coolidge, Shig Doi, Gerwin Eder, Walter Eschrich, Eddie Guy, Sam Handa, James M. Hanley, Joe Osamaru Hattori, Alois Herrmann, Marty Higgins, James Kanaya, Franz Kapfer, Shiro Kashino, Christopher R. Keegan, Young Oak Kim, M. Kimura, Vitus Kolbinger, Werner Kortenhaus, Hans von Luck, Tom Masamori, George

Miyashiro, Pierre Moulin, George Murphy, Henry Nakada, George Oiye, Allen Okamoto, George Oshita, Sammy Petty, Sherman Pratt, Glenn and Louise Rathbun, George Rebovich, Arthur Rodgers, Tadao Saito, Yaeko Sakamoto (Hattori), Herbert Sasaki, Joseph and Hannerose Schwieters, Franz Seebacher, Takashi Senzaki, Frank Shimada, Junji Shiroyama, Hugo Sommer, Frank Sotelo, Alvin "Bud" Spetz, Toni Stocker, Sakae Takahashi, Suguru Takahashi, Kazuo Takekawa, Clayton Thobro, Rudy Tokiwa, Jack Wilson, E. L. Wrenn, Jim Yamashita, Kiyoshi Yoshii, Hank Yoshitake

## SPECIAL THANKS

I would like to give special thanks to those who lent their invaluable expertise and assistance in researching this topic: Urban Bracken; Al Dietrick; Robert Faught; Tom Kawaguchi; Ed Moreno; George Nishinaka; Fred J. Phillips; Manfred Rommel; Sam Sakamoto; Gérard Seidl; Don Shearer; Carl Strom; Heinz Streffing.

**In the United States:** Eric Scott, the UCLA Map Library, Los Angeles; Robin Edward Cookson, The National Archives, Washington D.C.; Dr. Richard Sommers, and Pam Chaney, U.S. Army History Institute; Mr. Dennis Vetock, U.S. Army History Institute Reference Library; Carol J. Koenig, the U.S. Military Academy at West Point 36th Division Association; The Midwest Chapter, 36th Division Association; The 100th/442d Newsletter; The Watch on the Rhine, 3d Infantry Association Newsletter; The Western Region Newsletter, Society of the Third Infantry Division; The Cotton Balers, 7th Infantry Regiment Association Newsletter; INFORM, Minnesota Public Library.

**In Germany:** Archiv der Stadt Rendsburg; Oberstleutnant Diefenbach, Militärgeschichtliches Forschungsamt; Bundesarchiv, Militärarchiv Freiburg; Bundesarchiv, Abteil III, Berlin; Kameradenkreis der Gebirgstruppe; Verband Deutscher Soldaten, e.V.

**In Austria:** Österreichisches Staatsarchiv, Wien Salzburger Museum.

**In France:** Centre d'Histoire de la Résistance, Lyon Service Historique de l'Armée de Terre.

# Selected Bibliography

*Americans: The Story of the 442nd Combat Team.* Orville C. Shirey, Infantry Journal Press, 1946.

*Boyhood to War.* Dorothy Matsuo, Mutual Publishing, Honolulu, 1992.

*Go for Broke.* Chester Tanaka, Go for Broke, Inc., Richmond, CA, 1982.

*I Can Never Forget.* Thelma Chang, Sigi Productions, Honolulu, 1991.

*U.S. Army Samurais in Bruyères.* Pierre Moulin, Editions Gérard Louis, 1993.

*Bruyères: 50e Anniversaire de la Liberation.* Pierre Moulin, Editions Gérard Louis, 1994.

*Unlikely Liberators.* Masayo Umezawa Duus, University of Hawaii Press, 1983.

*Honor Bound.* Video production by Wendy Hanamura (KPIX, Channel 5), San Francisco, 1995.

*A Matter of Honor.* James M. Hanley, Vantage Press, New York, 1995.

*The History of the French First Army.* Général Jean de Lattre, Allan & Unwin, London, 1952.

*T-Patch to Victory.* Colonel Vincent M. Lockhart, Staked Plains Press, Canyon, TX, 1981.

*Five Years, Five Countries, Five Campaigns.* Clifford H. Peek, 141st Inf. Rgt. Assn., 1945.

*From Fedala to Berchtesgaden, The History of the 7th Infantry Regiment.* Nathan W. White, 1947.

*Inside Hitler's Headquarters 1939–45.* General Walter Warlimont, Presidio Press, Novato, CA 1962.

*Panzer Commander.* Hans von Luck, Dell Publishing, 1989.

Maps were reconstructed by the author, based on topographic maps provided by the UCLA Map Library, German and American maps and sketches and monthly unit histories (National Archives, RG

331 SHAEF, 6th Army Group, October/November 1944, folder 1, Wehrmacht maps of Oct. 16, 21, 23, 24, 25, 26, 27, 28, "Unternehmen Habicht," 12. 12.–14. 12. 44, as well as maps included in Military Studies).

# Index